Jürgen Beyerer, Alexey Pak (Eds.)

Proceedings of the 2013 Joint Workshop of Fraunhofer IOSB and Institute for Anthropomatics, Vision and Fusion Laboratory

AF140441

Karlsruher Schriften zur Anthropomatik
Band 17
Herausgeber: Prof. Dr.-Ing. Jürgen Beyerer

Lehrstuhl für Interaktive Echtzeitsysteme
Karlsruher Institut für Technologie

Fraunhofer-Institut für Optronik, Systemtechnik und
Bildauswertung IOSB Karlsruhe

Eine Übersicht über alle bisher in dieser Schriftenreihe
erschienenen Bände finden Sie am Ende des Buchs.

Proceedings of the 2013 Joint Workshop of Fraunhofer IOSB and Institute for Anthropomatics, Vision and Fusion Laboratory

Edited by
Jürgen Beyerer
Alexey Pak

Impressum

 Scientific
Publishing

Karlsruher Institut für Technologie (KIT)
KIT Scientific Publishing
Straße am Forum 2
D-76131 Karlsruhe

KIT Scientific Publishing is a registered trademark of Karlsruhe
Institute of Technology. Reprint using the book cover is not allowed.

www.ksp.kit.edu

Print on Demand 2014

ISSN 1863-6489
ISBN 978-3-7315-0212-8
DOI   10.5445/KSP/1000040668

Preface

In 2013, the annual joint workshop of the Fraunhofer Institute of Optronics, System Technologies and Image Exploitation (IOSB) and the Vision and Fusion Laboratory (IES) of the Institute for Anthropomatics, Karlsruhe Institute of Technology (KIT) has again been hosted by the town of Triberg-Nussbach in Germany.

For a week from July, 21 to 27 the PhD students of the both institutions delivered extended reports on the status of their research and participated in thorough discussions on topics ranging from computer vision and world modeling to data fusion and human-machine interaction. Most results and ideas presented at the workshop are collected in this book in the form of detailed technical reports. This volume provides a comprehensive and up-to-date overview of the research program of the IES Laboratory and the Fraunhofer IOSB.

The editors thank Miriam Ruf, Julius Pfrommer and other organizers for their efforts resulting in a pleasant and inspiring atmosphere throughout the week. We would also like to thank the doctoral students for writing and reviewing the technical reports as well as for responding to the comments and the suggestions of their colleagues.

Prof. Dr.-Ing. Jürgen Beyerer
Alexey Pak, PhD

Contents

Motion Field Segmentation and Appearance Change Detection for Hand Tracking from the Ego Perspective

Jan Hendrik Hammer

Vision and Fusion Laboratory
Institute for Anthropomatics
Karlsruhe Institute of Technology (KIT), Germany
jan.hammer@kit.edu

Technical Report IES-2013-01

Abstract: In this paper a novel method for moving object tracking is presented and applied in the context of hand tracking for mobile Augmented-Reality (AR) applications. AR glasses-like devices come with an integrated camera capturing the field of view of the user. Hand gestures are the most intuitive interaction modality for manipulating AR contents and hand tracking is the first step towards robust gesture recognition. The presented method fuses motion segmentation and appearance change detection in a new way to track hands in front of complex backgrounds under varying lighting conditions - without the need for previous color calibration. A comparison of this new algorithm with state-of-the-art tracking methods is conducted using a thorough evaluation methodology and challenging data sets containing different wiping hand gestures.

1 Introduction

Almost every month a new type of mobile Augmented-Reality (AR) device is announced. Many companies are working on the so called high-tech glasses offering optical see-through AR. The imagination of being able to visualize digital content everywhere in the users field of view allows for an unthinkable amount of applications - some of them would definitely make our life easier. To just take a picture, one wouldn't have to take out the mobile phone. To know where to go to, one would not have to look at the mobile phone. Information would just be there in the field of view (FOV) and not on some small display that needs to be carried and hold into the FOV every time one needs it. When looking at the AR game *Ingress*[1],

---

[1] http://www.ingress.com/

one sees how video see-through AR already changes the way people interact. This makes one think that one day people might not want to live in a world without AR - and their private AR glasses - anymore. Fortunately, we still have a few years before this might become reality, till the visualization capabilities of the head worn devices becomes good enough for daily usage.

Interaction with these devices will be realized using voice recognition, touch, eye tracking and hand gestures. Hand gestures are the most intuitive modality for manipulating AR contents visualized in the field of view. Therefore, the recognition of hand gestures is a must and robust hand tracking its basis. In the following sections we will first concentrate on related work (section 2). Then the new tracking approach is described in section 3. It is compared to several other hand tracking algorithms in section 5 using the evaluation framework of section 4. After the comparison this article is concluded in section 6.

2   Related Work

In mobile applications with a head-mounted camera, the background is not static. Hand localization can therefore not be achieved by simple frame subtraction as in [BRB09]. The lighting conditions may change all the time and direct sunlight can be illuminating the scene. Due to this, active sensors utilizing any kind of infrared illumination are no option. Accordingly, depth information is hard to get and with only one single RGB camera, scene segmentation becomes a difficult task and is often not performed. Gloves [WP09], markers [MM09], accelerates [PR11] or thermal cameras [AAHEM09] are used instead. But the optimal solution would be to not need to attach further devices to the hands of the user. 3D sensors are widely and successfully used for hand tracking [Oik12] because depth information easily results in an accurate segmentation of the scene. Unfortunately, available active sensors are to heavy for a light-weight head worn device and not sunlight-proof. A self-built passive stereo camera system would be the only option to create a more or less light-weight device, but this required effort in creating an new HMD or attaching the cameras to some existing device. Furthermore, a calibration of the two cameras would have to be performed and a robust stereo reconstruction algorithm to be developed. The latter one would heavily increase the computational load. Accordingly it is achievable to use only one single RGB camera and work without a more or less exact 3D reconstruction of the scene per frame. Therefore, Pisharady et al. [PVL13] proposed an interesting method for hand posture detection from single view even in front of a complex background. Unfortunately, their method is not real-time capable.

In [HB13] different hand tracking methods were compared to each other. The presented approaches use skin color detection based on a learned color distribution and motion information by optical flow estimation. Using our enhanced hand tracking benchmark, it turns out that skin color models need to be adapted to allow for robust tracking under challenging lighting conditions. But color model adaption is not trivial since the determination of an area to update with needs a correct image segmentation that can only be computed using sophisticated models like in Sun's *nLayers* approach [SSB12] which is also not real-time capable. One of the first steps of *nLayers* is to perform an initial flow field segmentation. This will also be utilized in our new approach described in the next section.

3   Moving Object Tracking using Motion and Color

The hand tracking approaches of [HB13] rely on a binary image segmentation. This image segmentation is achieved using skin-color detection. One algorithm called *tip*-tracking is a region-based approach illustrated in Figure3.1 where the skin-colored pixel are white. It computes the biggest blob of contiguous skin-colored pixels and then the tip of the hand is determined as follows: First, the uppermost skin-colored pixel is computed, whose vertical coordinate is the y-coordinated of the resulting tip position. Second, the mass value of all skin-colored pixels of the biggest blob with a y-coordinate in a specific range of the maximal height of the hand (all white pixels behind the green bar) is computed. The horizontal coordinate of this mass value is going to be the x-coordinate of the tip-tracking result, shown as green dot. Compared to the tracking of the center of the biggest blob, tip-tracking solves the hand-arm problem. Obviously, tip-tracking only works when the hand is reaching into the FOV from below. But for the given case of an HMD, we can assume this to be true, since gestures where the arm intersects the upper margin of the FOV would be completely unnatural. In [HB13] further methods, like particle filters with different observation and motion models, were compared to tip-tracking as well as the Camshift [Bra98] and Flocks of Features [KT04] algorithms.

The new tracking approach presented in the next two sections uses a completely different segmentation as basis.

3.1   Foreground Segmentation

With only one camera and an inhomogeneous background, it is not possible to perfectly segment the hands based on color information [AAHEM09]. But by using motion information, it is possible to distinguish between different objects in the

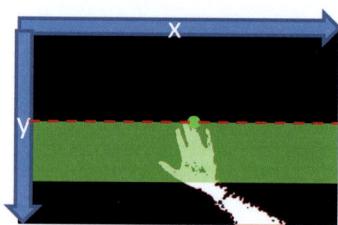

Figure 3.1: Region-based *tip*-tracking

scene. The motion information utilized in all results shown below is computed by the Graphics Processing Unit (GPU) version of the optical flow algorithm *Dual TV L1* [ZPB07] implemented in the library OpenCV[2]. The motion field contains the movement of each pixel to its position in the next frame.

The new hand tracking approach clusters the motion field. Therefore, k-Means with k=2 is utilized. One cluster is for the background motion and the other for the foreground. Affine motion models would be more precise for describing especially the background motion but, for the sake of simplicity, only a 2D vector is currently representing each cluster. Of course, this clustering only separates foreground from background correctly, when both, foreground and background, have a simple structure. Otherwise several motion layers would be needed and merged to figure out, what is background and what is foreground. For the data set used below we can assume, that this simple structure is given. When foreground and background are determined, the difference vector between foreground and background motion is computed. The first requirement for a foreground object like a moving hand is a high enough absolute value of this difference vector. Otherwise, both clusters describe the same background motion. For the computations below we used a value of $\sqrt{10}$. This means that a foreground motion is detected if the absolute value of the difference vector of both cluster motions is greater than $\sqrt{10}$. Additionally, we can fairly estimate that given the resolution of 752x480 pixels and usual distance of the hand to the camera the minimal size of the hand segment in pixels must be between 50,000 and 100,000 pixels. If the motion difference and pixel size requirement are both fulfilled, a hand may be visible in the foreground cluster.

What happens when a hand is moved into the field of view but hold still at some point of time t? Accordingly, the hand is not moving and no foreground motion is visible. In that case, no foreground cluster is estimated. Then, the new tracking approach assumes that the segmentation of the previous time step $t-1$ is still valid.

[2]http://opencv.org/

In fact, this is the case when the hand is not moved because the hand is still at the same position.

One important issue after the determination of the foreground segment is its warping into the present according to the motion field. Since the computed optical flow describes the motion from the previous frame at time $t - 1$ to the current frame at time t, the computed motion field clustering describes the segmentation at time $t - 1$. Because of that, the foreground segment must be warped using this flow field. The result is an approximated foreground segment of the current frame t.

The generated foreground segment can for example yield as segmentation basis for the tip-tracking algorithm or particle filters mentioned above. In the following sections we will only consider this foreground segmentation together with the tip-tracking approach.

3.2   Appearance Change Detection

The described approach works as long as the hand is completely visible. But when the hand is at the margins of the FOV sometimes only two-thirds of the hand are visible. Then the segmentation again does not find a foreground motion because of the requirement that the hand segment must contain a number of pixels in a certain range. In this case, the current estimation of the segmentation is computed by also using the previous segmentation with additional warping. But at the image margins another problem occurs: The optical flow is often corrupted at image margins and may make the segment stay at e.g. the lower margin although the hand has already left the image. To detect this situation, a color histogram is created using the RGB color values of the foreground segment. This histogram is compared to the color histogram of the previous foreground segment by computing the Hellinger distance [Hel09] of both histograms. If this distance value is above a certain threshold - in the given case 0.3 - then the color distribution has become too different and the hand is assumed to have left the image. This so called *Appearance Change Detection* of the foreground segment prevents from trusting wrong motion information at the image margins and brings color information into the game without the need for some calibration procedure before the tracking.

The Appearance Change Detection does not only make sense at image margins, it could be used as confidence value for the segment tracking. By allowing the color distributions to vary from frame to frame, illumination changes can be compensated for.

The following section describes the evaluation framework used in section 5 to compare different hand tracking approaches.

4 Evaluation Framework

Our evaluation methodology is based on the metrics for trajectory comparison of Needham and Boyle [NB03]. Using these makes a thorough evaluation of tracking results possible, since not only detection rates, like the hit rate, false alarm rate or precision of the detection results can be compared. Statistical measures as the mean of the deviations between two trajectories allow for precise conclusions.

4.1 Data sets

Since gesture recognition is the next step after a successful hand tracking, the current data sets consist of different wiping gestures recorded at 25 fps and a resolution of 752x480 pixels. Two persons performed a predetermined sequence of sixteen gestures under dark and light lighting conditions. Either no or one hand is visible at each point of time and the sequences of gestures were performed with the left and the right hand. In total, the benchmark consist of eight videos with more than 10,000 frames. In 40 % of the frames the hand is visible. During the development of different hand tracking methods, it turned out that detecting robustly that a hand has left the FOV is not trivial. Therefore, it is important to have long periods in the data sets which show the FOV when the hand has disappeared because then many false positives are produced if the leaving of the hand is not detected correctly. This could not be figured out if the video sequences ended directly after a performed gesture.

4.2 Ground Truth Annotation

The ground truth trajectories for the above described videos were labeled manually. A person selected the current position of the hand on each frame by estimating the center of the palm. Since this is somehow subjective, we compared the difference of different trajectories created by the same person. We measured an average distance of about seven pixels between corresponding trajectory points. Accordingly, a tracking result of less or about this value can be regarded as excellent. The average trajectories created by different people could show a higher average offset depending on the subjective impression what the center of the palm is. Due to the *shifted mean distance* this offset can be ignored without negatively affecting the evaluation.

4.3 Trajectory Comparison

Methods for trajectory comparison are needed to measure the accuracy of hand tracking results. The first requirement for a good tracking result is that it was correctly detected for each frame if a hand was visible or not. Therefore, high true positive rates, low false alarm rates, a high precision and a high F-measure are to be achieved. But these detection rates are not enough. Based on the methodology for trajectory comparison of Needham and Boyle [NB03], we compute furthermore the mean distance of corresponding trajectory points. But there is a difficulty when comparing different tracking algorithms. Some of them track the center of the hand and some the tip [HB13]. Resulting trajectories are therefore almost similar but shifted by some constant displacement. By compensating for this offset, the trajectories can be compared again. The mean distance of a ground truth trajectory and such a shifted tracking result is called *shifted mean distance* and taken into account when looking at the accuracy of a tracking result.

4.4 What is a good tracking result?

Finally, it comes to the following question: What is a good tracking result? For example, it is not important if the hand is already detected when only half of the fingers are visible. But it is important that the hand is tracked when completely visible. Similar to the appearing of the hand is the disappearing. Losing the hand, while it is still completely visible, is bad. But losing it, when it has partly disappeared, before it disappears completely, should not be regarded as tracking failure. Due to this, it turns out that for the described data sets a true positive rate of above 80 % is sufficient, since the frames, in which the hand is only partly visible while appearing or disappearing, are part of the reference trajectories. The false positive rate should be as low as possible and the F-measure as harmonic mean of recall and precision should be as high as possible. Additionally, the shifted mean distance should be as low as possible, but due to the subjective trajectory annotation (cf. section 4.2) shifted mean distances of less or about seven pixel per frame can be seen as excellent and equally good. The best tracking results for the shifted mean distance, a few of the algorithms reach on single sequences, have never been below 13 pixels. Even tracks with a shifted mean distance of up to 18 pixels would subjectively be considered as very good tracking that can be used for recognizing certain trajectory shapes for gesture recognition.

5   Evaluation

In the evaluation we take into account the best of our algorithms and test them on all eight sequences with 10,000 annotated frames:

- *Color-Tip*-Tracking: Region-based *tip*-tracking with skin-color segmentation [HB13]

- *Camshift* [Bra98]

- *Shape*-Particle: Particle Filter with *std* motion and *shape* observation model [HB13]

- *Flow*-Particle: Particle Filter with *flow* motion and *window* observation model [HB13]

- *Window-FoF*: Flocks-of-Features (FoF) Tracking with *window* observation model [HB13]

- *MotionSegAppearance*: Region-based *tip*-tracking with motion field segmentation and appearance change detection (cf. section 3)

The detection rates, including the true positive rate (TPR), the false positive rate (FPR), the precision (PREC) and the F-measure, and additionally the shifted mean distance averaged over all 10,000 frames are illustrated in table 5.1. All algorithms except *MotionSegAppearance* suffer from the problematic skin-color detection. Although for each of the lighting conditions a specific color model has been used, the skin color of the hand changes its appearance which is not covered by the learned model. As a consequence, the particles of the particle filter approaches cannot concentrate on the hand anymore and the algorithms cannot detect an appeared hand or loose it too often since the true positive rate is below 60 %. Hence, the particle filter approaches relying solely on skin color fail completely when based on the skin-color segmentation.

The *Color-Tip*-Tracking is surprisingly better than the particle filter variants, but again, the hand blob of contiguous skin-colored pixels often cannot be determined correctly and no hand is detected. This results in a too poor true positive rate of only 73 % regarding the notion of a good tracking result described in section 4.4. Furthermore, the biggest blob often does not contain the hand but parts of the arm only, what increases the shifted mean distance.

The Flocks of Features variant *Window-FoF* shows a very good true positive rate but can only reach this with a very high false positive rate of 23 % and a low precision of only 72 %. Additionally, the shifted mean distance averaged over all true positive frames is way too bad with 64 pixels. This shows that the performed tracking is not very accurate. When looking at the data, one finds out that often not the center of the hand is tracked but a part of the arm, and tracking is subjectively regarded as failure.

The *Camshift* algorithm reaches a true positive of above 80 % but similar to *Window-FoF* has a too high false positive rate of 16 % and a too low precision of only 76 %.

The new *MotionSegAppearance* method reaches a very good true positive rate of 94 %. It shows a false positive rate of 8 % which is not optimal. The F-measure of 91 % is the best of all approaches. The shifted mean distance is too high with 28 pixels but this is due to the fact that the shape of the foreground segmentation is changing according to the flow. Subjectively seen the track is trembling around the perfect trajectory. However, this tracking result is reached without any kind of color calibration and the most simple motion representation for a motion segment with only a 2D vector. Due to the big potentials for improvements and the already produced good detection rates, the new tracking approach can be considered as promising tracking approach.

	TPR	FPR	PREC	F1	Shft. dist.
Color-Tip-Tracking	0.73	0.00	0.99	0.84	21 px
Camshift	0.81	0.16	0.76	0.78	26 px
Shape-Particle	0.58	0.00	1.00	0.73	19 px
Flow-Particle	0.57	0.00	1.00	0.73	21 px
Window-FoF	0.93	0.23	0.72	0.81	64 px
MotionSegAppearance	0.94	0.08	0.89	0.91	28 px

Table 5.1: True positive rate (TPR), false positive rate (FPR), precision (PREC), F-measure and the shifted mean distance (Shft. dist.) results for the complete benchmark.

6 Conclusion

To sum up, we have shown a new 2D-hand tracking algorithm that does not need a learned skin-color model to track one hand robustly under varying lighting conditions. Therefore, it clusters the prevalent motion to get the foreground motion segment which is assumed to contain the hand. This segment is warped to get an approximation of the foreground segment at the always current point of time. To assert the correct detection of a leaving hand despite corrupted optical flow at image margins, a method named *Appearance Change Detection* was presented, which uses a comparison of color distributions to detect, if the object, associated with the tracked foreground segment, has left the field of view or not. Next steps are to improve the image segmentation by using more sophisticated segmentation procedures incorporating motion and color segmentation in parallel. Furthermore, it is absolutely necessary to use some kind of object recognition method to assert that the tracked object really is a hand. For this purpose, the benchmark needs to be enhanced with further sequences containing other moving objects and more people performing the gestures in front of even more complex backgrounds and challenging lighting conditions. Real-time capability is another important factor. Therefore, some parts of the system have to be parallelized on the GPU.

Bibliography

[AAHEM09] Jörg Appenrodt, Ayoub Al-Hamadi, Mahmoud Elmezain, and Bernd Michaelis. Data gathering for gesture recognition systems based on mono color-, stereo color- and thermal cameras. In *Proceedings of the 1st International Conference on Future Generation Information Technology*, FGIT '09, pages 78–86, Berlin, Heidelberg, 2009. Springer-Verlag.

[Bra98] Gary R. Bradski. Real time face and object tracking as a component of a perceptual user interface. In *Proceedings of the 4th IEEE Workshop on Applications of Computer Vision (WACV'98)*, WACV '98, pages 214–, Washington, DC, USA, 1998. IEEE Computer Society.

[BRB09] Thomas Bader, Rene Räpple, and Jürgen Beyerer. Fast invariant contour-based classification of hand symbols for hci. In *Computer analysis of images and patterns: 13th international conference, CAIP 2009, Münster, Germany, September 2-4, 2009 ; proceedings*, Lecture notes in computer science; 5702, pages 689–696. Springer, Berlin [u.a.], 2009.

[HB13] Jan Hendrik Hammer and Jürgen Beyerer. Robust hand tracking in realtime using a single head-mounted rgb camera. In Masaaki Kurosu, editor, *Human-Computer Interaction. Interaction Modalities and Techniques*, volume 8007 of *Lecture Notes in Computer Science*, pages 252–261. Springer Berlin Heidelberg, 2013.

[Hel09] E. Hellinger. Neue Begründung der Theorie quadratischer Formen von unendlichvielen Veränderlichen. *J. Reine Angew. Math.*, 136:210–271, 1909.

[KT04] M. Kölsch and M. Turk. Fast 2d hand tracking with flocks of features and multi-cue integration. In *Computer Vision and Pattern Recognition Workshop, 2004. CVPRW '04. Conference on*, page 158, june 2004.

[MM09] Pranav Mistry and Pattie Maes. Sixthsense: a wearable gestural interface. In *ACM SIGGRAPH ASIA 2009 Sketches*, SIGGRAPH ASIA '09, pages 11:1–11:1, New York, NY, USA, 2009. ACM.

[NB03]   Chris J. Needham and Roger D. Boyle. Performance evaluation metrics and statistics
            for positional tracker evaluation. In *Proceedings of the 3rd international conference on
            Computer vision systems*, ICVS'03, pages 278–289, Berlin, Heidelberg, 2003. Springer-
            Verlag.

[Oik12]   I. Oikonomidis. Tracking the articulated motion of two strongly interacting hands. In
            *Proceedings of the 2012 IEEE Conference on Computer Vision and Pattern Recognition
            (CVPR)*, CVPR '12, pages 1862–1869, Washington, DC, USA, 2012. IEEE Computer
            Society.

[PR11]   V.A. Prisacariu and I. Reid. Robust 3d hand tracking for human computer interac-
            tion. In *Automatic Face Gesture Recognition and Workshops (FG 2011), 2011 IEEE
            International Conference on*, pages 368 –375, march 2011.

[PVL13]   PramodKumar Pisharady, Prahlad Vadakkepat, and AiPoh Loh. Attention based de-
            tection and recognition of hand postures against complex backgrounds. *International
            Journal of Computer Vision*, 101:403–419, 2013.

[SSB12]   Deqing Sun, E.B. Sudderth, and M.J. Black. Layered segmentation and optical flow
            estimation over time. In *Computer Vision and Pattern Recognition (CVPR), 2012 IEEE
            Conference on*, pages 1768–1775, 2012.

[WP09]   Robert Y. Wang and Jovan Popović. Real-time hand-tracking with a color glove. *ACM
            Trans. Graph.*, 28(3):63:1–63:8, July 2009.

[ZPB07]   C. Zach, T. Pock, and H. Bischof. A duality based approach for realtime tv-l1 optical
            flow. In *Proceedings of the 29th DAGM conference on Pattern recognition*, pages 214–
            223, Berlin, Heidelberg, 2007. Springer-Verlag.

How to Describe Face Sequences for Fast Person Recognition

Christian Herrmann

Vision and Fusion Laboratory
Institute for Anthropomatics
Karlsruhe Institute of Technology (KIT), Germany
christian.herrmann@kit.edu

Technical Report IES-2013-02

Abstract: The evaluation of video material for forensic purposes is a time intensive and complex work. A common task is to identify or find persons in video footage. Computer vision based methods can help to reduce the manual effort. However, video databases in forensic applications are often rather large. This poses harsh requirements with respect to the processing speed of any automated recognition approach. Specifically, searching for persons needs to be much faster than real time. An analysis and evaluation of existing face recognition techniques is performed with respect to this requirement. Based on this result a promising approach is presented. The key concept is to use a cascade of the existing techniques and combine them in a way that the advantages of each one are used. This results in a significant speedup in processing time and additionally in a slight improvement in the recognition performance. Using this approach promises to help at the forensic search in video footage.

1 Introduction

With the increasing availability of video data in all kinds of shape, the interest in automatic analysis grows. Content-based video search is relevant in a wide area of applications. Ranging from sorting private holiday videos to professional analysis of surveillance material. A key interest is the search for known persons in the video data. As the human face is a discriminative feature for identity, the use of automated face recognition is useful for this task. The focus of this report is the forensic analysis of surveillance footage. Computer vision support promises to

Figure 1.1: Typical images from surveillance video. Containing several challenges like low resolution, different head poses, motion blur and noise.

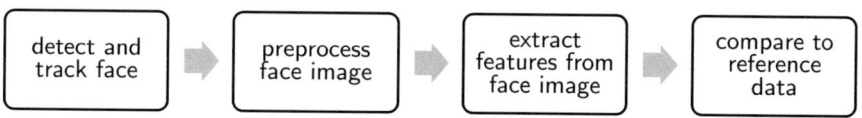

Figure 1.2: Flowchart showing the basic steps of a face recognition system.

speed up investigations which are based on video material. Compared to usual automated face recognition the main challenges for surveillance videos (see Fig. 1.1 for some sample images) are:

- *Unconstrained environment* – Head position, illumination and facial accessories may vary from video to video.

- *Large database* – The database may contain hours or days of video footage.

- *Low resolution* – Face sizes are typically well below 50 pixels.

In this report, the focus is on the large database while the two other challenges remain as side conditions. A research about the processing speed of different existing approaches is performed, and possibilities to address the problem are discussed.

The typical workflow for a face recognition system is shown in Fig. 1.2. In this report the first two steps are not considered. We assume that the face detection and tracking as well as a possible preprocessing is already done. The analysis will concentrate on the last two steps. Namely the feature extraction and the comparison of the extracted features. The wide variety of existing approaches will be discussed with respect to the main goal: fast recognition.

2   Problem Definition

Usually, in the field of automated face recognition two basic scenarios are known [PGM11]:

- *Verification / Authentication* – A reference identity is claimed and a sample face is provided. The task is to check if the sample face belongs to the claimed identity. This task requires a binary answer. A typical scenario is at border control where the sample face should be compared to a reference identity given by the passport.

- *Identification / Recognition* – A sample face is given and the task is to determine the most likely identity out of a predefined set of identities. This set is usually represented by a gallery which contains reference data for the face of each identity. This task requires an integer answer. A typical scenario is the recognition of a character in a movie.

Usually, automated face recognition compares the sample face to the reference face and calculates a score which measures the similarity between the faces. In the identification scenario the identity with the highest score is the result. For the verification a comparison of the score to a threshold is necessary and the verification is accepted if the score exceeds this threshold.

For the analysis of the introduced scenario of forensic analysis a few definitions are necessary. A video will be denoted by V and contains a sequence of F frames $f: V = (f_1, ..., f_F)$. One frame is an image vector of dimension d: $f \in [0, 1]^d$. A collection of B videos is denoted by $C = \{V_1, ..., V_B\}$. Each video V shows the face of exactly one person. Thus there exists a mapping $M : V \mapsto id$, where id is one identity in the set of M identities $I = \{id_1, ..., id_M\}$.

If the scenario of forensic analysis must be matched to one of the two previously defined scenarios, it can be understood as identification task (Fig. 2.1(a)). For each video in the database C, it must be checked, if it contains the requested person: $M(V_b) \stackrel{?}{=} id_{wanted}$ However, a threshold is necessary to generate the binary answer for each database video.

A different approach to look at the task of forensic analysis is the way of information retrieval. Given a large database of information, in this case video data C, a specific information should be found by some query information (Fig. 2.1(b)). Here, the wanted information R are all videos showing the specified identity from the query: $R = \{V_b \in C | M(V_b) = id_{wanted}\}$. By defining the problem like this, a binary decision can be avoided, and the usage of a threshold is obsolete. Instead, it is sufficient to rate the likelihood for each video in the database that it shows the specified identity. This results in a sorted list of the database videos with the most similar ones to the query pattern at the top of the list.

It should be noted, that the perception as information retrieval task is different from the recognition scenario. In recognition, a gallery G contains a well defined

(a)   (b)

Figure 2.1: Green boxes represent database videos and the blue box represents a reference video. (a) Identification performs an identification task for each database sample video to the reference video. (b) Retrieval poses one search request to the database with the reference video as search pattern.

and previously built set of data where the identity for each entry is clear. This means that the mapping $M : G \rightarrow I$ is known and used to categorize the videos by identity. For the database C in the presented scenario this is not true. There might be several videos V_i of one identity id_m in the database. But the information that the V_i belong together does not exist.

Considering the forensic analysis as information retrieval task, the respective performance measures can be used. As measure to rate the ranked result the average precision is used:

$$a = \sum_{k=1}^{B} p(k) \cdot \Delta r(k),$$

with the precision $p(k)$ at rank k and the difference for the recall $\Delta r(k)$ from rank $k-1$ to k: $\Delta r(k) = r(k) - r(k-1)$. Recall r and precision p result from the amount of true positives tp, false positives fp and false negatives fn up to rank k:

$$p(k) = \frac{tp(k)}{tp(k) + fp(k)},$$
$$r(k) = \frac{tp(k)}{tp(k) + fn(k)}.$$

It is $0 \leq a \leq 1$ for the average precision a. For $a = 1$ all relevant videos in the database, which show the wanted identity, are ranked at the topmost positions. The lower the relevant matches are ranked, the lower the average precision becomes. An important feature of the average precision is that it does not just represent the best match, but the whole ranking. Therefore, a relevant match at rank two in the list yields a better score than one at rank three. But both contribute to the score. This procedure fits our scenario of forensic analysis. Usually, the results will be

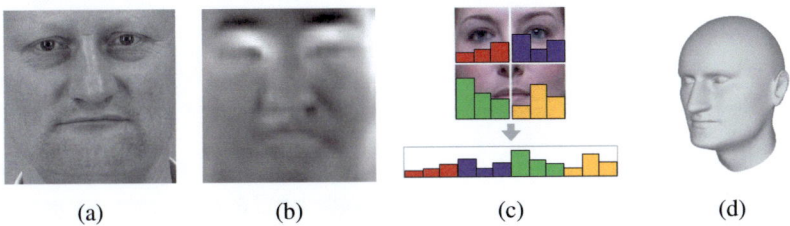

| (a) | (b) | (c) | (d) |

Figure 3.1: Different ways of representing a face: (a) intensity image, (b) in a subspace, (c) by local features, (d) 3D-model.

inspected by humans at the end. In this case two aspects are relevant. First, it is not sufficient to sort only one correct match to the top of the list, but as many as possible. Secondly, it is not a severe problem if a few wrong videos appear between the correct ones.

Building the mean out of N queries to the database, results in the mean average precision map:

$$map = \frac{1}{N} \sum_{i=1}^{N} a_i.$$

3 Face Model

Face recognition for videos can be split into two steps: modeling of the face and modeling of the temporal sequence. First, in this section the face modeling will be examined (step 3 in Fig. 1.2). This means to model the single frames f_j in a video V. In the next section the modeling of the sequence V as a collection of frames is discussed (step 4 in Fig. 1.2).

While there exists a large variety of possibilities to describe objects in images, a clear amount has established itself in the field of face recognition. The initial step is a brief discussion of the established approaches. The main concepts to describe a face in an image [LJ11] are presented in the following list and in Fig. 3.1:

- *Intensity image* – The intensity image of the face taken by the camera is used as face descriptor. This was already denoted as f before (Fig. 3.1(a)).

- *Subspace methods* – The intensity face image is projected into a pre-trained face subspace. The well-known Eigenfaces [TP91] and Fisher-faces [BHK97] approaches work this way. They use a PCA or an LDA respectively for the projection (Fig. 3.1(b)).

- *Local features* – The face is divided into several local patches. For each patch, features like Local Binary Patterns or Gabor features are extracted [ZJN07]. The combination of the patch features yields the face model (Fig. 3.1(c)).

- *Model based* – The face is represented by a 3D-model. An individual face model can be generated out of a 2D-image [BV03] (Fig. 3.1(d)).

The resulting model for a frame f will be denoted as $\tilde{f}$. Approximately, the complexity of the approaches increases from the top to the bottom of the list. With increasing complexity the necessary processing time increases as well. The processing time ranges from practically none for the intensity image, because $\tilde{f} = f$, to several seconds for the generation of an individual 3D-model for a specific face.

4   Sequence Model

Modeling a sequence of face images allows the step from still image face recognition to face recognition in video. Obviously, a sequence $\tilde{V}$ of face models $\tilde{f}_j$ contains more information than a single model, provided that the same image acquisition system is used. However, usually video data is of much worse quality than still image data. The loss of quality for video data mostly comes from lower resolution and a less constrained environment. Common techniques to create a sequence model $\overline{V}$ are:

- *Best shot* – The quality of each frame $\tilde{f}_j$ in the sequence is rated with respect to the face recognition task. The frame which seems suitable best for the recognition is selected: $\overline{V} = \tilde{f}_{best}$. This way, the task is reduced to still image face recognition.

- *Set of frames* – The frames of one video are interpreted as a set of vectors: $\overline{V} = \{\tilde{f}_j | j = 1..F\}$. Thus, comparing two videos means to compare two sets of vectors. An analysis for the most basic similarity measures was performed in [CMH$^+$11], showing that the Nearest Neighbor Distance seems to be the best.

- *Linear subspace* – All frames of a sequence together build a subspace in the image space. This subspace could be modeled, for example, by the affine or convex hull [CT10]. The Mutual Subspace Method (MSM) [YFM98, FY05] is the most basic one of the approaches. The similarity between subspaces in this case is measured by the principle angle between them.

- *Manifold* – Instead of assuming a linear subspace, the sequence is modeled as a nonlinear manifold. A big variety of manifold models and comparison approaches have been tested: e.g. LLE [HP09], Isomap [Yan02] or kernel based methods [CT10, SM11]. However, their high flexibility brings the risk of overfitting the data.

- *Probabilistic* – Two approaches fall in this category: distribution based and test based. In the first, a distribution of the frames in some space is determined and the similarity between videos is rated by standard distribution distances [ZC06]. The second possibility consists of drawing sample frames from the videos to test the identity hypothesis [DLZ$^+$13].

A short complexity analysis. Two steps need computation: model generation and model comparison. Model generation is the less important part as this needs to be done only once for a video database C. However, there is typically more than one search request to the database C. Thus, comparisons should have higher priority with respect to computation time. A simple way to estimate the cost for one comparison is the dimension D of the sequence model $\overline{V}$. Let $\widetilde{d}$ denote the dimension of one frame model $\widetilde{f_j}$. Then, the dimension D for the sequence model is usually the lowest for the best shot approach $D = \widetilde{d}$. The dimension D is the highest for the set of frames and the manifold approaches $D \geq F \cdot \widetilde{d}$, where at least all frames are part of the model. The dimension D of the other approaches is typically somewhere in between.

5   Possible improvements

Typically, set of frames based sequence modeling yields the best recognition results. But it is quite slow. Two possibilities are presented to reduce the dimension of the sequence model for set of frames based approaches. The first one is to perform a vector quantization. Practically this is done by understanding the sequence $\widetilde{V}$ as a set and clustering it. For each cluster, one representative vector is kept. However, this method looses information by omitting data from further processing. For this reason, the second approach is a content based reduction of the sequence model dimension D [Her13]. Similar frames are found based on the head pose and a fused representation of them is kept in the sequence model.

Another improvement to reduce the computation time is inspired by the most well-known application for a cascade, the Viola-Jones object detector [VJ01]. The approaches are comined in a cascade. Starting with the fastest method of sufficient performance in the first stage of the cascade and ending with the slowest and best-performing method n the last stage. Each stage in the cascade can either eliminate complete videos or some frames in each video. The remaining data is processed by the next stage. Formally speaking, let C^0 denote the initial database of videos V_b^0. A stage s with input

$$C^{s-1} = \{V_1^{s-1}, \dots, V_{B^{s-1}}^{s-1}\}$$

and

$$V_b^{s-1} = (f_1^{s-1}, \dots, f_{F_b^{s-1}}^{s-1})$$

has two processing options. The first is to reduce the number of videos, leading to the output

$$C^s = \{V_i^{s-1} \mid i \in N_v, N_v \subset \{1, \dots, B^{s-1}\}\}.$$

The second possibility is to identify and remove irrelevant frames from a sequence V_b^{s-1}. Thus, the output is

$$V_b^s = (f_i^{s-1} \mid i \in N_f, N_f \subset \{1, \dots, F_b^{s-1}\}).$$

Of course, a stage s can combine both processing options. Keeping track of the removed videos in each stage allows to create a full ranked list of the videos in the database with respect to the query. The difficulty in building a good cascade is to choose the right number of stages with their corresponding parameters. One possibility is to manually define performance requirements for each stage and then search for the approach that best fulfills them. This is mentioned in the original Viola-Jones detector design. There are attempts to automatize the design of a cascade for the binary classification case [SRB04]. However, they can not be transfered in a simple way to the information retrieval case and it is unclear if this is possible at all. This leaves the manual design as the only design option at the moment.

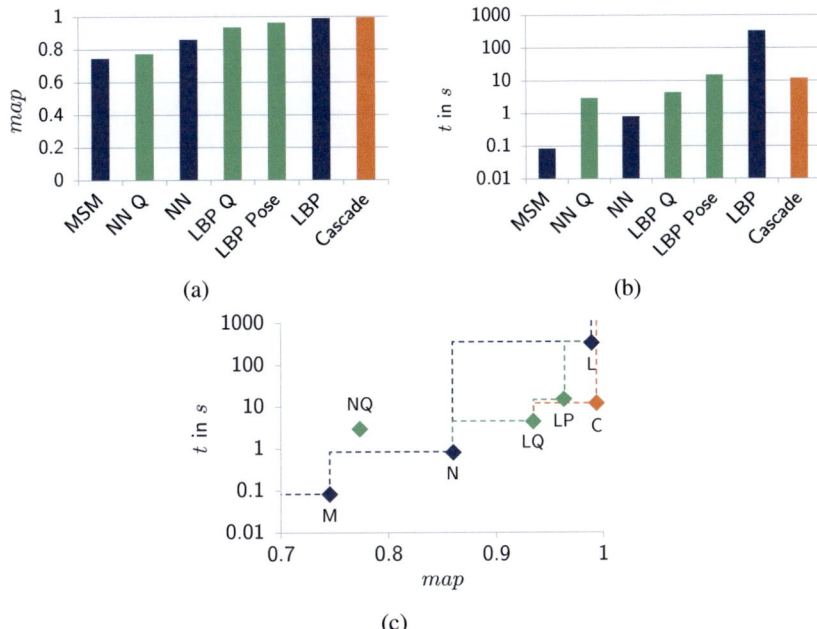

(a)

(b)

(c)

Figure 6.1: Comparison of different approaches. Basic approaches are blue, the ones using dimension reduction are green and the cascade approach is brown. The 'Q' denotes simple vector quantization and 'Pose' the content based dimension reduction. (a) mean average precision map, (b) average query time t and (c) comparison of map and t. Pay attention to the logarithmic scale of the time axis.

6   Evaluation

For evaluation, the combined Honda/UCSD dataset [LHYK03, LHYK05] is used. Face images are downscaled to 32 × 32 pixels. The dataset contains 92 videos of 35 persons. The evaluation was done using the leave-one-out strategy. This means to use one video as query and the remaining 91 as database. The mean average precision map is based on all 92 possible queries. The measured query time t consists of the actual time necessary for the database search t_s and the necessary time to prepare the query video t_p: $t = t_p + t_s$. It contains the whole time which is needed for one search in the database. In real world scenarios, the query video is usually not in the database and therefore not preprocessed. Thus, the time t_p to build the sequence model for the query video needs to be included.

Fig. 6.1 shows the measured results. As basic approaches, MSM with intensity images (MSM), nearest neighbor with intensity images (NN) and nearest neighbor with local binary patterns (LBP) were chosen. The three methods show the expected behavior: MSM being the fastest, but worst, LBP being the slowest, but best and NN in the middle. As can be seen in Fig. 6.1(c) all three have the right to exist because higher computation time correlates with higher recognition performance. Which one should be used depends on the processing time limits. Better approaches compared to the basic ones, would be below the dashed line, worse ones above. The better an approach is, reaching a high map in a small time t, the more to the lower right corner of the diagram it would be located.

Improving the set of frames based nearest neighbor method by quantization makes LBP faster (LBP Q), but not NN (NN Q). This is because the quantization time t_p of the query video is higher than the whole query time t for the pure NN. So NN Q is a useless approach. However, LBP Q is located between NN and LBP, both in terms of map and t. The head pose based dimension reduction of LBP (LBP Pose) yields better search results than LBP Q, but needs a little more processing time. At the end, it is located between LBP Q and pure LBP.

Finally, a cascade of the three basic approaches is considered. It uses MSM in the first, NN in the second and LBP in the last stage. The optimization of the cascade results in the following process: MSM sorts out about 30 percent of the videos, NN sorts out about 90 percent of the frames in each of the remaining videos and LBP is performed on the rest. This means that the LBP stage only has to process about 7 percent of the original data. The results show that the cascade approach renders the LBP Pose and the pure LBP approach useless as it is faster and yields a better map than both.

It should be noted, that all presented methods allow querying faster than real time. Each video in the dataset lasts about 10 seconds, making a total playtime of about 900 seconds. Even the slowest approach needs less than 400 seconds for one query.

7 Conclusion

A thorough analysis of basic face recognition techniques was given with respect to the scenario of forensic analysis. The mutual subspace method proved to be the fastest basic solution showing an acceptable performance. The best basic solution with respect to recognition performance uses the Local Binary Patterns. Several improvements to reduce the processing time were presented and evaluated. The most promising solution seems to be a cascade of basic face recognition techniques. The manual design of the cascade might be a drawback but also allows for situation specific adaptation. Altogether, the cascade achieved the highest recognition performance on the evaluated dataset while needing less computation time than most of the other approaches.

Bibliography

[BHK97]   P.N. Belhumeur, J.P. Hespanha, and D.J. Kriegman. Eigenfaces vs. fisherfaces: Recognition using class specific linear projection. *IEEE Transactions on Pattern Analysis and Machine Intelligence*, 19(7):711–720, 1997.

[BV03]   V. Blanz and T. Vetter. Face recognition based on fitting a 3d morphable model. *IEEE Transactions on Pattern Analysis and Machine Intelligence*, 25(9):1063–1074, 2003.

[CMH+11]   Shaokang Chen, Sandra Mau, Mehrtash T. Harandi, Conrad Sanderson, Abbas Bigdeli, and Brian C. Lovell. Face recognition from still images to video sequences: A local-feature-based framework. *EURASIP Journal on Image and Video Processing*, 2011, 2011.

[CT10]   H. Cevikalp and B. Triggs. Face recognition based on image sets. In *IEEE Conference on Computer Vision and Pattern Recognition*, pages 2567–2573. IEEE, 2010.

[DLZ+13]   Sihao Ding, Ying Li, Junda Zhu, Yuan F Zheng, and Dong Xuan. Robust video-based face recognition by sequential sample consensus. In *Advanced Video and Signal Based Surveillance (AVSS), 2013 10th IEEE International Conference on*, pages 336–341. IEEE, 2013.

[FY05]   K. Fukui and O. Yamaguchi. Face recognition using multi-viewpoint patterns for robot vision. *Robotics Research*, pages 192–201, 2005.

[Her13]   Christian Herrmann. Extending a local matching face recognition approach to low-resolution video. In *Advanced Video and Signal Based Surveillance (AVSS), 2013 10th IEEE International Conference on*, pages 460–465, 2013.

[HP09]   A. Hadid and M. Pietikäinen. Manifold learning for video-to-video face recognition. *Biometric ID Management and Multimodal Communication*, pages 9–16, 2009.

[LHYK03]   K.C. Lee, J. Ho, M.H. Yang, and D. Kriegman. Video-based face recognition using probabilistic appearance manifolds. *IEEE Conf. On Computer Vision and Pattern Recognition*, 1:313–320, 2003.

[LHYK05]   K.C. Lee, J. Ho, M.H. Yang, and D. Kriegman. Visual tracking and recognition using probabilistic appearance manifolds. *Computer Vision and Image Understanding*, 99(3):303–331, 2005.

[LJ11]   Stan Z. Li and Anil K. Jain. Introduction. *Handbook of Face Recognition*, pages 1–18, 2011.

[PGM11]   P. Jonathon Phillips, Patrick Grother, and Ross Micheals. Evaluation methods in face recognition. *Handbook of Face Recognition*, pages 551–574, 2011.

[SM11]   G. Shakhnarovich and B. Moghaddam. Face recognition in subspaces. *Handbook of Face Recognition*, pages 19–49, 2011.

[SRB04]   Jie Sun, James M Rehg, and Aaron Bobick. Automatic cascade training with perturbation bias. In *Computer Vision and Pattern Recognition, 2004. CVPR 2004. Proceedings of the 2004 IEEE Computer Society Conference on*, volume 2, pages II–276. IEEE, 2004.

[TP91]   M. Turk and A. Pentland. Eigenfaces for recognition. *Journal of cognitive neuroscience*, 3(1):71–86, 1991.

[VJ01]   Paul Viola and Michael Jones. Rapid object detection using a boosted cascade of simple features. In *IEEE Computer Society Conference on Computer Vision and Pattern Recognition, 2001. CVPR 2001*, volume 1, pages I–511. IEEE, 2001.

[Yan02]   M.H. Yang. Face recognition using extended isomap. In *International Conference on Image Processing. 2002*, volume 2, pages II–117. IEEE, 2002.

[YFM98]   O. Yamaguchi, K. Fukui, and K. Maeda. Face recognition using temporal image sequence. In *Third IEEE International Conference on Automatic Face and Gesture Recognition, 1998*, pages 318–323. IEEE, 1998.

[ZC06]   Shaohua Kevin Zhou and Rama Chellappa. From sample similarity to ensemble similarity: Probabilistic distance measures in reproducing kernel hilbert space. *IEEE Transactions on Pattern Analysis and Machine Intelligence*, 28(6):917–929, 2006.

[ZJN07]   Jie Zou, Qiang Ji, and George Nagy. A comparative study of local matching approach for face recognition. *IEEE Transactions on Image Processing*, 16(10):2617–2628, 2007.

Quantification of Uncertainties in a Distributed Parameter System using the Generalized Polynomial Chaos Expansion

Chettapong Janya-anurak

Vision and Fusion Laboratory
Institute for Anthropomatics
Karlsruhe Institute of Technology (KIT), Germany
janya@ies.uni-karlsruhe.de

Technical Report IES-2013-03

Abstract:
In many fields, active research is currently focused on quantification and simulation of model uncertainties. The latter are often described probabilistically, allowing for the accurate and detailed answers but necessitating extensive computations. Recently, the generalized polynomial chaos expansion (gPCE) has been proposed as an efficient approach to stochastic computing. In this report, we introduce the mathematical background of gPCE applied to a system described with partial differential equations (PDEs). The potential further benefits of gPCE are discussed and illustrated with synthetic examples.

1 Introduction

Nowadays the computer simulation based on mathematical models is commonly applied in every branch of natural science and engineering disciplines. These mathematical models are derived from physical laws in form of mathematical equations. However, due to the lack of knowledge and the inherent variability, there are always some deviations between the real measurement and the predicted value from a model. These can be considered as uncertainties in the model. The simulation of a mathematical model under considering the model uncertainties is an active research topic in many fields.

It is discussed in [Mat07] that the uncertainties can be described or quantified using different mathematical theories, such as fuzzy theory, evidence theory or stochastic theory. Expressing the uncertainties with a stochastic approach allows the mathematically most detailed description, hence it is widely applied in many areas. Nevertheless the intensive computation of a stochastic problem is still the major disadvantage of this approach.

In the last few years the generalized polynomial chaos expansion (gPC) has been proposed as an efficient methodology in the computing ot the uncertainties quantification. It is an extension of the original polynomial chaos expansion (PCE) proposed by Wiener in 1938 [Wie38]. The original Wiener's polynomial chaos employs *Hermite* polynomial to represent *Gaussian* random processes. The gPC extends the PCE towards some parametric statistical non-Gaussian distributions, based on the Askey scheme of orthogonal polynomials.

The adoptions of gPC in many stochastic problems were examined, for example, in the uncertainties propagation in PDE [XK04], in the calculation of Sobol's indices for the sensitivity analysis [CLMM09],[Sud08] and in Bayesian inference in inverse problem [Xiu10]. It was shown that the computational cost of gPC is, in many cases, lower compared to classical Monte Carlo methods.

In this technical report, we introduce the gPC and its application to the uncertainty quantification problem, both forward and inverse, especially for distributed parameter system. This report is organized as follows: In the section 2, the mathematical background for the gPC is described. The section 3 illustrates the application of gPC to the uncertainty quantification problem by means of examples. Conclusions and the directions of future works are presented in the section 4.

2 Uncertainty quantification with gPC

In 1938, Norbert Wiener introduced the *Polynomial Chaos* to represent the Gaussian processes by using a series of Hermite polynomials [Wie38]. Ghanem and Spanos applied the original PCE to quantify the uncertainty in solid mechanics systems by employing the PCE to the Finite-Element discretization [GS03]. Xiu and Karniadakis extended the PCE to some parametric non-Gaussian random processes [XK02] and named it *generalized Polynomial Chaos*. This section will introduce the basic concept of gPC and its application to the uncertainty propagation task.

2.1 Generalized Polynomial Chaos expansion

Consider an arbitrary real-valued random variable $Y = Y(\omega)$ according to some probability space $(\Omega, \mathcal{F}, \mathcal{P})$, with sample space Ω, σ-algebra $\mathcal{F}$, and probability measure $\mathcal{P}$. In addition, it is assumed that $Y(\omega)$ is square-integrable, i.e., $y \in L_2(\Omega) = \{y : \mathbb{E}(y^2) < \infty\}$, where

$$\mathbb{E}(Y) = \int_\Omega Y \, d\mathcal{P}$$

denotes the expectation of Y. Let $\xi(\omega)$ be another random variable with known probability distribution $p(\xi)$. In the Polynomial Chaos (PC) framework, the random variable Y is represented as a function of the random variable with known distribution ξ as:

$$Y(\omega) = f(\xi(\omega)) \tag{2.1}$$

Then the function $f(\xi)$ is expanded in a polynomial series of the random variable. The original polynomial chaos expansion (PCE), introduced by Norbert Wiener in [Wie38], decomposes the random variable Y by using Hermite polynomial series of Gaussian random variable as orthogonal basis.

$$Y(\omega) = f(\zeta(\omega)) = \sum_{k=0}^{\infty} a_k H_k(\zeta(\omega))$$

where $H_k(\zeta(\omega))$ denotes the Hermite polynomial of order k in term of normalized Gaussian random variables $\zeta(\omega)$. This expansion can be extended to the multivariate case. Given $\boldsymbol{\zeta}(\omega) = (\zeta_1, \zeta_2, \ldots, \zeta_d)$ a set of centered, normalized and mutually orthogonal Gaussian random variables, the PC expansion of random variable Y in the multivariate case yields:

$$Y(\omega) = a_0 H_0 + \sum_{i_1=1}^{\infty} a_{i_1} H_1\left(\zeta_{i_1}(\omega)\right) + \sum_{i_1=1}^{\infty} \sum_{i_2=1}^{i_1} a_{i_1 i_2} H_2\left(\zeta_{i_1}(\omega), \zeta_{i_2}(\omega)\right)$$

$$+ \sum_{i_1=1}^{\infty} \sum_{i_2=1}^{i_1} \sum_{i_3=1}^{i_2} a_{i_1 i_2 i_3} H_3\left(\zeta_{i_1}(\omega), \zeta_{i_2}(\omega), \zeta_{i_3}(\omega)\right) + \ldots$$

Cameron and Martin proved in [CM47] that the expression is convergent in the L_2-sense. Being a spectral polynomial expansion this expansion has an exponential convergent rate. However for non-Gaussian random variables, the expansion may exhibit low convergence rates and thus require a large number of truncation order. Therefore Xiu and Karniadakis [XK02] employed the Askey-scheme to generalize the original Wiener's PCE to some common non-Gaussian measure, which replaces the Hermite polynomial $\{H_k\}$ by other polynomials, denoted by $\{G_k\}$.

To distinguish between the original Hermite Chaos we use the notation $\xi(\omega) = (\xi_1, \xi_2, \ldots, \xi_d)$ for non-Gaussian random variables, with a known joint density $p(\xi) = \prod p_i(\xi_i)$. The Table 2.1 shows the correspondences between the distribution of the random variable and orthogonal polynomial family. The multivariate PC can be generalized to:

$$Y(\omega) = a_0 G_0 + \sum_{i_1=1}^{\infty} a_{i_1} G_1\left(\xi_{i_1}(\omega)\right) + \sum_{i_1=1}^{\infty} \sum_{i_2=1}^{i_1} a_{i_1 i_2} G_2\left(\xi_{i_1}(\omega), \xi_{i_2}(\omega)\right)$$
$$+ \sum_{i_1=1}^{\infty} \sum_{i_2=1}^{i_1} \sum_{i_3=1}^{i_2} a_{i_1 i_2 i_3} G_3\left(\xi_{i_1}(\omega), \xi_{i_2}(\omega), \xi_{i_3}(\omega)\right) + \ldots$$

In order to simplify the notation, we define a relation between functional $G()$ and the new functional $\Psi()$ by using multi-index notation $\underline{i} = (i_1, i_2, \ldots, i_d)$ with $|\underline{i}| = \sum_{\alpha=1}^{d} i_\alpha$ and rewrite the expansion as

$$Y(\omega) = \sum_{|\underline{i}|=0}^{\infty} \beta_{\underline{i}} \Psi_{\underline{i}}(\xi_1, \xi_2, \ldots, \xi_d) \tag{2.2}$$

Although the multi-index formulation is very clear, the single index is preferable to express the gPC expansion. The multi-index can be converted to the single index version, to do this the lexicographic ordering is the most widely adopted method. Using single index k the equation (2.2) is rewritten as

	Distribution	$p(\xi)$	gPC basis polynomials $\Psi(\xi)$	Support
Continuous	Gaussian		Hermite	$(-\infty, \infty)$
	Gamma		Laguerre	$[0, \infty)$
	Beta		Jacobi	$[a,b]$
	Uniform		Legendre	$[a,b]$
Discrete	Poisson		Chalier	$\{0,1,2,\ldots\}$
	Binomial		Krawtchouk	$\{0,1,2,\ldots,N\}$
	Negative binomial		Meixner	$\{0,1,2,\ldots\}$
	Hypergeometric		Hanh	$\{0,1,2,\ldots,N\}$

Table 2.1: Askey-Chaos corresponding to certain types of probability distributions

$$Y(\omega) = \sum_{k=0}^{\infty} \beta_k \Psi_k(\xi_1, \xi_2, \ldots, \xi_d)$$

where β_k are the deterministic expansion coefficients, and Ψ_k are polynomials, orthogonal in the L_2-space with regard to the inner product.

$$\langle \Psi_i, \Psi_j \rangle \equiv \int \Psi_j(\boldsymbol{\xi}) \Psi_i(\boldsymbol{\xi}) p(\boldsymbol{\xi}) d\boldsymbol{\xi} = \delta_{ij} \langle \Psi_i, \Psi_i \rangle$$

For practical reasons, this expansion is normally truncated to finite dimensions. Denoting N the order of the gPC expansion and $\{\phi_i\}_{i=0}^{N}$ the one-dimensional orthogonal polynomials degree up to order N from the Askey scheme, the multi-dimensional gPC basis $\Psi_{\underline{i}}$ is constructed by tensor products of the corresponding one-dimensional polynomials

$$\Psi_{\underline{i}}(\xi_1, \xi_2, \ldots, \xi_d) = \phi_{i_1}(\xi_1) \cdots \phi_{i_d}(\xi_d), 0 \le |\underline{i}| \le N$$

The finite dimensional decomposition of $Y(\omega)$ in the single-index form is

$$Y(\omega) \approx \sum_{k=0}^{P} \beta_k \Psi_k(\boldsymbol{\xi}(\omega))$$

where the basis dimension P is related to the dimension of the multivariate random variable d and the polynomial order N by the relation $P + 1 = \frac{(N+d)!}{N!d!}$.

2.2   Uncertainty Propagation

As shown in our previous works [JaBB11] and [Ja12], we focus on the uncertainty quantification of distributed parameter systems. Considering a distributed parameter system with the model $y = f(\boldsymbol{x}, t|\theta)$, where $\boldsymbol{x}$ denotes the spatial coordinate, t denotes time and θ is vector of parameters in the model. The uncertainties of the model are described by representing θ as random variable. For simplification θ is expressed by using a finite set of d independent random variables $\boldsymbol{\xi} = (\xi_1, \ldots, \xi_d)$ with a given joint probability density $p(\boldsymbol{\xi})$. Hence the output y is a functional of the random variable input and can be written in the form

$$y = f(\boldsymbol{x}, t, \boldsymbol{\xi}) \tag{2.3}$$

The uncertainty propagation is the studying of the response of the model outputs from the given probability distribution of the inputs. The targets of the uncertainty propagation analysis are normally:

1. Evaluating the reliability of the outputs.

2. Evaluating the statistical value as low-order moments of the outputs.

3. Assessing the complete probability distribution of the outputs.

Many probabilistic approaches are proposed to resolve these issues. For instance, most probable point-based methods such as first-order reliability method (FORM) or second-order reliability method (SORM) are used to evaluate the reliability. The simulation-based methods such as Monte-Carlo are generally adopted for the second and the third issues. Usually the calculation of the model outputs $f(x, t, \xi)$ for all samples from the distribution $p(\xi)$ can only be achieved with high computational effort. The PCE offers an efficient way to approximate the probability distribution and the moments of the outputs.

Formulation (2.3) is identical to equation (2.1) and therefore can be expanded with the PCE in form

$$y = \sum_{k=0}^{\infty} \beta_k(x, t)\Psi_k(\xi(\omega)) \approx \sum_{k=0}^{P} \beta_k(x, t)\Psi_k(\xi(\omega)) = y_P \qquad (2.4)$$

The advantage of PCE is the separation between the deterministic space and the stochastic space. The probability distribution $p(Y)$ is approximated by running the Monte Carlo with equation (2.4) as surrogate model. The PC model needs less effort than complete model. The statistical moments such as mean and variance are immediately calculated from gPC coefficients as shown in equation (2.5) and (2.6).

$$\mathbb{E}(y) = \mathbb{E}\left(\sum_{k=0}^{\infty} \beta_k\Psi_k(\xi(\omega))\right) \qquad (2.5)$$

$$= \sum_{k=0}^{\infty} \beta_k\mathbb{E}(\Psi_k(\xi(\omega)) \cdot 1)$$

$$= \sum_{k=0}^{\infty} \beta_k\mathbb{E}(\Psi_k(\xi(\omega)) \cdot \Psi_0)$$

$$\bar{y} = \beta_0$$

$$\sigma^2 = \mathbb{E}\left[(y(\boldsymbol{\xi}) - \bar{y})^2\right] \approx \mathbb{E}\left[(y_P(\boldsymbol{\xi}) - \bar{y})^2\right] \tag{2.6}$$

$$= \mathbb{E}\left[\left(\sum_{k=0}^{P} \beta_k \Psi_k(\boldsymbol{\xi}) - \beta_0\right)\left(\sum_{k=0}^{P} \beta_k \Psi_k(\boldsymbol{\xi}) - \beta_0\right)\right]$$

$$= \mathbb{E}\left[\left(\sum_{k=1}^{P} \beta_k \Psi_k(\boldsymbol{\xi})\right)\left(\sum_{k=1}^{P} \beta_k \Psi_k(\boldsymbol{\xi})\right)\right]$$

$$= \sum_{k=1}^{P}\sum_{l=1}^{P} \beta_k \beta_l \, \mathbb{E}\left[\Psi_k(\boldsymbol{\xi}) \cdot \Psi_l(\boldsymbol{\xi})\right]$$

$$\sigma^2 \approx \sum_{k=1}^{P} \beta_k^2 \, \|\Psi_k\|^2$$

2.3 Determination of PC coefficients

Since the gPC coefficients β_k characterize the process Y, we thus need the procedure to determine the gPC coefficients. In the community, three important approaches are proposed for the determination of the gPC coefficients, which are classified in an intrusive and a non-intrusive method. These three approaches are Galerkin projection, least square approximation and non-intrusive spectral projection (NISP). For the distributed parameter system, model (2.3) is generally described with differential equations governing the evolution. Solving the system of PDE with Finite Element method, formulation of equation (2.3) in the implicit form is preferable.

$$\mathcal{M}\left(y(\boldsymbol{x}, t), \boldsymbol{\xi}\right) = 0 \tag{2.7}$$

2.3.1 Galerkin Projection

Substituting the PCE expression with truncated order P (eq. (2.4)) to y in equation (2.7), the model equation is not satisfied anymore, but yields a residual. The residual has to be orthogonal to the space of expansion basis functions. It yields:

$$\left\langle \mathcal{M}\left(\sum_{k=0}^{P} \beta_k(\boldsymbol{x}, t)\Psi_k, \boldsymbol{\xi}\right), \Psi_k \right\rangle = 0, \qquad k = 0, \ldots, P$$

The Galerkin projection lead to a set of $P + 1$ coupled problems. It usually requires modification of the existing numerical code. If the model is complex, the Galerkin procedure can be difficult to implement and also not practical in general. To overcome the difficulties, in practice non-intrusive method (sometimes called collocation method as well) is applied more.

2.3.2 Least square approximation method

The gPC coefficients can be estimated by using regression method. Denoting $\left\{ \boldsymbol{\xi}^{(i)} \right\}$ a sample set of the random variables and $\boldsymbol{y} = \left\{ y^{(i)} \right\}$ the corresponding set of model output, so that it follows:

$$\mathcal{M}\left(y^{(i)}, \boldsymbol{\xi}^{(i)} \right) = 0, \ \forall i$$

Let us denote $\boldsymbol{\beta} = (\beta_0, \ldots, \beta_P)^T$ the vector of sought PC coefficients in the truncated expansion of the output y. Based on the sample set $\left\{ \boldsymbol{\xi}^{(i)} \right\}_{i=1}^n$ the optimal approximation $\hat{\boldsymbol{\beta}}$ of $\boldsymbol{\beta}$ can be obtained by solving the least squares problem

$$\hat{\boldsymbol{\beta}} = \arg\min_{\boldsymbol{\beta}} \sum_{i=1}^n \left(y^{(i)} - \sum_{k=0}^P \beta_k \Psi_k(\boldsymbol{\xi}^{(i)}) \right)^2 \qquad (2.8)$$

The well-known solution of the least square problem (2.8) is

$$\hat{\boldsymbol{\beta}} = \left(Z^T Z \right)^{-1} Z^T \boldsymbol{y},$$

where

$$Z = \begin{pmatrix} \Psi_0(\boldsymbol{\xi}^{(1)}) & \Psi_1(\boldsymbol{\xi}^{(1)}) & \cdots & \Psi_P(\boldsymbol{\xi}^{(1)}) \\ \Psi_0(\boldsymbol{\xi}^{(2)}) & \Psi_1(\boldsymbol{\xi}^{(2)}) & \cdots & \Psi_P(\boldsymbol{\xi}^{(2)}) \\ \vdots & \vdots & \ddots & \vdots \\ \Psi_0(\boldsymbol{\xi}^{(n)}) & \Psi_1(\boldsymbol{\xi}^{(n)}) & \cdots & \Psi_P(\boldsymbol{\xi}^{(n)}) \end{pmatrix}.$$

The sample set can be constructed by sample random sampling, Latin hypercube sampling etc. The methods from statistical learning are also applied to avoid the overfitting. For the d-dimensional multivariate random variable, an empirical rule for the optimal number of regression points is $n = P \cdot (d - 1)$ [Sud08].

2.3.3 Non-intrusive spectral projection (NISP)

On the contrary of the projection the residual to governing equation as Galerkin projection, the non-intrusive spectral projection (NISP) exploits the orthogonality of the gPC basis by projection to sampled model output, by taking the inner product of the output PC expansion with orthogonal polynomial Ψ_k

$$\langle y(\boldsymbol{\xi}), \Psi_k \rangle = \left\langle \sum_{k=0}^{P} \beta_k(\boldsymbol{x}, t)\Psi_k(\boldsymbol{\xi}), \Psi_k(\boldsymbol{\xi}) \right\rangle,$$

where the definition of inner product is:

$$\langle f(\boldsymbol{\xi}), g(\boldsymbol{\xi}) \rangle = \int_{\Omega^d} f(\boldsymbol{\xi})g(\boldsymbol{\xi})p(\boldsymbol{\xi})d\boldsymbol{\xi}.$$

Using the orthogonality property, it yields

$$\beta_k = \frac{\langle y(\boldsymbol{\xi}), \Psi_k(\boldsymbol{\xi}) \rangle}{\langle \Psi_k(\boldsymbol{\xi}), \Psi_k(\boldsymbol{\xi}) \rangle} = \frac{\langle y(\boldsymbol{\xi}), \Psi_k(\boldsymbol{\xi}) \rangle}{\|\Psi_k(\boldsymbol{\xi})\|^2}.$$

Thanks to the polynomial character of the Ψ_k, the inner product $\langle \Psi_k(\boldsymbol{\xi}), \Psi_k(\boldsymbol{\xi}) \rangle = \|\Psi_k(\boldsymbol{\xi})\|^2$ can be evaluated exactly. The determination of the PC coefficients is also the evaluation of $d-$dimensional integrals:

$$I_k \equiv \int_{\Omega^d} y(\boldsymbol{\xi})\Psi_k(\boldsymbol{\xi})p(\boldsymbol{\xi})d\boldsymbol{\xi} \qquad (2.9)$$

for $k = 0 \ldots k$, which is usually computed numerically. The numerical integration is the approximation of the equation (2.9) and has a generic form:

$$I_k \approx \sum_{i=1}^{n} y(\boldsymbol{\xi}^{(i)})\Psi_k(\boldsymbol{\xi}^{(i)})w^{(i)}$$

where $\boldsymbol{\xi}^{(i)}$, $w^{(i)}$ are the integration points and their corresponding weight, while n is the number of integration points. Numerical multi-dimensional integration can be found in many fields and various methods have been proposed. The integration methods possess specific advantages and disadvantages to be taken into account when selecting one of them. Some of the common integration methods are for example Monte-Carlo Sampling, Quasi-Monte-Carlo Sampling, Tensorization of one-dimensional quadrature formula and Cubature formula based on Smolyak's formula.

3   Numerical example

To illustrate the potential of gPC in the uncertainty quantification task, we select examples from Xiu's papers [XK04] and [MX09]. For studying the uncertainty quantification of distributed parameters system, we consider the initial boundary value problem (IBVP) of viscous Burgers' equation:

$$\frac{\partial u}{\partial t} + u\frac{\partial u}{\partial x} = \nu\frac{\partial^2 u}{\partial x^2}, \qquad x \in (-1, 1) \qquad (3.1)$$
$$u(-1) = 1 + \delta, \qquad u(1) = -1$$

where u is the solution of the field, $\delta > 0$ is a small perturbation to the left boundary condition $(x = -1)$ and $\nu > 0$ is the viscosity. The variables of interest are the stationary solution at some specific point x_s at steady state.

In this technical report, two examples are presented. At first we show the computation of the forward uncertainty propagation with gPC for system with distributed parameters. Then we demonstrate the gPC approach to Bayesian inference in inverse problem to estimate the parameter.

3.1   Uncertainty propagation of PDE system

Xiu has shown the application of gPC to this viscous Burger's equation in his work [XK04]. Instead of calling a computational expensive FEM-model, the gPC is used as surrogate model to approximate the probability distribution. Using the gPC, it only needs to calculate the value of the polynomials, which need less computation compared to computationally expensive FEM-model. The main computational cost of the gPC is the determination of the gPC coefficients. In [XK04] the intrusive Galerkin projection method is used to compute the gPC coefficient (see subsection 2.3.1). The gPC coefficients in this technical report are determined using the non-intrusive spectral projection method(see subsection 2.3.3).

The computation of the integration (eq. (2.9)) is done by means of the quadrature integration. The integration points and their corresponding weights depend on the various quadrature rules. The quadrature formula is specified by the probability distribution $p(\xi)$. Table 3.1 shows the quadrature formula corresponding to the certain types of probability distributions. For univariate random variable as in this example the normal quadrature is sufficed. But in case of multivariate random variable, the sparse-grid quadrature formulation is implemented to reduce the computational cost. More information about using sparse-grid in integration can be found in [NR96].

Distribution $p(\xi)$	Domain Ω	Weight	Quadrature
Uniform	[-1,1]	1	Gauss-Legendre or Clenshaw-Curtis
Gaussian	$(-\infty,\infty)$	$e^{-\frac{(x-\alpha)^2}{\beta^2}}$	Gauss-Hermite
Gamma	$[0,\infty)$	e^{-ax}	Gauss-Laguerre
Beta	[-1,1]	$(1-x)^\alpha(1+x)^\beta$	Gauss-Jacobi

Table 3.1: Quadrature formula corresponding to certain types of probability distributions

We study the propagation of the perturbation δ at the left boundary in the viscous Burger's equation. The perturbation is considered as a random variable with the given the probability density function $p(\delta)$, which is assumed to be a uniform distribution $p(\delta) = \mathcal{U}(0,0.1)$. In this subsection we consider the solutions at the points $x_s \in \{0.6, 0.7, 0.8, 0.9\}$ as the outputs of the system.

The probability density functions of the outputs are generated from Monte-Carlo simulation. For each sampling of δ from $\mathcal{U}(0,0.1)$, the IBVP (3.1) is solved by Finite Element Method. Setting $\nu = 0.05$, the surface plot of the PDF of the solutions via Monte-Carlo is illustrated in the Figure 3.1(a) and the probability density functions of the solutions at $x = 0.6, 0.7, 0.8$ and 0.9 are shown in the figure 3.1(b).

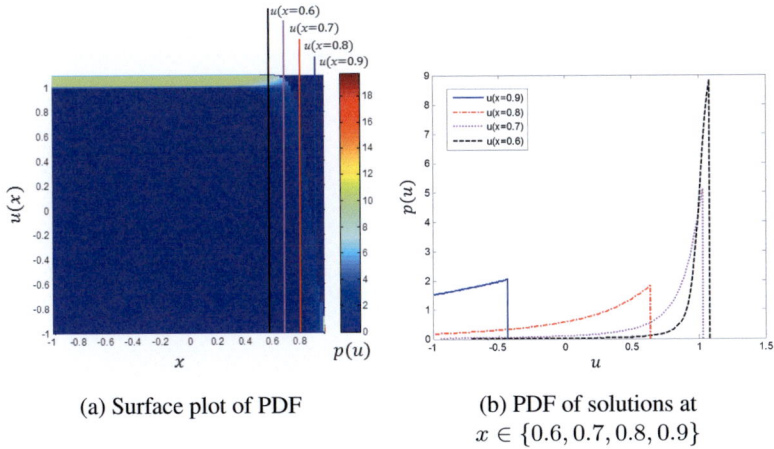

(a) Surface plot of PDF

(b) PDF of solutions at $x \in \{0.6, 0.7, 0.8, 0.9\}$

Figure 3.1: Stochastic solutions of viscous Burger's Equation by Monte Carlo

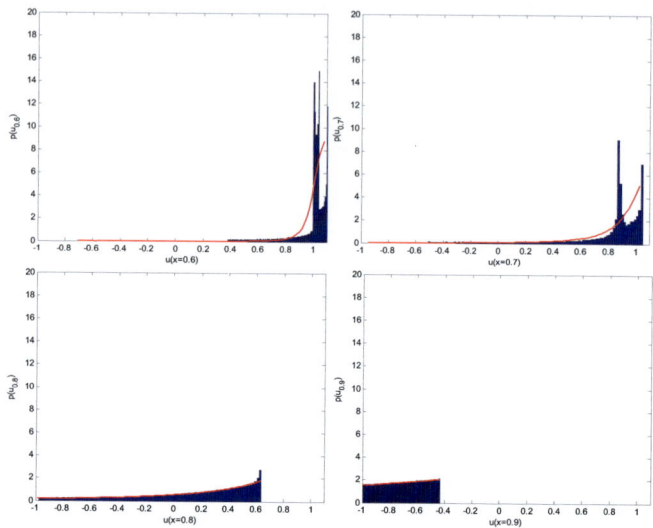

Figure 3.2: Probability density function at various locations with gPC order 4

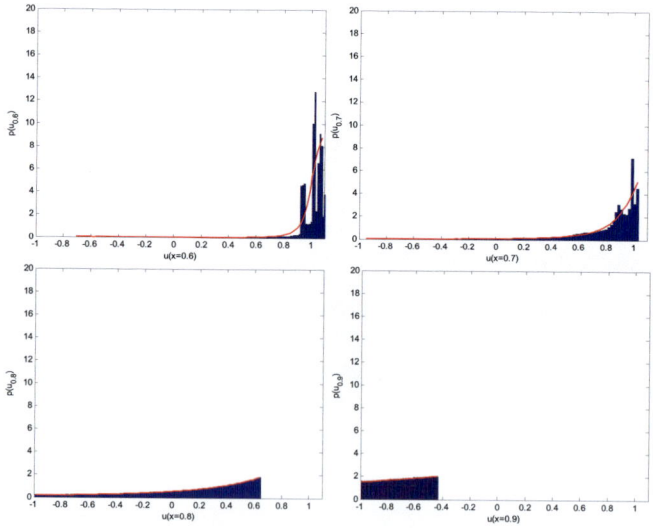

Figure 3.3: Probability density function at various location with gPC order 8

For the uniform distribution, the Legendre polynomial is used as orthogonal polynomial (see table 2.1) and the Gauss-Legendre quadrature formula is applied (see table 3.1) for integrating the equation (2.9). The approximation of the probability distributions for different orders of truncation of gPC, $N = 4$ and $N = 8$, are shown in Figure 3.2 and 3.3 respectively. For comparison the red lines indicate the probability densities calculated from the full model.

It is shown, that the gPC can approximate the PDF of the solutions at the points $x = 0.8$ and 0.9 very well. It is also obvious, that the gPC with high truncated order offer the better approximations. But it also shows the stochastic Gibbs phenomenon at the points $x = 0.6$ and 0.7 where numerical oscillations occur and they do not disappear as the truncated order increased. This numerical artifact arises from using globally smooth polynomial basis function to approximate a discontinuous function. More discussion about Gibbs phenomenon can be found in [GS97].

Despite the numerical artifacts, the gPC approch still has an advantage of computational effort. The full model had to be calculated only at some quadrature points to build the gPC coefficients, compared to Monte Carlo method that the full model had to be computed for all sample points. In this example, the gPC approach took time about 120 s compared to Monte Carlo simulation spending about 4 hours for 1000 sampling points.

3.2 gPC Approach to Bayesian Inference in Inverse Problem

In science and engineering the model parameters are commonly estimated from a given limited number of observations. Such a problem is called inverse problem, and there exist various methods for the inverse problem. The Bayesian approach to the inverse problem provides a quantitative assessment of uncertainty in the inverse solution simultaneously. Despite of many advantages, the Bayesian approach to inverse problem normally requires tremendous computational efforts. The gPC can be an effective tool to reduce the computation of the Bayesian approach as presented in [MX09].

We use our implementation to solve the example from the paper with some modification. In the last subsection, we show the application of gPC to compute the PDF of u by giving PDF of δ. For the inverse problem, our example is formulated as:

Given noisy observations y_i of the steady-state value of the solution at some specific point $u(x_s)$, what is the initial perturbation δ at the left boundary ?

The noisy observations are modeled as additive measurement noise:

$$y_i = u(x_s) + e_i, i = 1, \ldots, n_o$$

In the Bayesian setting, we seek the posterior density of δ condition on the observations y. The Bayes' rule has the form

$$\pi_{post}(\delta|y) = \frac{\pi(y|\delta)\pi_{pr}(\delta)}{\int \pi(y|\delta)\pi_{pr}(\delta)d\delta},$$

where the Likelihood is

$$\pi(y|\delta) = \prod_{i=1}^{n_o} \pi_e \left(y_i - y_m(\delta) \right).$$

In this example, the measurement noise is assumed to be Gaussian, $e_i \sim \mathcal{N}(0, \sigma^2)$, the likelihood for Gaussian noise is formulated as:

$$\pi(y|\delta) = \prod_{i=1}^{n_o} \exp \left(-\frac{1}{2\sigma^2} \|y_i - y_m(\delta)\|^2 \right).$$

In common $y_m(\delta)$ have to be computed with a full model such as FEM model, which needs a huge effort for the computation of Bayesian approach. The gPC can be adopt as surrogate model to approximate the full model as

$$y_m(\delta) \approx \tilde{y}_m(\delta) = \sum_{k=0}^{P} \beta_k \Psi_k(\delta).$$

Therefore, the approximation of the likelihood is

$$\pi(y|\delta) = \prod_{i=1}^{n_o} \exp \left(-\frac{1}{2\sigma^2} \left\| y_i - \sum_{k=0}^{P} \beta_k \Psi_k(\delta) \right\|^2 \right).$$

All parameters are exact the same as the example from the last subsection, the observations, the solution of the forward model for $\delta = 0.05$ and the observations at $x = 0.8$ with $\sigma = 0.05$, are shown in the figure 3.4(a). Assuming the prior distribution to be uniform $\pi_{pr}(\delta) = \mathcal{U}(0, 0.1)$, the gPC-approximation of the posterior distribution of δ are presented in Figure 3.4(b). For comparison, the exact posterior density is also calculated using FEM-model. The resulting densities illustrate that the approximated posterior distribution with gPC order 4 is slightly different from the exact posterior distribution with the full model. The approximation of gPC at truncated order 8 is hardly distinguishable from the exact posterior density. This can imply the convergence of the gPC-based Bayesian algorithm. More information about the convergence and the proof in the sense of Kullback-Leibler divergence can be found in [MX09].

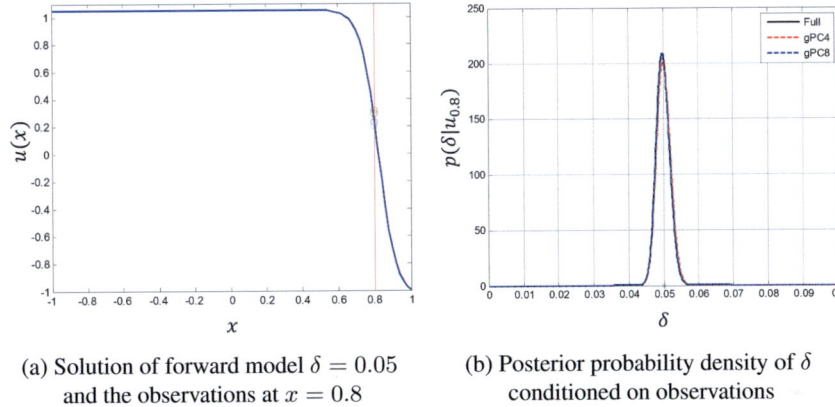

(a) Solution of forward model $\delta = 0.05$ and the observations at $x = 0.8$

(b) Posterior probability density of δ conditioned on observations

Figure 3.4: Result of gPC approach for Bayesian inference

4   Conclusion

The simulation of a mathematical model under considering the model uncertainties offers more information for model users. The stochastic approach to quantify the uncertainties is a powerful tool to analyze the system. However, solving the stochastic problems requires tremendous computational effort. The generalized polynomial chaos (gPC) expansion is proposed as an effective methodology to overcome this difficulty. In this technical report the mathematical foundations for gPC are introduced. The applications of the forward as well as inverse uncertainty quantification are discussed by means of numerical examples. It is also shown that the gPC can be used as surrogate model to approximate the full model, which causes a reduction of computation time.

Nevertheless many studys of gPC showed the application only to academic examles. Moreover the application of gPC is limited to some parametric probability density function. Recently the polynomial chaos received a data-driven generalization under the name arbitrary polynomial chaos (aPC) [ON12]. The aPC generalizes the polynomial chaos techniques towards arbitrary probability distributions from the data set. Applying the gPC to real practical cases and using the aPC to quantify the uncertainty will be the direction of our future research topic.

Bibliography

[CLMM09] Thierry Crestaux, Olivier Le Maitre, and Jean-Marc Martinez. Polynomial chaos expansion for sensitivity analysis. *Reliability Engineering & System Safety*, 94(7):1161–1172, 2009.

[CM47] R. H. Cameron and W. T. Martin. The orthogonal development of non-linear functionals in series of fourier-hermite functionals. *Annals of Mathematics*, 48(2):p 385–392, 1947.

[GS97] David Gottlieb and Chi-Wang Shu. On the gibbs phenomenon and its resolution. *SIAM review*, 39(4):644–668, 1997.

[GS03] Roger Ghanem and Pol D Spanos. *Stochastic finite elements: a spectral approach*. DoverPublications. com, 2003.

[Ja12] Chettapong Janya-anurak. Statistical inverse problem of partial differential equation: an example with stationary 1d heat conduction problem. Technical report, Vision and Fusion Laboratory, Institute for Anthropomatics, Karlsruhe Institute of Technology (KIT), Karlsruhe, 2012.

[JaBB11] Chettapong Janya-anurak, Hannes Birkhofer, and Thomas Bernard. Numerical sensitivity analysis of a complex glass forming process by means of local perturbations. In *Proceedings of COMSOL Conference*, Stuttgart, 2011.

[Mat07] Hermann G. Matthies. Quantifying uncertainty: Modern computational representation of probability and applications. In Adnan Ibrahimbegovic and Ivica Kozar, editors, *Extreme Man-Made and Natural Hazards in Dynamics of Structures*, NATO Security through Science Series, pages 105–135. Springer Netherlands, 2007.

[MX09] Youssef Marzouk and Dongbin Xiu. A stochastic collocation approach to bayesian inference in inverse problems. *Communications in Computational Physics*, 6:826–847, 2009.

[NR96] Erich Novak and Klaus Ritter. High dimensional integration of smooth functions over cubes. *Numerische Mathematik*, 75(1):79–97, 1996.

[ON12] S Oladyshkin and W Nowak. Data-driven uncertainty quantification using the arbitrary polynomial chaos expansion. *Reliability Engineering & System Safety*, 106:179–190, 2012.

[Sud08] Bruno Sudret. Global sensitivity analysis using polynomial chaos expansions. *Reliability Engineering & System Safety*, 93(7):964–979, 2008.

[Wie38] Norbert Wiener. The homogeneous chaos. *American Journal of Mathematics*, 60(4):897–936, 1938.

[Xiu10] Dongbin Xiu. *Numerical methods for stochastic computations: A spectral method approach*. Princeton University Press, Princeton and N.J, 2010.

[XK02] Dongbin Xiu and George Em Karniadakis. The wiener–askey polynomial chaos for stochastic differential equations. *SIAM Journal on Scientific Computing*, 24(2):619–644, 2002.

[XK04] Dongbin Xiu and George Em Karniadakis. Supersensitivity due to uncertain boundary conditions. *International journal for numerical methods in engineering*, 61(12):2114–2138, 2004.

Wavelet Filter Bank Optimization for Classification of Deflectometry Measuring Data

Tan-Toan Le

Institute for Applied Research
Pforzheim University, Germany
tan-toan.le@hs-pforzheim.de

Technical Report IES-2013-04

Abstract: With the invention of the deflectometry, a method for defect detection and classification on specular surface was presented. Even though several improvements took place in this field since then, automatic classification of data gained by deflectometry method is still a challenge in image processing. An idea based on wavelet filter banks to classify deflectometry measuring data is presented in this paper. The advantage of wavelets is their ability to analyze multi-resolution signals, which is useful for detecting defect in various sizes. Different from other works based on wavelets method for specular surface presented before, the wavelet filter banks presented here are optimized for each defect class to obtain good features for classification. Besides the new optimized wavelet filter bank, the classification possibility of standard wavelet families is also regarded in this paper. For classification purposes a classifier based on Bayes' theorem is applied.

1 Introduction

In recent years, deflectometry has become more and more important in the image processing, since it was first introduced in the 1980s [KL81]. This area remains however object of many recent researches, for example in [BHLO12], [RKJ11], [KS08]. One of the topics is to classify correctly a defect despite of its scales. The classification should therefore be performed by the multi-resolution analysis of the deflectometry measuring data. The wavelet analysis would be an appropriate method for such a mission owing to its ability to decompose signals in different scales. There are several methods using wavelets for evaluating specular surfaces introduced before. Ghorai et al. [GMGD12] used several standard wavelet families to extract features on specular surface. Wavelets was also used to smooth images from specular surfaces as proposed in [ZDL$^+$11]. In this work, we propose a novel approach, where the wavelet filter bank is directly optimized on the defect obtained by deflectometry measurement.

The paper is organized as follows: in Section 2 theory of wavelets is introduced. In Section 3 and 4 methods for optimizing M-channel biorthogonal wavelet filter bank together with the application of standard wavelet families are presented. A conclusion as well as an outlook for further work is made in the last Section.

2   Wavelets - An Introduction

A signal s can be decomposed and later perfectly reconstructed by an *orthogonal basis*, where the two vectors $\{\varphi^{2n}, \varphi^{2n+1}\}$ of the basis are orthogonal to each other as for example in Figure 2.1. φ^{2n} and φ^{2n+1} must however not be always orthogonal, like in Figure 2.2. In this case, a perfect reconstruction from decomposed parts of s can only take place, if there exists another basis $\{\tilde{\varphi}^{2n}, \tilde{\varphi}^{2n+1}\}$, with $(\tilde{\varphi}^{2n} \perp \varphi^{2n+1})$ as well as $(\tilde{\varphi}^{2n+1} \perp \varphi^{2n})$, which together are called *biorthogonal basis*.

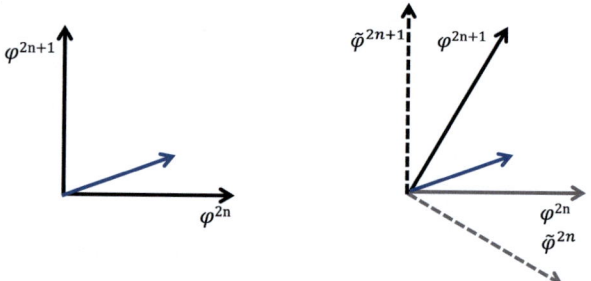

Figure 2.1: Orthogonal Basis   **Figure 2.2**: Biorthogonal Basis

A function $\Psi(t)$ called *mother wavelet* analyses a time-continuous signal $f(t) \in L^2(\mathbb{R})$ as follows:

$$d_b^a = \int\limits_{-\infty}^{\infty} f(t)\Psi^*{}_b^a(t)dt \quad \text{with } a \in \mathbb{R}^+, b \in \mathbb{R},$$

where

$$\Psi_b^a(t) = \frac{1}{\sqrt{a}}\Psi(\frac{t-b}{a}).$$

The function $\Psi(t)$ is shrunk in case $a < 1$ and stretched for $a > 1$. a and b are thereby called as *dilation-* and *translation-factor* respectively, while d_b^a are *analysis coefficients* in relation to a and b. Because an analysis with all combinations of $\{a \in \mathbb{R}^+\}$ and $\{b \in \mathbb{R}\}$ is highly redundant, the *dyadic wavelet transformation* was introduced with $\{a = 2^j, b = k.2^j (j, k \in \mathbb{Z})\}$. The dilation and transformation of $\Psi(t)$ become in this case:

$$\Psi_k^j(t) = \frac{1}{\sqrt{2^j}} \Psi(\frac{t}{2^j} - k).$$

A *scaling function* $\Phi(t)$ builds together with the *wavelet function* $\Psi(t)$ a vector space, where a multi-resolution analysis of a function $f(t)$ is possible. By increasing the scale j, more details of f should be gained. The idea here is to project a vector space $\mathbf{V^j}$ into subspaces $\mathbf{V^{j+1}}$ and $\mathbf{W^{j+1}}$:

$$\mathbf{V^j} = \mathbf{V^{j+1}} \oplus \mathbf{W^{j+1}} \text{ and } \mathbf{V^{j+1}} \perp \mathbf{W^{j+1}},$$

where $\mathbf{V^{j+1}}$ and $\mathbf{W^{j+1}}$ are stretched by Φ_k^{j+1} and Ψ_k^{j+1} respectively. On a scale $(j+1)$, f is approximated by Φ with coefficients:

$$a_k^{j+1} = \langle f(u), \frac{1}{\sqrt{2^{j+1}}} \Phi(\frac{u}{2^{j+1}} - k) \rangle.$$

The difference between the approximations of f on scale j and $(j+1)$ is considered as *detail coefficients*:

$$d_k^{j+1} = \langle f(u), \frac{1}{\sqrt{2^{j+1}}} \Psi(\frac{u}{2^{j+1}} - k) \rangle.$$

After some mathematical transformations, it can be proved that $\Psi(t)$ and $\Phi(t)$ are equivalent to a filter bank with filters h and g, where:

$$h(n) = \langle \Phi(u), \sqrt{2}\Phi(2u - n) \rangle \text{ and } g(n) = \langle \Psi(u), \sqrt{2}\Phi(2u - n) \rangle.$$

The multi-resolution analysis can therefore also be performed by an appropriate filter bank. In general, the dilation- and translation factors of $\Psi(t)$ are discretized by M:

$$\Psi_k^j(t) = \frac{1}{\sqrt{M^j}} \Psi(\frac{t}{M^j} - k).$$

There will be $(M - 1)$ *wavelet functions* $\Psi_{k,i}^j(t)$ (with $i = 1, ..., M - 1$) and one *scaling function* $\Phi_k^j(t)$, which stretches the subspace $\mathbf{W_i^j}$ and $\mathbf{V_i^j}$ respectively. The vector space $\mathbf{V^j}$ is in this case calculated as:

$$\mathbf{V^j} = \oplus_{i=1}^{M-1} \mathbf{W_i^{j+1}} \oplus_{i=1}^{M-1} \mathbf{W_i^{j+2}} \oplus_{i=1}^{M-1} \mathbf{W_i^{j+3}} ...$$

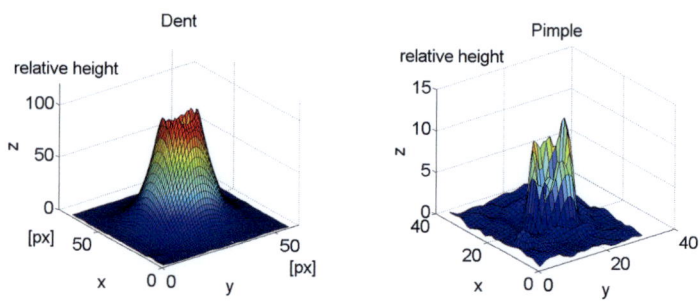

Figure 3.1: Typical form of dent and pimple

On a scale j, a function $f(t)$ is analyzed as:

$$f(t) = \sum_k \langle f(t), \Phi_k^j(t)\rangle {\Phi'}_k^j(t) + \sum_i \sum_k \langle f(t), \Psi_{k,i}^j(t)\rangle {\Psi'}_{k,i}^j(t),$$

where ${\Phi'}_k^j(t)$ is the biorthogonal basis to $\Phi_k^j(t)$. As in case $M = 2$ it can also be proved that:

$$\Phi(t) = \sqrt{M} \sum_{n=-\infty}^{\infty} h_0(n)\Phi(M.t-n) \text{ and } \Psi_i(t) = \sqrt{M} \sum_{n=-\infty}^{\infty} h_i(n)\Phi(M.t-n).$$

This means that there is always a filter bank with M channels $h_i(n)$ ($i = 0, ..., M - 1$) equivalent to the set of wavelet functions $\Psi(t)$ and scaling function $\Phi(t)$. A multiscale analysis of a signal $f(t)$ can therefore also be performed with the help of this M-channel filter bank.

3   Wavelet Filter Banks for Deflectometry Data

3.1   Comparison between Standard Wavelet Families

Firstly, the existing standard wavelet families were used for classification and the results were compared. As observed, there are two typical defect forms on our test surfaces, *dent* and *pimple*. Extracted from the reconstructed images obtained by deflectometry measuring, typical form of defects class *dent* and *pimple* are shown in Figure 3.1.

The wavelet coefficients in the area of a dent and a pimple, which are obtained by filtering deflectometry data with different standard wavelet families, are also

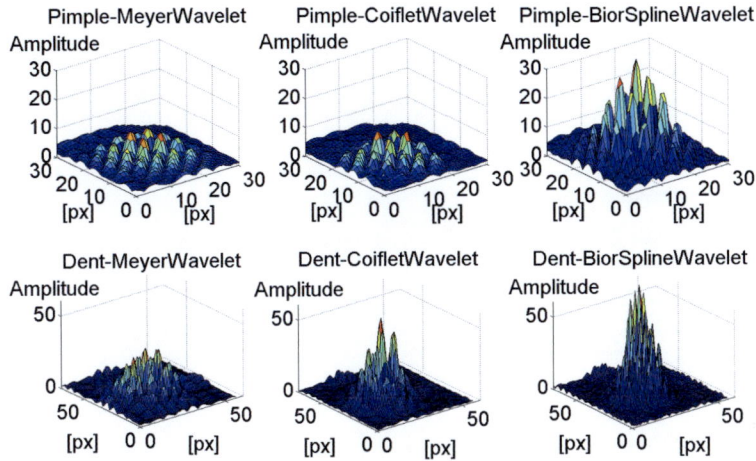

Figure 3.2: Wavelet coefficients in defect's area

extracted. For example in Figure 3.2, the filtering results with the wavelet families *Meyer*, *Coiflet* and *Biorthogonal spline wavelets* (first-, second- and third column in the Figure respectively) are shown. One can see that the *Biorthogonal spline wavelets* presented by Cohen et al. [CDF06] deliver coefficients with higher amplitude in comparison to other wavelet families. A defect detection and classification based on these coefficients should be therefore better than with coefficients from other standard wavelet families. Besides these wavelet families, the performances of other standard wavelet families were also considered and analyzed. A quantitative result of detection can be found in table 3.3.

Among the standard wavelet families, the filter bank with *Biorthogonal spline wavelets* seems to be best appropriate for detection and classification purpose of dent and pimple. This wavelet family can later be considered as a reference for our optimized wavelet filter banks.

3.2 Optimized Biorthogonal Wavelet Filter Banks

A general method for designing biorthogonal wavelet filter banks is presented in this Section. In the first step the object class to be detected on the surface was extracted, so that a typical curve can be presented. Based on this curve, a filter h_0 could be designed, which represents the defect and has impulse responses with the same course as the defect. Then other filters h_i are optimized, which create

	Pimple	Dent
Daubechies Wavelet db4	Detection on Scale 3	Detection on Scale 7
Symlet Wavelet	Detection on Scale 3	Good Detection on Scale 9
Complex Gaussian (absolute value)	Good Detection on Scale 2	Detection on Scale 7
Biorthogonale Spline Wavelets	Good Detection on Scale 3	Good Detection on Scale 7
Meyer Wavelet	Detection on Scale 1	Good Detection on Scale 3
Complex Shannon (absolute value)	Detection on Scale 3	Detection on Scale 7

Figure 3.3: Compare between standard wavelet families

together with h_0 a filter bank with biorthogonal property. This filter bank is used later to classify data from deflectometry measuring.

The optimization problem turns now into creating a biorthogonal wavelet filter bank with M channels. The first $(M-1)$ channels are given, which are normally defect filters.

Using an M-channel filter bank, an analyzed signal will be perfectly reconstructed from its wavelet coefficients, if the determinant $\Delta_P(z)$ of the polyphase-matrix $P(z)$ of the filters $\boldsymbol{h}_t$ ($t = 0, .., M-1$) consists of only a single term z^{-n_0} [Gre96]. $P(z)$ has the form:

$$P_{ij}(z) = z^{-j} H_{ij}(z^M).$$

Here $H_{ij}(z^M)$ is the jth polyphase component of the ith filter [Vet86]. Its determinant $\Delta_P(z)$ can be calculated as:

$$\Delta_P(z) = c_0 z^{-M\frac{M-1}{2}} + \ldots + c_{N-M} z^{-[MN - M\frac{M+1}{2}]}, \qquad (3.1)$$

with the constants c_m, $m = 0, \ldots, N - M$.

3.2.1 Quality criteria for filter bank design

For an M-channel filter bank consisting of $(M-1)$ filters $\boldsymbol{h}_t$ ($t = 0, \ldots, M-2$), a filter $\boldsymbol{h}_{M-1}$, which is biorthogonal to all $\boldsymbol{h}_t$, is constructed. In order to match the biorthogonal wavelet filter bank to a given defect class, a quality criterion Q is defined as the Euclidean distance between the filter h_i of the defect class C_i and the filter to be constructed h_{M-1}:

$$Q = \|h_i - h_{M-1}\|^2.$$

By maximizing the quality criterion Q, the filter h_{M-1} will be optimized to be as different from the given defect class as possible. Due to the condition for PR above, all the constants c_j in (3.1) except one need to be set to zero. The constants c_j are weighted sums of coefficients of the filter h_{M-1} to be constructed:

$$c_j = \sum_{n=0}^{N-1} a_{mn} h_{M-1}(n).$$

The construction of h_{M-1} can thus be considered as optimizing the quality criterion Q under the constraint that the condition for PR is fulfilled. As a linear system, the set of $(N - M)$ equations $c_j \overset{!}{=} 0$, which contain the filter coefficients $h_{M-1}(n)$, $(n = 0, \ldots, N - 1)$, is optimized with respect to Q. In order to solve this optimization problem a Lagrange function with Lagrange multiplier λ is defined as:

$$L(h_{M-1}, \lambda) = \frac{1}{2} Q - \lambda^T [A h_{M-1} - 0].$$

The optimum can be found by solving the derivation equations:

$$\nabla_{h_{M-1}, \lambda} L(h_{M-1}, \lambda) \overset{!}{=} 0.$$

This way, we define the coefficients of filter h_{M-1}, which are biorthogonal to given filters h_t $(t = 0, \ldots, M - 2)$. Using the approach described above, a typical curve of each defect class is at first extracted and then used to create a representative filter. Figure 3.4 shows the impulse response of a dent filter with length 8 as well as its associated biorthogonal wavelet filter.

After the coefficients of all filters h_t have been defined, a filter bank for the stationary wavelet transform is created based on these filters. Each surface is analyzed with a filter bank, which results in a wavelet packet tree. Each coefficient node d_k is numbered consecutively, as shown in Figure 3.5 for the case of a 3-channel filter bank in 2 scales. On the wavelet packet tree, different branch variations, which also mean the different nodes combinations, can be chosen. Each branch variation has its own meaning of wavelet analysis. For example the nodes set $\{d_1, d_4\}$ in Figure 3.5 would be appropriate for classifying defects of class C_1. Meanwhile $\{d_2, d_8\}$ should analyze defects of class C_2 better. In Figure 3.6 the results obtained by the two first transformation scales of a dent are shown. It can be seen, that the filter has a quite good correlation with the defect.

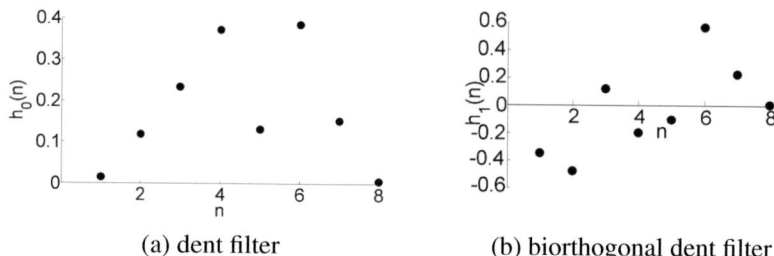

(a) dent filter   (b) biorthogonal dent filter

Figure 3.4: Impulse responses of a dent filter.

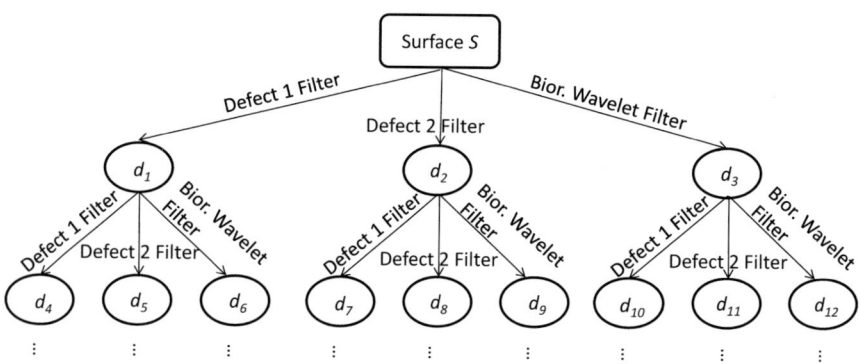

Figure 3.5: Wavelet packet tree in case $M=3$

3.2.2 Classification and results

Based on the wavelet packet trees created in the last step, the nodes on this tree can be considered as features for classification purpose. To classify a point (x, y) on the surface S, a set of nodes at the same point $d_k(x, y)$ are chosen to create a feature vector d. Based on the idea presented in [ZLGH12], a suitable classifier can be set up. The parameters μ_i and σ_i are considered as mean and standard deviation of each coefficient on the class C_i for all selected nodes in a feature vector d. The Bayes' theorem defines the probability p for vector d belonging to class C_i as:

$$p(\mu_i, \sigma_i | d) = \frac{p(d|\mu_i, \sigma_i) p(\mu_i, \sigma_i)}{p(d)}.$$

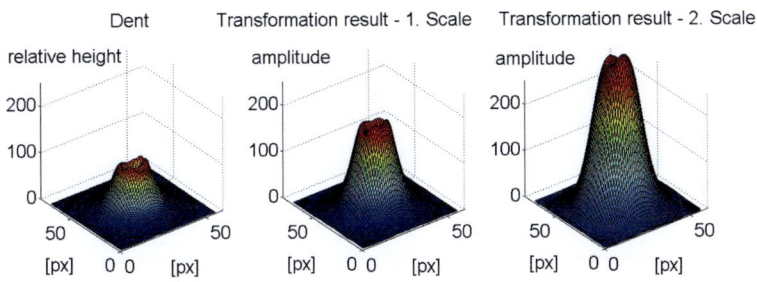

Figure 3.6: Dent and his transformation results

The distribution of coefficients can be considered as Laplace [ZLGH12]. The likelihood for class C_i can therefore be modelled as the product of a univariate Laplace distribution:

$$p(d|\mu_i, \sigma_i) = \prod_k \frac{1}{\sigma_{i,k}\sqrt{2\pi}}\exp(-\frac{1}{2}\frac{|d_k - \mu_{i,k}|}{\sigma_{i,k}^2}).$$

For each class C_i the parameters μ_i and σ_i are learned with a training set.

Applying this approach to several M-channel biorthogonal wavelet filter banks found in the last step, we receive classification results for the classes *pimple* and *dent*. The standard wavelet family *biorthogonal spline wavelet* (see Section 3.1), which delivered best results under standard wavelet families, was used as reference. An extract for the accuracy results of each class using 4 filter bank systems is shown in table 3.1:

- Two systems with two channels ($M = 2$): one consisting of a filter adapted on *dent* and its associated biorthogonal wavelet filter; one consisting of a filter adapted on *pimple* and its associated biorthogonal wavelet filter,

- A three channel system ($M = 3$) for the case of a filter, which is biorthogonal to both *dent* and *pimple*, and

- A 4-channel system ($M = 4$) as a combination of the two systems with two channels above.

is shown in table 3.1. It's recalled that the nodes on the wavelet packet tree were numbered as in Figure 3.5. With the help of optimized biorthogonal wavelet filter

			accuracy			
			surface one		surface two	
standard wavelet			C_d	C_p	C_d	C_p
biorthogonal spline wavelet 3.5			34.7%	80.9%	96.8%	94.9%
M	**adapted an**	**selected nodes**	C_d	C_p	C_d	C_p
2	C_d	1	97.8%	98.2%	99.7%	96.4%
2	C_d	1, 3	99.3%	96.7%	99.6%	96.1%
2	C_d	1, 3, 4	99.6%	96.1%	99.4%	95.6%
2	C_p	1	62.2%	84.6%	99.7%	96.5%
3	C_d, C_p	1, 2	96.3%	94.4%	99.7%	96.5%
3	C_d, C_p	1, 2, 4, 5, 7, 8	97.4%	95.7%	99.2%	95.2%
4	C_d, C_p	1, 2	96.9%	93.7%	99.7%	96.5%

Table 3.1: Classification accuracy using standard wavelet and optimized wavelets

banks, the classification accuracy for the class *dent* reached up to 99% on the two testing surfaces, and for the class *pimple* up to 98% on the first surface, as well as 97% on the second one. Compared to the standard *Biorthogonal Spline Wavelets*, the classification results were improved significantly for both defect classes.

4   Conclusion

A new method for classification data obtained by deflectometry measuring by designing an optimized M-channel biorthogonal wavelet filter bank was presented. The optimized wavelet filter banks have delivered higher accuracy rates and shown thereby his benefit compared to filter bank with standard wavelet families. For a better correlation between filter and defect in various sizes, an application of optimized wavelet filter bank with rational scaling factors is conceivable. Further work could therefore be the combination of the presented approach with rational sampling factors to further improve classification result. The method should also be evaluated with more test samples.

This work was part of a project financed by the Baden-Württemberg Stiftung.

Bibliography

[Bal08]   J. Balzer. *Regularisierung des Deflektometrieproblems – Grundlagen und Anwendung.* PhD thesis, Universität Karlsruhe (TH), 2008.

[BHLO12]   A. Burla, T. Haist, W. Lyda, and W. Osten. Genetic programming applied to automatic algorithm design in multi-scale inspection systems. *Optical Engineering*, 51:067001-1–067001-13, 2012.

[CDF06]   A. Cohen, I. Daubechies, and J.C. Feauveau. Biorthogonal bases of compactly supported wavelets. *Communications on Pure and Applied Mathematics*, 45(5):485–560, 2006.

[GMGD12]   S. Ghorai, A. Mukherjee, M. Gangadaran, and P. K. Dutta. Automatic defect detection on hot-rolled flat steel products. *IEEE Trans. Instrumentation and Measurement*, PP:1–10, 2012.

[Gre96]   T. Greiner. Orthogonal and biorthogonal texture-matched wavelet filterbanks for hierarchical texture analysis. *Signal Processing*, 54(1):1–22, 1996.

[KL81]   O. Kafri and A. Livnat. Reflective surface analysis using moiré deflectometry. *Applied Optics*, 20(18):3098–3100, 1981.

[KS08]   Kiriakos N Kutulakos and Eron Steger. A theory of refractive and specular 3d shape by light-path triangulation. *International Journal of Computer Vision*, 76(1):13–29, 2008.

[RKJ11]   L. Rosenboom, T. Kreis, and W. Jüptner. Surface description and defect detection by wavelet analysis. *Measurement Science and Technology*, 22:1–9, 2011.

[Vet86]   M. Vetterli. Filter banks allowing perfect reconstruction. *Signal Processing*, 10(3):219–244, 1986.

[WMHB09]   S. Werling, M. Mai, M. Heizmann, and J. Beyerer. Inspection of specular and partially specular surfaces. *Metrology and Measurement Systems*, 16:415–431, 2009.

[ZDL+11]   X.-W. Zhang, Y.-Q. Ding, Y.-Y. Lv, A.-Y. Shi, and R.-Y. Liang. A vision inspection system for the surface defects of strongly reflected metal based on multi-class svm. *Expert Systems with Applications*, 38:5930–5939, 2011.

[ZLGH12]   M. Ziebarth, T.-T. Le, T. Greiner, and M. Heizmann. Inspektion spiegelnder Oberflächen mit Wavelet-basierten Verfahren. In Michael Puente León, Fernando; Heizmann, editor, *Forum Bildverarbeitung 2012*, pages 167–180, Regensburg, Deutschland, November 2012. KIT Scientific Publishing.

Local Shape From Specular Flow

Alexey Pak

Vision and Fusion Laboratory
Institute for Anthropomatics
Karlsruhe Institute of Technology (KIT), Germany
alexey.pak@ies.uni-karlsruhe.de

Technical Report IES-2013-05

Abstract: In this report, we consider the challenging problem of recovering a specular shape from the continuous observation during motion. We find that under certain constraints, the information contained in the perceived optical flow (also known as specular flow) is sufficient to locally reconstruct a surface and its first- and second-order derivatives. We further consider the effect of measurement errors and the practical implementation issues.

1 Introduction

In the field of computer vision, specularities have always been a challenge for the 3D reconstruction methods. On the one hand, specular objects have no intrinsic texture suitable for stereo matching. On the other hand, the high sensitivity of the specular reflection to the small variations in the surface inclination allows for a very precise inspection of mirror surfaces. In particular, the techniques of the precision deflectometric inspection of specular objects have matured enough to rival the accuracy of the more established (and expensive) interferometry [FOKH12]. The more general problem of multi-view specular reconstruction has recently seen some practical (albeit computationally expensive) solutions [Pak12, WORK13]. Recently, Liu et al [LHS13] suggested that the knowledge of the derivatives of the registration data may considerably simplify the deflectometric reconstruction.

These state-of-the-art techniques evaluate the camera images of a reflection of some calibrated screen in the studied object, while the screen displays a series of encoded patterns. This setup naturally assumes that the studied object, the camera and the projection screen remain static (do not move) during the entire registration session, which may require a few dozen coded pattern projections. For that purpose, some industrial implementations use precision robots that position the sensors near a fixed object and maintain the chosen configuration during the projections. Obviuosly, the industry would welcome a more dynamic inspection method with e.g. objects moving on a transporter band through the control station (as it is presently done during the inspection by human workers).

There already exist several methods for the industrial on-line inspection based on specularities. However, the shape reconstruction in those cases is either based on complicated precision hardware and per-line registration [WASS12a], or is not performed at all [TAM+12]. Another option is to exploit the perceived optical flow, or the field of displacements of texture points as seen by the camera under certain motion. Such methods (known as shape-from-specular flow) have been studied in the context of the global variational reconstruction [LBRB08], and in [AVBSZ07, AVZBS10, VZGBS11] in a special setup, where a telecentric camera is fixed with respect to the object, and the infinitely remote textured environment undergoes a global rotation. The flow field could be obtained from the camera images with the common algorithms (possibly with some minor modifications [AZBS11]). The resulting system of coupled linear partial differential equations is discretized and solved with the standard tools.

While very elegant mathematically, such approach is not ideally suited for the common industrial settings. A more realistic observation would use some less-exotic camera, moving along some trajectory with respect to the object, while the environment is located far enough and does not rotate. In this formulation, the problem receives an extra dimensional parameter (the distance between the camera and the object) and the resulting system of second-order coupled non-linear equations is much harder to integrate. It should be noted though, that this problem is routinely solved by humans who e.g. notice minor surface defects while walking near a standing car!

In this report we investigate a scenario, where a pin-hole camera moves along a known linear trajectory near the object. Inspired by the work of Liu et al [LHS13], we attempt to simplify the reconstruction by providing additional data: namely, we assume that in addition to the specular flow its derivatives with respect to the camera coordinates are known. We show that in this case, the problem can be solved exactly, resulting in a local surface representation *for each individual camera ray*.

2 Notation and geometry

In the setup shown in Fig. 2.1, the moving camera C makes two subsequent observations of the specular object O, such that at the time moment $t = 0$ the projection

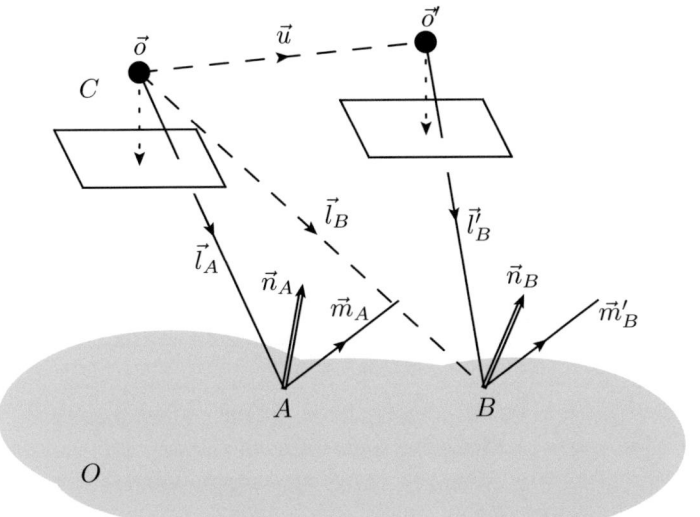

Figure 2.1: Geometry of the specular flow problem

center of the camera is located at the point $\vec{o}$, and at the moment $t = 1$ it moves to $\vec{o}'$ without rotation (i.e. the directions of the camera remain the same).[1] The shift vector $\vec{u} = \vec{o}' - \vec{o}$ is a known parameter.

Let us first consider the time moment $t = 0$ and the ray that hits the surface at some arbitrary point A. Without losing generality, we may assume that $\vec{o} = (0, 0, 0)$, and that the sensor's x and y directions and the main camera direction are collinear with the global x, y, and z axes, respectively. We also postulate that the camera sensor is located exactly at the unit distance from the projection center, so that a ray corresponding to the sensor point (x, y) has direction $\vec{v}(x, y) = (x, y, 1)$. Under these assumptions, the point A, projected to the sensor point (x_A, y_A), has 3D coordinates $\vec{l}_A = \vec{l}(x_A, y_A)$, where $\vec{l}(x, y) = \vec{v}(x, y) \cdot s(x, y)$, and $s(x, y)$ is the scalar depth function.

Under the technical assumption of a sufficiently smooth surface, and assuming that $\vec{l}(x, y)$ is close to the central ray (i.e. that $x, y \ll 1$), the depth function is

$$s(x, y) = s_0 + s_x x + s_y y + s_{xx}\frac{x^2}{2} + s_{yy}\frac{y^2}{2} + s_{xy}xy + \mathcal{O}(x^3, y^3, x^2y, y^2x).$$

At any surface point, vectors $\partial \vec{l}/\partial x$ and $\partial \vec{l}/\partial y$ describe the motion of $\vec{l}$ as x and y change, and are thus tangential to the surface. The outer (un-normalized) normal

---

[1]In what follows, the primed quantities will correspond to the time moment $t = 1$.

vector at A is then $\vec{n}_A = \vec{n}(x_A, y_A)$, with

$$\vec{n}(x, y) = \frac{\partial \vec{l}(x, y)}{\partial y} \times \frac{\partial \vec{l}(x, y)}{\partial x} \tag{2.1}$$
$$= (s_0 s_x, s_0 s_y, -s_0^2) + x(s_x^2 + s_0 s_{xx}, s_0 s_{xy} + s_x s_y, -3s_0 s_x)$$
$$+ y(s_0 s_{xy} + s_x s_y, s_y^2 + s_0 s_{yy}, -3s_0 s_y) + \mathcal{O}(x^2, y^2, xy).$$

Given the sight ray $\vec{l}_A$ and the normal vector $\vec{n}_A$, the reflected ray direction at A could be easily found as $\vec{m}_A = \vec{l}_A - 2\vec{n}_A(\vec{n}_A \cdot \vec{l}_A)/(\vec{n}_A \cdot \vec{n}_A)$. (The corresponding expression in terms of x_A, y_A is needed through the 1-st order, and is easy to find but bulky. We thus refrain from citing it here.)

Let us now switch to the time moment $t = 1$. The camera located at $\vec{o}' = \vec{o} + \vec{u}$ with $\vec{u} = (u_1, u_2, u_3)$ will observe some different point B, with the corresponding sight ray $\vec{l}'_B = \vec{l}_B - \vec{u}$, where $\vec{l}_B$ is the sight ray to point B as it was observed at $t = 0$. The corresponding sensor coordinates (at $t = 0$) would be (x_B, y_B) (not to be confused with the sensor coordinates at $t = 1$, x'_B and y'_B), and $\vec{l}_B = \vec{l}(x_B, y_B)$. Provided that also $x_B, y_B \ll 1$, the normal vector at B will be given by $\vec{n}_B = \vec{n}(x_B, y_B)$, according to the same Eq. (2.1). Since the normal vector at B does not change with time, we may compute the reflected ray direction, as viewed at $t = 1$ by the camera: $\vec{m}'_B = \vec{l}'_B - 2\vec{n}_B(\vec{n}_B \cdot \vec{l}'_B)/(\vec{n}_B \cdot \vec{n}_B)$.

3   Specular flow and surface constraints

So far, we have specified no relation between the points A and B. Let us now require that the specular flow transforms the point A to B, i.e. that the perceived value (color, or texture feature) observed by the camera in the direction of point A at $t = 0$ is identical with the value observed at point B later at $t = 1$. If this value originates from the background, and this background is located far enough (or, more precisely, that the distance between the points A and B is much smaller than the distance to the reflected background), then this requirement is equivalent to the condition

$$\vec{m}_A = \alpha \cdot \vec{m}'_B,$$

where the factor α accounts for the freedom in the normalization of $\vec{m}$. This system of three equations constrains the three unknowns: α, x_B, and y_B. The solution can be obtained in closed form and expanded in x_A, y_A, and the components of $\vec{u}$.

Substituting the found x_B and y_B into $\vec{l}_B$ and $\vec{l}'_B$, we find the sensor coordinates of the point B at the time moment $t = 1$:

$$(x'_B, y'_B) = \left(\frac{(\vec{l}'_B)_1}{(\vec{l}'_B)_3}, \frac{(\vec{l}'_B)_2}{(\vec{l}'_B)_3} \right).$$

The perceived specular flow, obtained from the two camera images, is by definition $\vec{f} = (f_1, f_2) = (x'_B - x_A, y'_B - y_A)$. Evaluating this result at $(x_A, y_A) = (0, 0)$ gives us then the value of the flow displacement vector exactly in the middle of the sensor. However, if we consistently expand all quantities to the first order in x_A and y_A, we may also find the derivatives of the specular flow, $\partial \vec{f} / \partial x_A$ and $\partial \vec{f} / \partial y_A$ at the same point $(0, 0)$.

The resulting expressions are relatively cumbersome but have a simple structure:

$$\vec{f}(0,0) = \frac{(\vec{u} \cdot N_1)}{D}, \quad \frac{\partial \vec{f}}{\partial x_A}(0,0) = \frac{(\vec{u} \cdot N_2)}{s_0 \cdot D}, \quad \frac{\partial \vec{f}}{\partial y_A}(0,0) = \frac{(\vec{u} \cdot N_3)}{s_0 \cdot D}, \quad (3.1)$$

where D and the elements of the 3x2-matrices N_i are polynomials (of the 6-th power at most) in the six shape parameters $(s_0, ..., s_{xy})$.

Given some measured values of the LHS vectors in Eq. (3.1), we may solve these six equations for those parameters and thus completely constrain the surface. Note that unlike the previous results on specular flow (e.g., [VZGBS11]), our result is local and does not require one to solve a global system of differential equations, nor any boundary conditions or regularization data.

Our choice to reconstruct surface in the single point $(x_A, y_A) = (0, 0)$ in fact does not diminish the applicability of the result. Given some specular flow field over a large camera sensor, one may rotate the system of coordinates and adjust the flow parameters to match the geometry of Fig. 2.1 for each pixel. (Of course, the computed depth field and its derivatives should then be accordingly rotated back and adjusted to the original notation.) In a similar fashion, one may correct for the rotation of the camera between the two positions, and thus apply this method for the absolutely arbitrary camera trajectories. The only real remaining constraint is that the object must not rotate with respect to the background between the camera shots. The corresponding generic transformations and parameterizations will be discussed in more details in a forthcoming publication.

4 Absolute surface reconstruction

Finding a closed-form solution of Eq. (3.1) seems to be impossible at the moment. However, the equations can be solved numerically to any required accuracy. We indeed have performed several numerical experiments and checked that given some simulated specular flow at one point, the solution with Wolfram Mathematica's numerical solver (NSolve[]) returns the answer reproducing the ground truth. In addition to that solution, those equations appear to have quite a few spurious complex and real-valued solutions. However, with a decent gradient-descent solver (Mathematica's FindRoot[], or solvers from the GSL library) and a close-enough initialization, the solution is fast, and the result unique and coinciding with the ground truth.

In realistic conditions, the measured optical flow fields and their derivatives will always contain some error. Moreover, the six input parameters are strongly correlated due to the optical flow calculation method, which usually attempts to smooth out the gradients in the flow field. If we combine the shape parameters $s_0, ..., s_{xy}$ into a six-dimensional vector $\vec{s}$, and the input parameters $f_1, ..., \partial f_2/\partial y_A$ into a six-dimensional vector $\vec{g}$, then the Eq. (3.1) will have the form $\vec{F}(\vec{s}) = \vec{g}$. If the uncertainty in $\vec{g}$ is $\delta\vec{g}$, then the resulting uncertainty in $\vec{s}$ will be $\delta\vec{s} = \delta\vec{g}\left(\frac{\partial F_i}{\partial s_j}\right)^{-1}$. Further, if the 6-by-6 correlation matrix of $\delta\vec{g}$ is C_g, the corresponding correlation matrix C_s of $\delta\vec{s}$ will be given by

$$C_s^{-1} = \left(\frac{\partial F_i}{\partial s_j}\right) C_g^{-1} \left(\frac{\partial F_i}{\partial s_j}\right)^T,$$

the solution of Eq. (3.1) and its uncertainty shape could be obtained by finding

$$\vec{s}^* = \arg\min_{\vec{s}}\left\{\left(\vec{F}(\vec{s}) - \vec{g}\right) C_g^{-1} \left(\vec{F}(\vec{s}) - \vec{g}\right)^T\right\}.$$

The derivatives of $\vec{F}$ can be easily computed analytically from Eqs. (3.1) and evaluated numerically in any point. In fact, their knowledge will also improve the performance of the gradient descent solver, and after the solution has been found, C_s can be provided as the estimate of its accuracy. At this point, given multiple pixels with the correlated estimates of the depth and its derivatives in each point, one still has to employ some global fitting method of the sufficient order to fit the most accurate global smooth function.

5 Conclusion and outlook

In this report, we present the theoretical basis of the novel method to reconstruct specular surfaces from uncalibrated natural specular flow under the linear motion of the camera. By exploiting the derivatives of the flow field, we are able to completely reconstruct the local profile of the surface near the central ray. The method easily generalizes to an arbitrary (known) motion of the camera and the sensor pixels further away from the center. In the near future, we plan to apply the method to the real observation data and study its numerical stability in further details.

Bibliography

[AVBSZ07]   Yair Adato, Yuriy Vasilyev, Ohad Ben-Shahar, and Todd Zickler. Toward a theory of shape from specular flow. Proc. ICCV, 2007.

[AVZBS10]   Yair Adato, Yuriy Vasilyev, Todd Zickler, and Ohad Ben-Shahar. Shape from specular flow. *IEEE Transactions On Pattern Analysis and Machine Intelligence*, 32:2054 – 2070, 2010.

[AZBS11]   Yair Adato, Todd Zickler, and Ohad Ben-Shahar. A polar representation of motion and implications for optical flow. Proc. CVPR, 2011.

[FOKH12]   Christian Faber, Evelyn Olesch, Roman Krobot, and Gerd Häusler. Deflectometry challenges interferometry: the competition gets tougher! Proc. SPIE 8493, Interferometry XVI: Techniques and Analysis, pages 84930R–84930R–15, 2012.

[LBRB08]   J. Lellmann, J. Balzer, A. Rieder, and J. Beyerer. Shape from specular reflection and optical flow. *Int J. Comput. Vis.*, 80:226–241, 2008.

[LHS13]   Miaomiao Liu, Richard Hartley, and Mathieu Salzmann. Mirror surface reconstruction from a single image. Proc. CVPR, 2013.

[Pak12]   Alexey Pak. Recovering shapes of specular objects in motion via normal vector map consistency. Proc. SPIE 8493, Interferometry XVI: Techniques and Analysis, pages 84930T–84930T–8, 2012.

[TAM+12]   J. Tornero, L. Armesto, M. Mora, N. Montes, A. Herraez, and J. Asensio. Detección de defectos en carrocerías de vehículos basado en visión artificial: Diseño e implantación. *Revista Iberoamericana de Automática e Informática industrial*, 9:93–104, 2012.

[VZGBS11]   Yuriy Vasilyev, Todd Zickler, Steven Gortler, and Ohad Ben-Shahar. Shape from specular flow: Is one flow enough? Proc. CVPR, pages 2561–2568, 2011.

[WASS12a]   R. D. Wedowski, G. A. Atkinson, M. L. Smith, and L. N. Smith. Dynamic deflectometry: A novel approach for the on-line reconstruction of specular freeform surfaces. *Optics and Lasers in Engineering*, 50:1765–1778, 2012.

[WORK13]   M. Weinmann, A. Osep, R. Ruiters, and R. Klein. Multi-view normal field integration for 3d reconstruction of mirroring objects. Proceedings of the International Conference on Computer Vision (ICCV), 2013.

Information and Control in Cyber-Physical Production Systems

Julius Pfrommer

Vision and Fusion Laboratory
Institute for Anthropomatics
Karlsruhe Institute of Technology (KIT), Germany
julius.pfrommer@kit.edu

Technical Report IES-2013-06

Abstract: Computation and communication have become cheap and near-ubiquitous. In the domain of manufacturing automation, this led to the development of Cyber-Physical Production Systems (CPPS). Traditionally, the control infrastructure of manufacturing systems ensured the correct execution of predetermined processes. In CPPS, detailed knowledge about the system dynamics and the current runtime state allow more flexible control approaches to adapt the system behavior to changing tasks and conditions. In this work, we discuss principles for driving CPPS consisting of many heterogeneous components. For this, we identify the four fundamental approaches for information modeling and control of CPPS, as well as their consequences concerning the system design and operation.

1 Introduction

Norbert Wiener described his vision of cybernetics as the conjunction of control and communication [Wie48]. And indeed, control and communication relations between system components have been tightly linked in the past. Today, communication can be done nearly *structureless*. All participants are part of a shared global network in which interactions can be freely established by the participants themselves on an ad-hoc basis. But this extra flexibility remains unused if the control infrastructure is not adopted accordingly. Lunze and Grüne [LG14] describe the transition from the current *networks of information* to *networks of action* of interacting subsystems. In this work, we expand on this view in the context of automated manufacturing systems. This domain lends itself conveniently as a test case for a broader class of networked systems, since a) it currently undergoes the

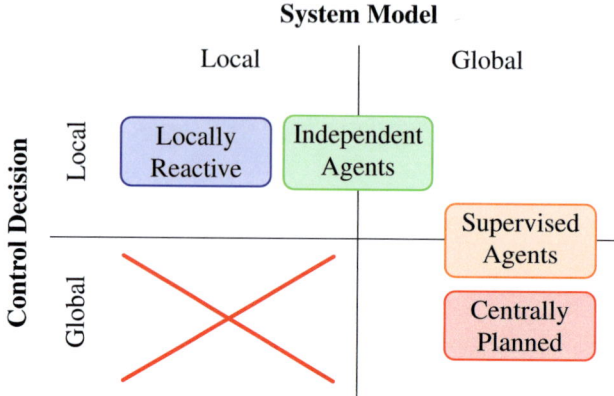

Figure 1.1: Organizational principles for CPPS control.

transition towards fully networked system-wide communication, b) it has an intrinsic interest in optimizing efficiency whilst c) enhancing its operational flexibility to adapt to changing tasks, external conditions and internal structural transformations, and d) every (individual) part of the system is usually well-defined and can be captured in a behavioral model.[1]

Given the freedom to establish communication between any two system components, two separate but interlinked design decisions need to be made:

> "Who holds information about the system and its current state?"
> "Who is making control decisions and who is affected by them?"

We classify the possible answers into two broad categories. Either a central authority is responsible (global within the considered context), or the responsibility is distributed among several components (local). Within this framework, we identify four fundamental organizational principles for manufacturing control in CPPS (see Figure 1.1). Note that the lower left quadrant is marked inaccessible, as it is not sensible to derive global control decisions from a system model with only a local scope. The following sections each discuss one of the four organizational principles in detail.

---

[1]We assume discrete manufacturing processes, where the actions performed by system components are deterministic. This renders the problem formulations and optimization techniques quite different from continuous or hybrid systems, where only few discrete state and control variables are considered.

2 Local Reactive Control

Traditionally, it was time-consuming to adapt automated manufacturing systems to new products or product variants. Machines and tools had to be adjusted (and reprogrammed) manually and the correct interplay of the manufacturing system components had to be assured. Today, the combination of fast changes between machine configurations (under various names, such as Single-Minute Exchange of Die, SMED) and tracking of individual products within a manufacturing system using auto-identification (Auto-ID, [MSC$^+$03]), e.g. by visual recognition of barcodes on the products or RFID-based solutions, is mainstream technology.[2]

Being able to interleave the production of different products (or product variants) is considered advantageous also in settings where lot sizes are generally large. For example, it is essential to the reduction of waste according to the Lean Manufacturing principle (i.e. the Toyota Production System, TPS [Ōno88]). It also enables the automation of mass-customized production tasks. If, say, a customer wants a custom engraving on his tablet computer, the Auto-ID tag on the product would be read locally at the engraving machine and the task completed accordingly.

The Auto-ID paradigm does not explicitly require coordination between machines other than the information transmitted via the products themselves. In case of the engraving example, decisions about production steps are made locally as a reaction to local sensor inputs (reading the product tag). In the context of this paper, we denote this approach as *local reactive control*.

Local reactive control works well for production settings with highly decoupled decision problems, i.e. if system components do not need to coordinate their actions other than at their direct interfaces. It has the advantage of not requiring a global system model containing an up-to-date representation of the current system state. On the downside, the actions taken independently by system components might be suboptimal. If a machine is blocked longer than usual, e.g. during some elaborate work requested by a product or by an unexpected downtime, it has no means to communicate this up- or downstream so that other system components may react accordingly. For example by sending products to a redundant resource of the same type instead.

Information Model: Local   **Decision Making:** Local

---

[2]In the Auto-ID paradigm, the work pieces themselves carry their identification as well as metadata. We do not distinguish cases when the metadata is contained in the Auto-ID mechanism itself and when it can be retrieved from a central storage based on the ID.

3   Central planning of automation tasks

The central planning approach aims to optimize manufacturing operations across multiple resources (machines and equipment) by specifying their actions and interactions in a detailed plan. The planning authority needs to known the initial system state and the system dynamics in order to accurately predict future system states as part of the planning mechanism. The result is a sequence of actions to be performed by the available resources. Traditionally, problem formulations based on mathematical programming have been used for manufacturing planning [Pin12]. However, solutions are often approximated with heuristics due to a high problem complexity and time constraints.

One of the main goals of CPPS is to make better use of flexibility in manufacturing. Currently, there are two well-researched approaches to handle flexibility in scheduling. In the *Flexible Job-Shop* problem, every job (production of a specific part) is accomplished by executing a set of tasks (first milling, then drilling, then painting...) in a fixed order. Flexibility is introduced by defining groups of resources that could all be used to accomplish a certain task. The *Flexible Open-Shop* problem is similar, but defines jobs whose tasks can be run in any order. The assumption of these scheduling models was that products can move freely between any two resources. But when plant logistics (like conveyor belts, buffer space, etc.) are considered as part of the system dynamics, the solution space becomes more complex. First, the use of transportation equipment needs to be adequately modeled. This includes the need for further cooperation between the actions of resources. For every execution of a transportation operation, the source, the transportation equipment, and the target resource need to be aligned. Second, the order in which tasks (including transportation) are executed are neither completely predefined for each product type (this would render the system non-flexible) nor freely chosen (as there are additional constraints imposed by the plant topology). Jobs rather become graphs of operations and their precedence constraints (see e.g. [AKM03]). Lastly, the assembly of several (possibly customized) parts into one final product is quite difficult to model with classical scheduling tools, as merging of several workpieces gives rise to a second level of coordination between parts. To take all these properties of modern manufacturing operations into account, we present a novel approach to capture the system dynamics of CPPS in Section 3.1.

Information Model: Global   **Decision Making:** Global

3.1 A discrete event model for the system dynamics of CPPS

In the following, we present a novel formalism to capture the system dynamics of CPPS. All automated tasks (product transformation, transportation, tooling, etc.) are part of a single formalism that also handles the temporal coordination for concurrent execution (parallelism) on many resources.

Products $p \in P$ denote product types and not individual physical objects (including intermediary products occurring only during production). Resources $r \in R$ represent actual machines. For every resource, we define a set of states S_r the resource might reside in. A state describes the resource's mode of operation, configuration, and contained product.

$$s = (m, c, p) \in S_r \subseteq M \times C_r \times (P \cup \varnothing)$$

The possible modes of operation $m \in M$ are the same for every resource and describe basic conditions, such as "running", "halted", "in maintenance", etc. On the contrary, resource configurations $c \in C_r$ are defined individually. E.g. for a mobile robot, the configuration might denote a position, whilst the configuration of a NC-mill might indicate the type of milling head that is currently used. The approach of having products *contained* in a resource lets us model product transformations and movements. The empty set $\varnothing$ denotes the absence of a product, i.e. the resource is currently empty. The state of a specific resource at a specific point in time is

$$\sigma = (s, t) \in S_r \times \mathbb{R} \, .$$

We write $s(\sigma)$ for the untimed state component of a timed state σ. Similar notation is used to directly access the components of the untimed state. Thus, $c(\sigma)$ denotes the resource configuration of a resource $r(\sigma)$ at time $t(\sigma)$. The overall system state is described by the vector $\boldsymbol{\sigma}$, containing a timed state for each resource. Its semantic is the next time $t(\boldsymbol{\sigma}_r)$ at which resource r will reach a known state $s(\boldsymbol{\sigma}_r)$. Until then, the resource executes an *action* whose inner workings remain opaque from the outside. Actions are defined by the set of participating resources $\mathcal{R}$, and the respective pre- and post-states $\boldsymbol{s}_r^{pre}$, $\boldsymbol{s}_r^{post}$ and timing conditions $\boldsymbol{t}_r^{slack}$ and $\boldsymbol{t}_r^{dur}$ for each resource $r \in \mathcal{R}$.

$$a = (\mathcal{R}, \boldsymbol{s}^{pre}, \boldsymbol{s}^{post}, \boldsymbol{t}^{slack}, \boldsymbol{t}^{dur})$$

The time slack $\boldsymbol{t}_r^{slack}$ gives the amount of time a particular resource r has left – after the beginning of action a's execution – to reach the required pre-state $\boldsymbol{s}^{pre}$. This is motivated by actions where the interaction between resources is not immediate, but can occur later during the execution. The duration until an action is finished for $r \in \mathcal{R}$ (after a possible slack time) is given by $\boldsymbol{t}_r^{dur}$.

Seeing every action a as a symbol from the alphabet of actions A, a sequence of actions forms a word $w = a_1 a_2 \ldots$ Concatenation of an action a to a sequence of actions w is written as $w \circ a$. Given an initial system state $\sigma(\epsilon)$ (ϵ being the empty word), the execution of an action a_1 results in a new system state $\sigma(a_1)$, where the (timed) states of the resources $r \in \mathcal{R}(a_1)$ are changed. Now, the next action a_2 can be applied to reach $\sigma(a_1 \circ a_2)$, and so on. The single rule that governs the state transition between any $\sigma(w)$ and $\sigma(w \circ a)$ consists of the following pre- and post-condition:

$$\frac{\forall r \in \mathcal{R}(a),\ s(\sigma_r(w)) = s_r^{pre}(a)}{t^{start} = \max\{t(\sigma_r(w)) - t_r^{slack}(a) \mid r \in \mathcal{R}(a)\}}$$

$$\sigma_r(w \circ a) = \begin{cases} \left(s_r^{post}(a), t^{start} + t_r^{slack}(a) + t_r^{dur}(a)\right), & \text{if } r \in \mathcal{R}(a) \\ \sigma_r(w), & \text{else} \end{cases}$$

If the pre-condition is fulfilled, then action a can be executed to reach the new state $\sigma(w \circ a)$ given by the post-condition. Note that the above transition rule can be used to describe the entire system dynamics of a production system, including the

- transformation of work-pieces (products), the

- transportation and storage of products,

- concurrency, e.g. the parallel execution of actions and the synchronization of resources who collaborate as part of a single action, and

- changes to resource modes (maintenance ...) and configurations (e.g. tooling actions, or changing the position of a mobile robot) that might occur as part of a manufacturing task (transformation/transportation of a product) or as a dedicated action,

in a single formalism. Here, all actions are assumed to be deterministic. Future work might consider the possibility of non-determinism for the time until an action completes as well as uncertainty of action outcomes (e.g. the probability of a machine break-down or quality problems).

The presented system model, where discrete actions influence a world state is conceptionally close to McCarthy's Situation Calculus [Rei01]. The biggest difference is a narrower definition of the applicability of actions based on specific resources and their states and the handling of time. However, many results from the literature based on the Situation Calculus still apply. In a preliminary investigation, we implemented a planning mechanism based on the presented formalism. The input is a description of the system's *capabilities* (available actions) and the *goals* that

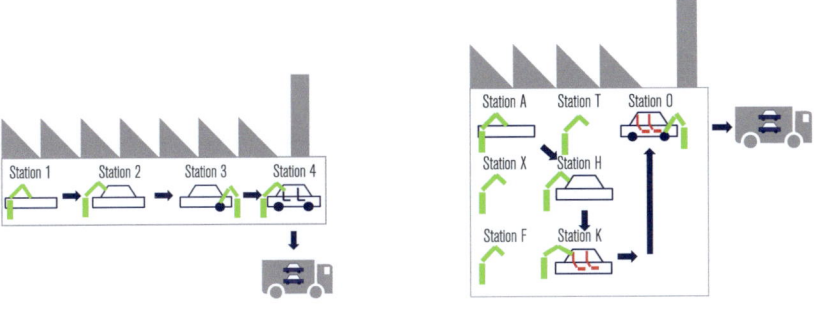

(a) Today: fixed assembly line   (b) Tomorrow: flexible assembly system

Figure 4.1: Individualized production of the future according to [KWH13]

shall be achieved. The planner then performs a forward-search in the state-space to find the best (according to some cost function) sequence of actions that achieves the goal. Unexpected changes to the system state (like a machine breakdown or quality problems…) are handled gracefully in a replanning step (e.g. by delaying some actions or even re-routing products on the fly).

In recent years, the performance of planning algorithms for exploring state spaces has been improved by several orders of magnitude for important example domains (see [Hof11] for an introduction). However, planning times remain a challenge for online replanning in large settings. To some extend, this also applies to traditional scheduling methods and heuristic solvers. Thus, from a computation perspective, it seems worthwhile to pursue decentralized organization paradigms, where the optimization problems are split into subproblems that can be solved independently.

4 Independent Agents

In the future, the automotive OEMs will produce more car types with shorter life-cycles. And their offer will encompass not only gasoline and diesel engines of various sizes, but also hybrid and electric ones. Since the powertrain has a huge impact on the car body design, car configurations will differ more profoundly, and few manufacturing processes will remain identical for all cars, even within the same type.

Figure 4.1 shows a currently debated vision for manufacturing systems of the future. Fixed assembly lines are replaced by assembly stations that are visited by products depending on their type and desired configuration. This organizational paradigm lends itself conveniently to agent-based approaches [Lei09]. Individual products[3] have the ability to decide themselves about actions (in terms of transportation and transformation) they request from the system. Instead of executing a centrally predefined action sequence, product agents pursue their own goals and act selfishly. The hope for agent-based manufacturing systems is that flexibility will increase due to self-organizing behavior of agents and that the overall system performance remains "good" event though optimization on a global scale (concerning the ensemble of all agents over a long-term time horizon) is omitted. The actual system performance is not only the result of an individual agent's actions, but emerges from the interplay of all agents. In order to coordinate their actions (e.g. the sequence in which agents enter a production station), agents need to communicate and share information. For this, auction mechanisms have been used in the past [WWWMM01].

Necessarily, the agents need to have some internal knowledge about the production system, its current state, as well as their direct surrounding. Since products are unlikely to be equipped with all the sensors necessary for this task, additional information needs to be provided by some outside authority. The overview figure 1.1 indicated that agent-based systems can provide a global or local system state model to the agents. The information received by the agents influences their ability to predict the effects of their choices and the sophistication of their interaction.

Even though many applications of agent-based technology in manufacturing settings have been developed [SWH06], only few industrial applications have prevailed beyond an experimental stage. In the following, we discuss two main reasons for the lack of industry adoption: 1) efficiency losses in settings where large-scale agent-coordination would be necessary and 2) lack of a predictable system behavior and missing guarantees on the minimum system performance.

Figure 4.2 depicts a well-known example of suboptimal agent behavior. It also exemplifies that the overall system dynamics emerging from individual selfish choices can be nonintuitive, especially with regards to the introduction of topology changes. Thus, before deciding on the use of agent-based control, it would be helpful to know bounds for a possible efficiency loss. In many settings, it is possible to state this so-called *cost of anarchy* [Rou05]). However, in flexible manufacturing operations, there is often times the possibility of deadlocks where circular dependencies block resources indefinitely. So a single action of a single agent (after which a deadlock can no longer be avoided) might have devastating consequences on the overall system performance. This makes it challenging to apply the cost of anarchy-principle to find guaranteed performance bounds. If the behavior of agent-based systems is not predefined but emerging during runtime,

---

[3]Or a virtual object representing a product in the relevant software.

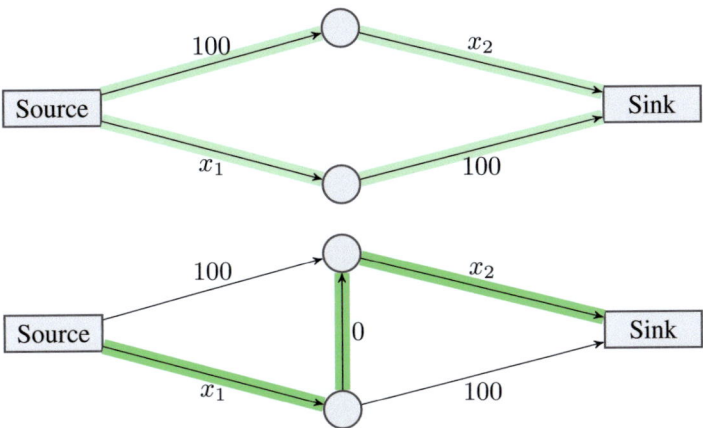

Figure 4.2: Braess Paradox [Bra68]. Assume that one hundred agents intend to traverse over the depicted network from the source to the sink with minimum time delay. The time delay per edge is either a fixed value or equal to the number of agents traversing over this edge (due to congestion, denoted with a variable x_i). By adding an additional edge as in the below graph, the delay per agent increases from 150 to 200 due to uncoordinated and selfish agent behavior.

how then shall forecasts for business decisions, interactions with customers and for personnel staffing be made?

Some of these uncertainties can be mitigated by a careful system design, buffer stock strategy, and so on. But, depending on the application, it might still turn out advantageous to restrict some of the decisions that agents can make by introducing a supervisory instance that can reduce the negative impact of uncoordinated behavior.

Information Model: Local/Global   **Decision Making:** Local

5   Supervised Agents

A planning and control mechanism for an entire production system and agents who are free to pursue their own goals are on the opposite sides of the spectrum of centralized and decentralized control of CPPS. We denote the mixed approaches, trying to mitigate the downsides of independent agents and centralized optimization, as supervised agents[4]. They try to improve the overall system performance by setting guidelines to the agents decisions based on the runtime system state. Essentially, we are limiting the set of choices that agents can take in a particular situation.

Consider an agent-based CPPS that is subject to possible deadlocks. There are two ways to overcome this problem. Either by *statically* limiting the choices of agents in a way that the Coffman conditions [CES71] necessary for deadlocks to occur never hold. But this could considerably reduce the system flexibility and performance. Or by *dynamically* checking for each agents decision whether it might lead to a deadlock in the future and removing it from the set of possible choices if necessary. For this, a detailed and up-to-date system state needs to be centrally available. In Section 5.1, we discuss such a method based on symbolic model checking to distinguish between *safe* and *unsafe* system states (where a deadlock can no longer be prevented) in discrete event systems.

To reduce the complexity of the system dynamics model, we can partition a CPPS into subsystems (e.g. a sequence of machines linked by conveyor belts that can be seen as performing a single production step) that take the role of resources in the planning process or deadlock prevention techniques. Still, we need to deal with the interfaces between subsystems and the necessity for coordination arising from this. The interfaces between subsystems of CPPS can be classified as follows:

Unbuffered Interface Using an unbuffered interface, products who leave subsystem *a* directly enter an adjacent subsystem *b*. Since this relation does not offer any *slack* in terms of the order in which input products are processed, the two subsystems need to be coordinated on a very fine-grained level.

Buffered Interface A buffered interface (e.g. parts being dropped in a wire-mesh box) allows for simple decoupling of subsystems. In the best case, the upstream subsystem can completely neglect the order in which it delivers products. But there exist also cases, when the exact sequence in which products enter the downstream subsystems is relevant. For example, if several custom parts need to be matched into one final product. Then, buffered decoupling is only temporal, but per-product relations still need to be taken into regard.

Random Access Buffered Interface More advanced technical solutions might allow to explicitly select elements from a storage buffer. This allows subsystem to schedule their production more independently. But also Random

---

[4]Some author call this approach "hybrid agent negotiation" between a set of heterarchical agents and a hierarchical supervisory structure. See for example [WLMF06].

Access Buffered Interfaces there may occur deadlocks. Consider a situation where the buffer between two subsystems is full. The downstream subsystem needs to get a specific workpiece in order to continue production. The upstream subsystem could deliver the workpiece. But the buffer – needed for the transfer – is full and cannot take in another product before the downstream system has removed one first.

In total, the supervised agents approach is based on local decision-making. An additional supervisory infrastructure knows about the systems dynamics and current system state from a global perspective and can set guidelines or coordinate between local agents. For this, some form of abstraction might be put into place to reduce the burden for communication and computation. The problem of deadlocks – and the possibility of using supervisory control to prevent it – was mentioned several times so far. In the following subsection, we discuss a method from model checking that can be used for this purpose.

Information Model: Global   **Decision Making:** Local/Global

5.1   Preventing deadlocks via agent supervisory control

The number of possible states of a system suffers combinatorial explosion in the number of system components. In their seminal paper, Burch et al. [BCM+92] showed how to use model checking on very large discrete event systems without enumerating all possible states. They apply logical transformations directly to a compressed representation of sets (Binary Decision Diagrams, BDD [Bry92]) to reason about system states and possible transitions between them.

Algorithm 5.1 Computation of deadlock-prone states in a discrete event system

---

Require: Q: set of all possible system states, Q_g: set of goal states, e.g. an *empty* manufacturing system, T: possible transitions between system states

1: **procedure** BACKWARDRESTRICTEDSTATES(Q, Q_g, T)
2:     $k \leftarrow 0, \ X_0 \leftarrow Q_m$ // X_k are the states with a path to Q_g
3:     **repeat**
4:         $k \leftarrow k + 1$
5:         $X_k = X_{k-1} \cup \{q \in Q | \exists q' \in X_{k-1} : (q, q') \in T\}$
6:     **until** $X_{k+1} = X_k$ // A fixpoint has been reached
7:     **return** $Q \backslash X_k$ // States without a path to Q_g are restricted
8: **end procedure**

Algorithm 5.1 shows a procedure used to compile a list of unsafe states from which deadlocks can no longer be avoided. It assumes as input a set of possible states Q, a set of target states Q_m that shall be reached eventually and a set of possible operations that result in a transition between system states $T \subseteq Q \times Q$. All of them can be given in their compressed form as BDD. Binary operations on them are linear in the length of the BDD (and not in the size of the sets they represent). The algorithm starts at the goal states (for example an "empty" production system where no partially finished products remain in the system). It then computes backwards the set of states that can reach the goal states in 1 step. These are added to the set of "good" states as they obviously do not lead to a deadlock. This backwards search is continued until a fixed point is reached: No additional system states exist that can reach one of the goal states by applying operations from T. For a more in-depth discussion and ways to speed up the computation even more, see [VFL06]. Note that there exist other techniques for model checking that do not necessarily depend on BDDs for state encoding [BCCZ99].

6 Conclusion

In this work, we presented four organizational principles for the design and control of CPPS. It became clear that central planning of operations still poses computational problems. On the other hand, local control of uncoordinated subsystems may lead to inefficiencies and even deadlocks. To prevent these inefficiencies from happening, one needs to introduce a system model that holds the current state during runtime. This trade-off between the system performance and the technical complexity of the control infrastructure raises a range of questions that need to be answered individually for each CPPS: Which information has to be stored at least about each component? Are there ways to abstract from single resources to subsystems in order to lessen the amount of required data exchange and computation? Can the system be adequately modeled deterministically (with replanning after unexpected events) or is it necessary to address uncertainty about the system state and -dynamics in the model used for control? We considered the organizational principles presented here only in the context of automated production systems. However, similar questions arise in several domains of the manufacturing industry. For example in the supply chain, or on the different hierarchical levels of an enterprise. It is unlikely that a single organizational paradigm will be used in all of these contexts. Then, appropriate interfaces need to be introduced. Linking, for example, a make-or-buy decision for parts of a customized product order to the actual execution of automated manufacturing procedures in a CPPS. Of course, humans are to remain an integral part of this decision making process on the higher levels.

Bibliography

[AKM03]   Yasmina Abdeddaïm, Abdelkarim Kerbaa, and Oded Maler. Task graph scheduling using timed automata. In *Parallel and Distributed Processing Symposium, 2003. Proceedings. International*, pages 8–15. IEEE, 2003.

[BCCZ99]   Armin Biere, Alessandro Cimatti, Edmund Clarke, and Yunshan Zhu. *Symbolic model checking without BDDs.* Springer, 1999.

[BCM+92]   Jerry R Burch, Edmund M Clarke, Kenneth L McMillan, David L Dill, and Lain-Jinn Hwang. Symbolic model checking: 10^{20} states and beyond. *Information and computation*, 98(2):142–170, 1992.

[Bra68]   Dietrich Braess. Über ein Paradoxon aus der Verkehrsplanung. *Unternehmensforschung*, 12(1):258–268, 1968.

[Bry92]   Randal E Bryant. Symbolic boolean manipulation with ordered binary-decision diagrams. *ACM Computing Surveys (CSUR)*, 24(3):293–318, 1992.

[CES71]   Edward G Coffman, Melanie Elphick, and Arie Shoshani. System deadlocks. *ACM Computing Surveys (CSUR)*, 3(2):67–78, 1971.

[Hof11]   Jörg Hoffmann. Everything you always wanted to know about planning. In *KI 2011: Advances in Artificial Intelligence*, pages 1–13. Springer, 2011.

[KWH13]   H Kagermann, W Wahlster, and J Helbig. Umsetzungsempfehlungen für das Zukunftsprojekt Industrie 4.0–Abschlussbericht des Arbeitskreises Industrie 4.0. *Forschungsunion im Stifterverband für die Deutsche Wissenschaft. Berlin*, 2013.

[Lei09]   Paulo Leitão. Agent-based distributed manufacturing control: A state-of-the-art survey. *Engineering Applications of Artificial Intelligence*, 22(7):979–991, 2009.

[LG14]   J Lunze and L Grüne. Introduction to networked control systems. In *Control Theory of Digitally Networked Dynamic Systems*, pages 1–30. Springer, 2014.

[MSC+03]   Duncan McFarlane, Sanjay Sarma, Jin Lung Chirn, CY Wong, and Kevin Ashton. Auto id systems and intelligent manufacturing control. *Engineering Applications of Artificial Intelligence*, 16(4):365–376, 2003.

[Ōno88]   Taiichi Ōno. *Toyota production system: beyond large-scale production.* Productivity press, 1988.

[Pin12]   Michael Pinedo. *Scheduling: theory, algorithms, and systems.* Springer, 2012.

[Rei01]   Raymond Reiter. *Knowledge in action: logical foundations for specifying and implementing dynamical systems*, volume 16. Cambridge Univ Press, 2001.

[Rou05]   Tim Roughgarden. *Selfish routing and the price of anarchy.* MIT press, 2005.

[SWH06]   Weiming Shen, Lihui Wang, and Qi Hao. Agent-based distributed manufacturing process planning and scheduling: a state-of-the-art survey. *Systems, Man, and Cybernetics, Part C: Applications and Reviews, IEEE Transactions on*, 36(4):563–577, 2006.

[VFL06]   Arash Vahidi, Martin Fabian, and Bengt Lennartson. Efficient supervisory synthesis of large systems. *Control engineering practice*, 14(10):1157–1167, 2006.

[Wie48]   Norbert Wiener. Cybernetics; or control and communication in the animal and the machine. 1948.

[WLMF06]   TN Wong, CW Leung, KL Mak, and Richard YK Fung.   Dynamic shopfloor
              scheduling in multi-agent manufacturing systems. *Expert Systems with Applications*,
              31(3):486–494, 2006.

[WWWMM01] Michael P Wellman, William E Walsh, Peter R Wurman, and Jeffrey K MacKie-
              Mason.   Auction protocols for decentralized scheduling.   *Games and Economic
              Behavior*, 35(1):271–303, 2001.

Face Alignment and Multi-Frame Super-Resolution

Chengchao Qu

Vision and Fusion Laboratory
Institute for Anthropomatics
Karlsruhe Institute of Technology (KIT), Germany
qu@kit.edu

Technical Report IES-2013-07

Abstract:
In many computer vision, image processing and pattern recognition tasks, resolution plays a crucial role in the quality of the algorithm. Image super-resolution, which combines a sequence of low-resolution images to generate an artificial image with increased resolution and reduced blur, provides an effective solution. Regarding super-resolution of facial images with a wide range of facial expressions and pose changes, however, registration of multiple frames becomes more difficult. To handle this problem in this work, a face alignment approach optimized for low-resolution images is employed. After fusing the normalized images on the reference frame, a robust image super-resolution and deblurring algorithm is applied, producing visually superior results compared to traditional interpolation-based image resizing techniques.

1 Introduction

Facial image analysis has been an important research topic in the computer vision and pattern recognition community for decades. Recently, in the wake of increasing demand in video security, biometric tasks for low-resolution images from surveillance cameras at a distance have gained greater popularity. Even with HD devices, subjects located far away appear to be of low resolution in the capture of wide-angle surveillance scenario. Moreover, without subject's cooperation, as well as under indoor low-light conditions, poor image quality, *e.g.*, motion blur, interlacing, low-light noise, *etc.*, is another major disadvantageous condition for face recognition algorithms. Due to these deciding factors, a minimal resolution for face recognition, or a general definition of low-resolution facial images does not exist, since such a boundary varies among different datasets and methods. Nevertheless, for images smaller than 32×24 pixels, or with an interocular distance (IOD) of less than 10 pixels, it is almost at the limits of conventional face recognition methods [WMJW+13].

Super-resolution is considered to be a straightforward approach to break the resolution limitation caused by optical and sensor restrictions. As a preprocessing step, it provides super-resolved images for the later stages as if they were working on real high-resolution data. Based on the number of the low-resolution input images, super-resolution can be categorized into two main classes, multi-frame and single-frame super-resolution, which, according to their technical approaches, are also referred to as reconstruction-based and example-based or learning-based methods in the literature.

This work concentrates on the multi-frame case due to its data-driven property, as no prior knowledge for super-resolving facial appearance is needed. For the multi-frame approach, image registration has a huge impact on the final output. Image artifacts occur at the places where texture is erroneously combined. Unlike planar motion of rigid objects, faces embed a rich set of motion (*e.g.*, rotation) and deformation (*e.g.*, facial expression), which cannot be effectively modeled by simple parameterized transformations. In this paper, this non-rigid problem is addressed by using a novel registration model with a resolution-aware Constrained Local Model (CLM) for low-resolution faces. After aligning each face in the given low-resolution sequence, pixels are warped onto the reference frame with the help of triangulation, so that a point cloud denser than the original input frame is generated. Finally, denoising and deblurring are applied to remove averaging effect and noises caused by illumination difference or registration error among the frames. A flow diagram of our proposed system is illustrated in Figure 1.1.

The rest of the paper is organized as follows: Brief introduction and literature review of face alignment and super-resolution, followed by our proposed framework, are presented in §2 and §3 respectively. The experimental setup and results are discussed in §4. In the end, we conclude our work and discuss future research directions in §5.

2   Low-Resolution Face Alignment

Face alignment (or facial feature registration) of images in standard resolution has been extensively studied for decades. It is a crucial step in facial image analysis for the latter processing stages, *e.g.*, face recognition, pose estimation and expression analysis, *etc.* Despite the broad applications with improving performance, due to the ill-posed problem brought by low-resolution images, most existing work concentrating on standard-quality facial images is not directly usable and sees a

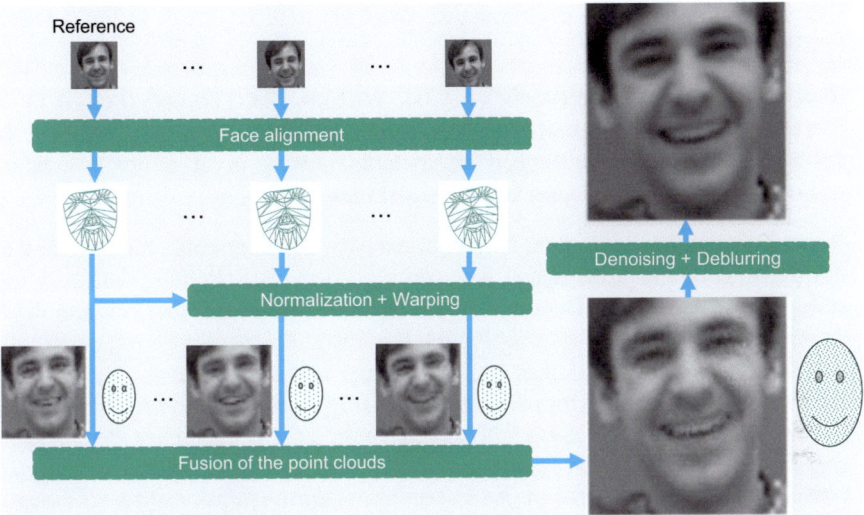

Figure 1.1: Flow diagram of the proposed multi-frame super-resolution framework using face alignment

huge performance drop when the resolution decreases, *e.g.*, when images are acquired by web cameras or closed-circuit televisions (CCTVs). This work addresses this issue by proposing a resolution-aware approach with a mixture of feature descriptors. Difficulties in low-resolution deformable model fitting under changing conditions are resolved.

2.1 Related Work

Since the seminal work of Cootes *et al.* for Active Shape Model (ASM) [CTCG95], as well as its extension Active Appearance Model (AAM) [CET98], fitting 2D images with a statistical deformable shape model has attracted vast interest in the community for years. ASM exploits the image patches around a number of predefined points, which are placed at certain characteristic facial feature landmarks. AAM also employs texture information of the whole face region as a complement to the shape model. Joint optimization searches the best fit between the actual shape and appearance and the synthesized ones from the trained model. However, because of the much larger parameter space, the holistic approach is more prone to local minima. It also lacks the capability to generalize well on unseen data and is thus outperformed by discriminative methods with regard to fitting accuracy [CC06, Liu09].

Recently, some ASM approaches [CC06, WLC08, SLC11], called CLM in the literature, utilize an ensemble of local patch experts and jointly estimate the optimized update for their shape parameters, showing good ability in handling occlusion, global illumination variation, and unseen data.

When fitting to low-resolution images, most existing deformable model fitting algorithms encounter a mismatch between high-resolution training data and low-resolution test images. Dedeoğlu *et al.* [DBK06] point out that original AAM causes loss of quality when warping the low-resolution image onto the reference coordinate frame. Instead, they present a fitting algorithm by reversely modeling the low-resolution image formation process using high-resolution AAM. Liu *et al.* [LTW06] propose an enhancement method for iteratively correcting the AAM fitting procedure and manual annotations, which removes inconsistency in landmark labeling. The improved face model and multi-resolution fitting yield robust results. However, the above generative approaches using holistic appearance features are shown to be more error-prone on unseen data compared to discriminative models [Liu09], *e.g.*, CLM. The benefit of a multi-resolution statistical deformable model is also verified by Hu *et al.* [HCKC12], in which a resolution-aware 3D Morphable Model (3DMM) [BV99] is built with different number of 3D vertices for fitting under various resolutions.

We approach the task of fitting deformable face models to low-resolution images by extending the CLM with a 4-level pyramid for the discriminative patch model. The appropriate pyramid level is automatically selected according to the current shape estimate. Moreover, a number of possible feature descriptors for extracting local patch experts in CLM are investigated and compared to each other.

2.2   Resolution-Aware Constrained Local Model

Assume that we have a dataset with annotated landmarks for each image. A shape denotes the location of these predefined landmarks in a fixed order. Many deformable model fitting algorithms make use of a linear subspace to model non-rigid shapes, which is named Point Distribution Model (PDM). PDM consists of a compact linear subspace shape model with its variation learned using Principal Component Analysis (PCA) on the training data. In order to fit the landmarks to an image, the area around each landmark is exploited. This forms the other component of CLM—the local patch model.

The patch model is a square matrix with its center being placed at the respective landmark. It stores a discriminative texture model around this landmark learned from the dataset. Given the estimate of the current landmark location, the patch model is applied to the underlying image patch, revealing a likelihood response. A discriminative patch model realization is formulated by Wang *et al.* in [WLC08], where the positive and negative training patch samples are first trained with linear Support Vector Machine (SVM), followed by a logistic regressor. Saragih *et al.* [SLC11] outline an efficient CLM fitting strategy with regard to the parametric approximation of the patch model and propose the robust regularized landmark mean-shift algorithm. Our low-resolution face alignment method also builds on this framework.

Traditional CLM approaches do not take account of the resolution of the input images. Given an initial guess of the landmark estimate, the search window around the landmark is rescaled and warped according to the shape-free reference, *i.e.*, the PDM mean shape. For normal fitting tasks, the image resolution is often adequate, meaning that the face in the image is equal to or larger than the reference shape. Therefore, the image is downscaled to the reference size, discarding higher frequency spectrum to match the trained patch experts. However, when the image becomes smaller, the situation changes significantly. Mismatch between the high-resolution trained patch model and the interpolated upsized low-resolution images must be taken into account.

We address the critical impact of resolution mismatch by incorporating a pyramid patch model into the existing CLM framework. A facial image is smoothed and bilinearly downsampled, producing a 4-level pyramid for CLM training. When fitting images, the patch model of the most closest size with reference to the current shape estimate is selected. This model selection step ensures a similar frequency spectrum between model and image, avoiding outliers brought by high-resolution model. Furthermore, at low resolution, images lose a great amount of texture data dependent on decimation scale. To make the most out of the remaining pictorial information, we also employ a number of feature descriptors alongside the raw intensity of the image to add robustness under different conditions. Gradient, Modified Census Transform (MCT), and Laplacian filter are incorporated into the patch model to obtain illumination-invariant and high-passed features. We have already detailed this approach in [QMS13]. Interested readers are thus referred to the original paper. Example fittings on public datasets are given in Figure 2.1.

Figure 2.1: Example fitting results of the proposed low-resolution face alignment algorithm

3 Multi-Frame Super-Resolution

High-quality images are always desired in most imaging applications. Although with the progress of digital imaging technology, better and cheaper optical sensors and objectives come into existence from day to day, high-resolution images are not always available in some areas, *e.g.*, surveillance video, medical and satellite imagery, *etc.* To break the optical limitation on spatial resolution of the image, research on super-resolution came into existence since early 90's. As one of the most active research topics in the past years, approaches on super-resolution span from frequency domain to spatial domain, and from signal processing techniques to machine learning algorithms. In contrast, domain-specific tasks with respect to deformable objects, *e.g.*, human faces, have received very little attention. The reason therefor is the difficulty of registration for low-resolution non-rigid objects between frames. A global assumption for motion is not or only partially satisfied here. This paper presents a novel approach to register low-resolution facial images using the face alignment method demonstrated in §2.

3.1 Related Work

In low-resolution images, high-frequency information from the scene is lost during the degradation process when obtained by the image sensor. If those aliased images are artificially upscaled, *e.g.*, using image interpolation techniques, high-frequency components cannot be recovered since no additional information is provided. Super-resolution solves this ill-posed problem by combining non-redundant information from multiple low-resolution frames of the same scene. Figure 3.1 illustrates the basic idea of multi-frame super-resolution inspired by the low-resolution observation process. When multiple low-resolution images are recorded, small motion of the scene with respect to the sensor produces subpixel shifts in the high-resolution image coordinate. When sampled at a lower frequency, they are mapped to the low-resolution image coordinate with the same integer pixel shift. If these subpixel offsets are registered precisely, the non-redundant information

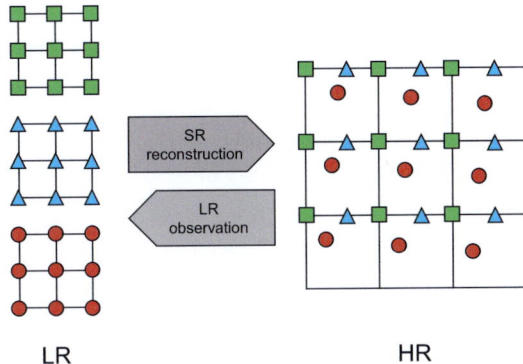

LR   HR

Figure 3.1: Multi-frame super-resolution reconstruction: low-resolution frames with subpixel shifts are registered on the higher-resolution image raster

can be recovered and super-resolution beyond the limitation of the optical system is possible.

Existing multi-frame super-resolution frameworks [IP91, SS96, HBA97, FREM04, UPWB10] employ simple motion models or just assume that motion is known in prior. The non-rigid property of faces, *i.e.*, deformation caused by expressions changes, blinking, talking, *etc.*, fails their observation models when super-resolving facial images. Current multi-frame approaches try to overcome this challenge with diverse motion estimation and compensation algorithms.

Yu and Bhanu [YB06] handle different parts of the faces non-uniformly. Faces are segmented into 5 regions, *i.e.*, left/right eyebrows, left/right eye and mouth, and tracked respectively in the low-resolution video. Fine registration is done using an optical flow method, while patches with lower matching score are discarded from the super-resolution process. This step helps remove misalignment and large deformations. Visually superior results after applying the Iterative Back-Projection (IBP) [IP91] algorithm to the warped patches compared to uniform reconstruction are demonstrated.

Another non-rigid registration method is presented by Yu and Bhanu later in [YB08]. Unlike the segmentation approach in [YB06], Free Form Deformation (FFD) based on B-spline with embedded low-resolution imaging model deforms the input image so that the difference to the reference image is minimized according to some energy functions. The proposed FFD approach shows promising performance in dealing with complicated deformations of human faces. However, a direct comparison to the previous method [YB06] is not given in the paper.

Recently, a real-time super-resolution method with optical flow motion estimation based on robust total least squares is published by Schuchert and Oser [SO12]. The structure tensor approach is embedded in a recursive coarse-to-fine manner, estimating the covariance matrices propagated through the pyramid, which, as motion and confidence measure, are combined with the multi-frame super-resolution approach [FREM04] to enhance the quality of facial image super-resolution.

Since the image registration problem, as a critical component to the multi-frame methods, is yet to be solved, some researchers choose to go another way. Single-frame super-resolution, originated by Baker and Kanade [BK02], is also known as *face hallucination*. The essence of those learning-based methods is to study the relationship between low-resolution and high-resolution image patches. In face hallucination, the super-resolution process is formulated as a Maximum a Posteriori (MAP) estimation to obtain high-frequency components from parent structures using a pyramid derivative set of features instead of raw data. Liu *et al.* [LSF07] treat the MAP formulation in two steps, where the first step uses Eigenfaces [TP91] to produce a smooth global face, followed by high-frequency residue face learned by the training data. Additionally, single-frame super-resolution can also be interpreted as manifold learning to model the correspondence in the low-dimensional subspace [YWHM10].

Although precise registration is not required with example-based algorithms, pose remains a big problem. Mortazavian *et al.* [MKC09] fit a 3DMM [BV99] to low-resolution facial images, and perform pose normalization before face hallucination. Bilgazyev *et al.* [BESK11] also employ ASM for face alignment, but only the global motion (*i.e.*, scale, rotation and translation) is estimated before applying example-based super-resolution [YWHM10].

3.2   Registration

Low-resolution face alignment, introduced in §2, returns the position of the landmarks on the image coordinate. Figure 3.2 demonstrates an example fitting result of 66 landmarks on low-resolution video data with facial expression (smile) and pose change (roll). Compared to 3DMM with typically more than 50000 vertices, our sparse landmarks are able to offer relatively rough registration inside the triangulated areas. These triangles can be generated with Delaunay triangulation on the predefined landmarks in prior.

In multi-frame super-resolution, the low-resolution images to be combined should have as little difference to the reference image as possible in order to suppress artifacts to a minimal level. In computer vision, the most straightforward method for face normalization is the piecewise affine warp. The piecewise affine warp

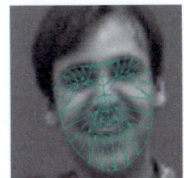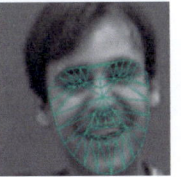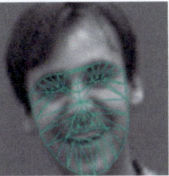

Figure 3.2: Example faces aligned with our resolution-aware CLM in §2

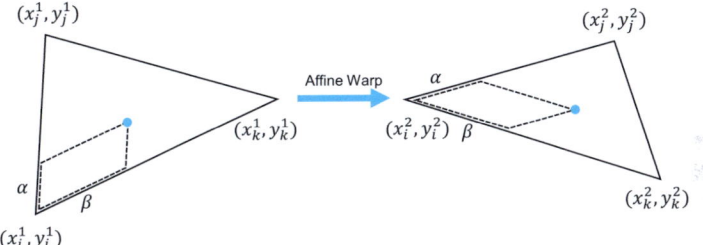

Figure 3.3: Piecewise affine warp

projects each pixel inside a source triangle to the respective location of the destination triangle. As depicted in Figure 3.3, each pixel $\mathbf{x}^1 = (x^1, y^1)^\top$ in a triangle $((x_i^1, y_i^1)^\top, (x_j^1, y_j^1)^\top, (x_k^1, y_k^1)^\top)$ of the base mesh, based on barycentric coordinate, it is uniquely represented by

$$\mathbf{x}^1 = (x_i^1, y_i^1)^\top + \alpha \left((x_j^1, y_j^1)^\top - (x_i^1, y_i^1)^\top\right) + \beta \left((x_k^1, y_k^1)^\top - (x_i^1, y_i^1)^\top\right).$$

In the destination mesh, it is mapped onto the corresponding triangle at

$$\mathbf{x}^2 = (x_i^2, y_i^2)^\top + \alpha \left((x_j^2, y_j^2)^\top - (x_i^2, y_i^2)^\top\right) + \beta \left((x_k^2, y_k^2)^\top - (x_i^2, y_i^2)^\top\right).$$

Afterwards, all low-resolution images are warped to the normalized image. An example of the registration result is seen in Figure 1.1.

Since the core realization [SLC11] for our face alignment approach outputs the estimated 3D coordinate of the fitted landmarks, the 3D coordinates of all pixels inside the face region, *i.e.*, the convex hull of the triangles, can be calculated using the barycentric projection. In this way, a 3D point cloud for each frame is produced. The normalized sparse point clouds are then fused on the reference frame, yielding a denser point cloud for super-resolution.

3.3 Super-Resolution

In consequence of interpolating during piecewise affine warp and averaging of multiple point clouds, a natural process of the blurring effect occurs. The fast and robust multi-frame super-resolution technique of Farsiu *et al.* [FREM04] is integrated in our framework. We denote $\mathbf{x}$ as the high-resolution image and $\mathbf{y}_i$ ($i \in \{1, 2, \ldots, N\}$) as the registered low-resolution frames bilinearly interpolated from the 3D point clouds. The low-resolution image acquisition process can be formulated as

$$\mathbf{y}_i = \mathbf{DHF}_i\mathbf{x} + \mathbf{v}_i,$$

where $\mathbf{F}_i$ is the geometric motion operator between the high-resolution frame $\mathbf{x}$ and low-resolution frame $\mathbf{y}_i$. The blurring matrix $\mathbf{H}$ simulates the camera's point spread function (PSF), where a Gaussian kernel is applied here for approximation. $\mathbf{D}$ means the downsampling decimation operator and $\mathbf{v}_i$ is the additional system noise. Farsiu *et al.* [FREM04] estimate the super-resolved image $\hat{\mathbf{x}}$ by minimizing the modeled degradation image and the actual observations as

$$\hat{\mathbf{x}} = \arg\min_{\mathbf{x}}\left\{\sum_{i=1}^{N}||\mathbf{DHF}_i\mathbf{x} - \mathbf{y}_i||_1^1 + \lambda\mathbf{\Upsilon}(\mathbf{x})\right\}, \qquad (3.1)$$

where the regularization term $\mathbf{\Upsilon}(\mathbf{x})$ uses ℓ_1-based Bilateral Total Variation (BTV) to preserve sharp edges while denoising super-resolution artifacts. The conventional ℓ_2-based least square approaches are proven to be non-robust against inappropriate modeling and registration errors, compared to the ℓ_1 norm employed in Eq. (3.1) [FREM04]. The solution to this function is broken into two steps. First, a blurred version of the high-resolution image $\mathbf{z} = \mathbf{Hx}$ is determined by median operator on the low-resolution point clouds on the high-resolution grid, then $\mathbf{z}$ is deblurred iteratively. One is referred to [FREM04] for details.

4 Experimental Results

In this section, we demonstrate the effectiveness of the proposed multi-frame super-resolution approach with a low-resolution video of a face registered by our face alignment method.

The progressive fusion procedure of the normalized point clouds is shown in Figure 4.1. In the original reference point cloud, the pixels are very sparse and the face is hardly visible on the black background. The more the input point clouds are registered and fused onto the reference frame, the brighter the result point cloud is,

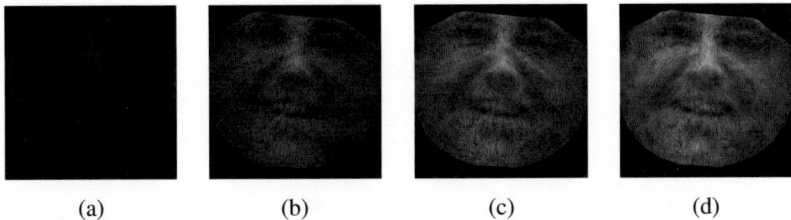

(a) (b) (c) (d)

Figure 4.1: Fusion results of (a) 1 (b) 4 (c) 7 and (d) 10 sparse point clouds

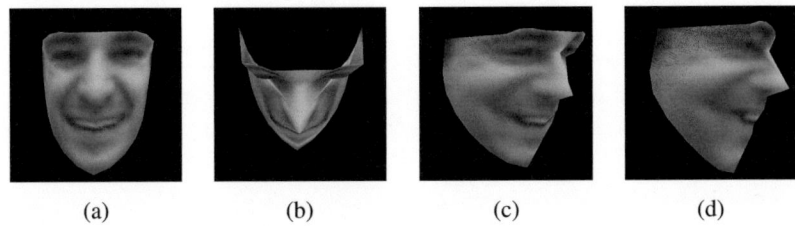

(a) (b) (c) (d)

Figure 4.2: Dense 3D point clouds after registration and fusion in (a) frontal (b) top (c) half profile and (d) profile view

because the "holes" in the point cloud are gradually "filled" with more and more pixels from the subsequent frames. In doing so, more detail is incorporated into the super-resolution image. Note that due to imprecise face registration regarding to large expression changes, or illumination variation, the final point cloud contains some outliers, which can also be seen in the interpolated 2D image in Figure 1.1. These outliers are later removed in the denoising step of super-resolution.

Figure 4.2 reveals the super-resolved 3D point cloud in different views. With 3D registration, it is possible to generate novel views. However, with the rough mesh based on the sparse landmarks from face alignment, the degree of freedom is rather constrained. For example, there is no landmarks on the flat area of the cheek. Hence from the top view in Figure 4.2(b), the large structureless triangles make the face look very unrealistic. Since the video is recorded mostly in frontal view, few pixels near the contour of the face are visible, therefore a lot of "holes" are seen in the profile view (see Figure 4.2(d)).

Figure 4.3 compares the performance of our super-resolution algorithm with the original low-resolution image upscaled with bilinear interpolation. IOD of the original image is approximately 15 pixels. More details and increased sharpness of edges at facial features, *e.g.*, eyes and mouth, are reconstructed with our approach. Noise, which is common in low-resolution images, is also suppressed with the

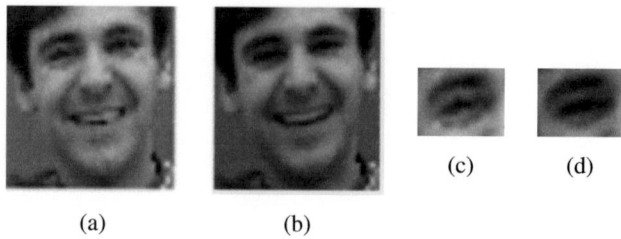

Figure 4.3: Example low-resolution image in (a) and our super-resolution result in (b), as well as details of the right eye in (c) and (d) respectively

regularized multi-frame super-resolution algorithm. This result justifies the feasibility of our proposed face super-resolution framework using face alignment as registration method.

5   Conclusions and Future Work

This paper presents a novel framework for multi-frame facial texture super-resolution. Our resolution-aware face alignment method is applied to the low-resolution video to address the difficulties in deformable object registration of low-resolution images. On the basis of the fitted sparse landmarks, pixels are warped to the reference grid using piecewise affine warp in the triangulated mesh. A fast and robust multi-frame super-resolution method is integrated, yielding visually better results.

The robustness of registration plays an important part in super-resolution. Just one pixel error of the landmark in the low-resolution image could lead to error of several pixels in the high-resolution grid. Therefore, a better low-resolution face alignment algorithm with state-of-the-art performance is under research. It is also remarked that the current approach with sparse facial landmarks only allows a limit degree of pose and facial expression variation. A realistic morphable model fitting [MKC09] might provide greater capability in handling these situations. However, the efficiency of the 3DMM-based approaches must be taken into account for online applications. Furthermore, single-frame super-resolution [BK02, LSF07, YWHM10] could show another direction for super-resolving faces, as the trouble of precise multi-frame registration does not exist any more.

Bibliography

[BESK11]   Emil Bilgazyev, Boris Efraty, Shishir K. Shah, and Ioannis A. Kakadiaris. Improved face recognition using super-resolution. In *Proceedings of the International Joint Conference on Biometrics (IJCB)*, pages 1–7, 2011.

[BK02]   Simon Baker and Takeo Kanade. Limits on super-resolution and how to break them. *IEEE Transactions on Pattern Analysis and Machine Intelligence*, 24(9):1167–1183, 2002.

[BV99]   Volker Blanz and Thomas Vetter. A morphable model for the synthesis of 3D faces. In *Proceedings of the International Conference and Exhibition on Computer Graphics and Interactive Techniques (SIGGRAPH)*, pages 187–194, 1999.

[CC06]   David Cristinacce and Timothy F. Cootes. Feature detection and tracking with constrained local models. In *Proceedings of the British Machine Vision Conference (BMVC)*, pages 929–938, 2006.

[CET98]   Timothy F. Cootes, Gareth J. Edwards, and Christopher J. Taylor. Active appearance models. In *Proceedings of the European Conference on Computer Vision (ECCV)*, volume 2, pages 484–498, 1998.

[CTCG95]   Timothy F. Cootes, Christopher J. Taylor, David H. Cooper, and Jim Graham. Active shape models-their training and application. *Computer Vision and Image Understanding*, 61(1):38–59, 1995.

[DBK06]   Göksel Dedeoğlu, Simon Baker, and Takeo Kanade. Resolution-aware fitting of active appearance models to low-resolution images. In *Proceedings of the European Conference on Computer Vision (ECCV)*, volume II, pages 83–97, 2006.

[FREM04]   Sina Farsiu, M. Dirk Robinson, Michael Elad, and Peyman Milanfar. Fast and robust multiframe super resolution. *IEEE Transactions on Image Processing*, 13(10):1327–1344, 2004.

[HBA97]   Russell C. Hardie, Kenneth J. Barnard, and Ernest E. Armstrong. Joint map registration and high-resolution image estimation using a sequence of undersampled images. *IEEE Transactions on Image Processing*, 6(12):1621–1633, 1997.

[HCKC12]   Guosheng Hu, Chi-Ho Chan, Josef Kittler, and Bill Christmas. Resolution-aware 3D morphable model. In *Proceedings of the British Machine Vision Conference (BMVC)*, pages 1–10, 2012.

[IP91]   Michal Irani and Shmuel Peleg. Improving resolution by image registration. *CVGIP: Graphical Models and Image Processing*, 53(3):231–239, April 1991.

[Liu09]   Xiaoming Liu. Discriminative face alignment. *IEEE Transactions on Pattern Analysis and Machine Intelligence*, 31(11):1941–1954, 2009.

[LSF07]   Ce Liu, Heung-Yeung Shum, and William T. Freeman. Face hallucination: Theory and practice. *International Journal of Computer Vision*, 75(1):115–134, 2007.

[LTW06]   Xiaoming Liu, Peter H. Tu, and Frederick W. Wheeler. Face model fitting on low resolution images. In *Proceedings of the British Machine Vision Conference (BMVC)*, pages 1079–1088, 2006.

[MKC09]   Pouria Mortazavian, Josef Kittler, and William J. Christmas. 3D-assisted facial texture super-resolution. In *Proceedings of the British Machine Vision Conference (BMVC)*, pages 1–11, 2009.

[QMS13]   Chengchao Qu, Eduardo Monari, and Tobias Schuchert. Resolution-aware constrained local model with mixture of local experts. In *Workshop on Low-Resolution Face Analysis (LRFA) in conjunction with the IEEE International Conference on Advanced Video and Signal Based Surveillance (AVSS)*, pages 454–459, 2013.

[SLC11]   Jason M. Saragih, Simon Lucey, and Jeffrey F. Cohn. Deformable model fitting by regularized landmark mean-shift. *International Journal of Computer Vision*, 91:200–215, 2011.

[SO12]   Tobias Schuchert and Fabian Oser. Optical flow estimation with confidence measures for super-resolution based on recursive robust total least squares. In *Proceedings of the International Conference on Pattern Recognition Applications and Methods (ICPRAM)*, pages 463–469, 2012.

[SS96]   Richard R. Schultz and Robert L. Stevenson. Extraction of high-resolution frames from video sequences. *IEEE Transactions on Image Processing*, 5(6):996–1011, 1996.

[TP91]   Matthew A. Turk and Alex P. Pentland. Face recognition using eigenfaces. In *Proceedings of the IEEE Conference on Computer Vision and Pattern Recognition (CVPR)*, pages 586–591, 1991.

[UPWB10]   Markus Unger, Thomas Pock, Manuel Werlberger, and Horst Bischof. A convex approach for variational super-resolution. In *Proceedings of the DAGM conference on Pattern recognition*, pages 313–322, Berlin, Heidelberg, 2010. Springer-Verlag.

[WLC08]   Yang Wang, Simon Lucey, and Jeffrey F. Cohn. Enforcing convexity for improved alignment with constrained local models. In *Proceedings of the IEEE Conference on Computer Vision and Pattern Recognition (CVPR)*, pages 1–8, 2008.

[WMJW+13] Zhifei Wang, Zhenjiang Miao, Q.M. Jonathan Wu, Yanli Wan, and Zhen Tang. Low-resolution face recognition: a review. *The Visual Computer*, pages 1–28, 2013.

[YB06]   Jiangang Yu and Bir Bhanu. Super-resolution restoration of facial images in video. In *Proceedings of the International Conference on Pattern Recognition (ICPR)*, volume 4, pages 342–345, 2006.

[YB08]   Jiangang Yu and Bir Bhanu. Super-resolution of facial images in video with expression changes. In *Proceedings of the IEEE International Conference on Advanced Video and Signal Based Surveillance (AVSS)*, pages 184–191, 2008.

[YWHM10]   Jianchao Yang, John Wright, Thomas S. Huang, and Yi Ma. Image super-resolution via sparse representation. *IEEE Transactions on Image Processing*, 19(11):2861–2873, 2010.

Automatic Selection of Optical Filters for Classification in Hyperspectral Images

Matthias Richter

Vision and Fusion Laboratory
Institute for Anthropomatics
Karlsruhe Institute of Technology (KIT), Germany
matthias.richter@kit.edu

Technical Report IES-2013-08

Abstract:
  The color of a material is one of the most frequently used feature in automated visual inspection systems. While it is sufficient for many "easy" tasks, more complex materials such as food-stuffs and minerals usually require more complex features. Spectral "signatures" in the near infrared or UV spectrum have proven useful, but hyperspectral imaging devices are still too costly and too slow for industrial application. Therefore, off-the-shelve cameras and optical filters are used to extract characteristic features from the spectra. While the visual inspection community has acknowledged the benefits of this method, relatively few works are concerned with automatic selection of suitable filters. In a novel approach, filter selection is generalized as *feature* selection problem. In contrast to existing methods, this method can be used to select the best out of a large given set of filters, e.g. from a catalogue. This meta-method is exemplified by application of feature selection methods based on linear discriminant analysis, information theory and boosting.

1 Introduction

At the present time, automated visual inspection of bulk materials is primarily achieved by utilizing color information. This approach ensures high throughput and economic feasibility, but hits a wall when the materials under inspection are of similar color (low *inter-class* variance) or when the material of one class occupies large regions of the color space (large *inter-class* variance). Both is commonly the case with organic materials, like fruit and crop, but also applies to inorganic substances such as minerals and alloys. Often, reliable discrimination is still possible by exploiting reflectance-characteristics outside of the visible spectrum, especially the near infrared and ultraviolet spectral bands, or by utilizing narrow banded, faint fluorescence and luminescence effects. One might be tempted to use the full "spectral fingerprint" of a material for classification by including a hyperspectral imaging device in the inspection pipeline. However, such devices are more expensive, have a low spatial resolution and require brighter illumination or longer exposure times than off-the-shelve industrial cameras. Furthermore, these devices produce much higher data volume, which in turn increases the time required for data transfer and processing. These factors make such a solution impractical in an industrial settings.

A common workaround solution combines off-the-shelve cameras with optical filters. The spectral signatures of the materials under inspection are obtained in the laboratory or from a spectral database and analysed to determine the discriminative wavelength bands. Suitable optical filters are manufactured or acquired accordingly. The resulting visual inspection system uses only the reduced, usually one- to four-channel image to perform it's task. This approach is all the more attractive, since existing solutions can often be repurposed with minimal effort.

There are two general methods to determine the filters: top-down (design) and bottom-up (selection). In the *design* approach, filter transmission functions are designed based on the results of the analysis and realized using e.g. thin-film optical filters [Mac01]. The resulting solution is optimal for the task at hand, but – depending on the complexity of the transmission function – relatively expensive. *Selection*, on the other hand, chooses the best few filters from a pool of possibilities. While the pool may contain arbitrary transmission functions, an interesting case emerges when it is matched with optical filters in a catalogue. This solution is often sub-optimal, but since the filters can be mass-produced, it is generally more cost-effective than the design approach. This work focuses on the second approach, selection, for application in an industrial setting.

1.1 Related Work

The visual inspection community has long since acknowledged the usefulness of filter selection based on hyperspectral imaging. For example, Kleynen et at. selected a combination of four bandpass filters from a pool of 24 possibilities in order to detect defects in "Jonagold" apple fruits [KLD03]. They rated each combination using the correct classification rate of a quadratic discriminant analysis classifier on the filtered spectra. In [PLK+08], Piron et al. use a similar method to select up to four filters (out of 22) to discriminate weeds from crop. While this exhaustive search works well with a small pool of filters, it does not scale well due to combinatory explosion.

Other approaches do not focus on finding the best performing filter combination, but rather, identify the most discriminative wavelengths to guide a subsequent (manual) filter selection. Osborne et al. use the regression coefficients obtained in partial least squares analysis as proxy to rank wavelengths by their relative importance [OKJ97]. This approach can be used to select both an optimum (with respect to discriminative power), or fixed number of wavelengths. In [FVG01], Feyaerts and van Gool rank wavelengths using the Fisher criterion, i.e. the ratio of variability between, and variability within classes. The highest ranking wavelength is selected automatically, while lower ranking wavelengths are only considered when they are positioned "sufficiently far" from the already selected ones. Similarly, Chao et al. perform a stepwise selection according to the Fisher criterion in a five-class classification problem [CCHP01]. However, unlike Feyaerts and van Gool, the ranking in each step is computed with respect to the already selected wavelengths. Similar ideas can be found in the remote sensing field: Pal uses (i) coefficients of the weight vector of a support vector machine and (ii) model parameters in sparse multinomial regression to create a ranking. The intuition is that, similar to the approach of Osborne et al., both methods encode the relative importance of each wavelength [Pal09, Pal12]. Guo et al. utilize mutual information of each band with a set of key-spectra that they expect to find in the hyperspectral images [GGDN06].

Alternative methods lend ideas from filter design: De Backer et al. parametrize a set of band-pass filters by their central wavelength and band-width [DBKDS05]. The parameters are jointly optimized by adaptive simulated annealing using the Bhattacharya bound (which is an upper bound on the Bayes error) as merit function. Similarly, Nakauchi et al. optimize band-pass parameters – lower and upper wavelength – by a global, random sampling based search followed by local optimization [NNY12]. In both steps the Fisher criterion serves as merit function.

All these band selection and parameter optimization approaches indeed show promising theoretical developments in their respective application areas. However, there is no guarantee that matching *physical* optical filters are available or even realizable in an economically feasible way. Therefore it is worth to take a step back and look at the problem in a different light.

2   Methods

Filter selection can be formalized in the following way: Given a set of filter transmission functions $\mathcal{F}$, a ground truth dataset $\mathcal{T}$, and a merit function $\gamma(\cdot, \cdot)$, the goal is to select an optimal set of filters, i.e. $\mathcal{S} \subseteq \mathcal{F}$ so that $\gamma(\mathcal{S}, \mathcal{T})$ is at a maximum.

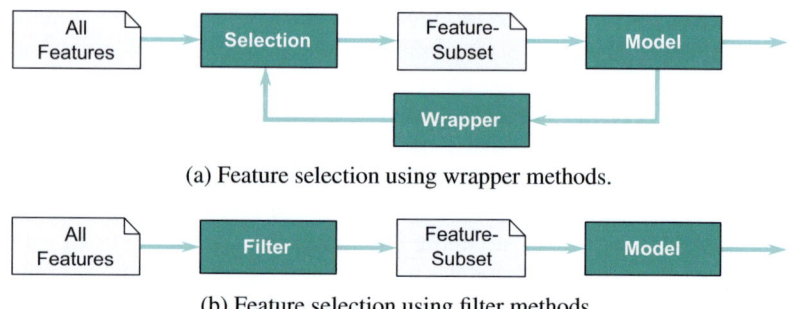

(a) Feature selection using wrapper methods.

(b) Feature selection using filter methods.

Figure 2.1: Schema of feature selection by wrapper and filter methods.

By simply replacing the words "filter transmission functions" with "features" one arrives at a formal definition of *feature selection* as known in the machine learning community. This is an important insight, as it allows to use the numerous methods found in literature. Generally, these methods can be divided into three classes: wrapper, filter and embedded methods.

Wrapper methods select a feature-subset according to some selection parameters or feature ranking. A model is trained using the subset, and the model's prediction performance is used to re-parametrize or re-rank the feature selection. The process is repeated until some stopping criterion is reached. While this is a straightforward method, it is prone to overfitting the chosen predictor: the feature selection may not work as well when using a different method.

Filter methods on the other hand select a subset according to some classifier-independent, objective criterion. Since the election contains the (globally) most relevant features, it is expected to work equally well on different classifiers. However, the selection may be suboptimal when a specific model is concerned.

Finally, in embedded methods the feature selection process is embedded in the learning algorithm in a fundamental way – hence the name. Popular examples of such algorithms are random forests [Bre01] and multinomial logistic regression with sparsity constraints.

2.1 Preliminary Considerations

Before showing the application of wrapper, filter and embedded methods in the context of optical filter selection, it is necessary to fill in some details of the above definition: The ground truth dataset $\mathcal{T}$ consists of N training samples $(\mathbf{s}_i, y_i)$, where $\mathbf{s}_i \in \mathbb{R}^b$ is a measured point spectrum with b bands, and $y_i = \pm 1$ denotes the associated class. The K filter transmission functions (i.e. features) $f \in \mathcal{F}$ map a given measurement to a scalar, $f : \mathbb{R}^b \to \mathbb{R}$, where $g = f(\mathbf{s})$ represents the response of the filter f to the spectrum $\mathbf{s}$. A selection of features is a subset $\mathcal{S} \subseteq \mathcal{F}$; the complement $\overline{S} = \mathcal{F} \setminus \mathcal{S}$ contains the $K - |\mathcal{S}|$ unselected features. To enable a concise notation, $\mathbf{f}_\mathcal{S} = (f_1, \ldots, f_S)^\top$ is used to denote the vector of features in the selection $\mathcal{S}$.

Some methods require discrete features to be efficiently computable. The discretization of the feature f_k will be denoted h_k, where in this work

$$h_k(\mathbf{s}) = \begin{cases} 1 & \text{if } f_k(\mathbf{s}) \leq \tau_k \\ -1 & \text{otherwise.} \end{cases}$$

The threshold τ_k can be determined arbitrarily, e.g. through random selection or to minimize classification error of a classifier using $(f_k(\mathbf{s_i}), y_i)$ as training data.

Note that the filter functions f_k can be chosen arbitrarily; if only one band is extracted, the resulting method will in fact be a band selection technique.

2.2 Wrapper Methods

A simple wrapper method can be derived from Fisher's linear discriminant analysis (LDA). Briefly, LDA determines a projection direction $\mathbf{w}$ that maximizes class separation of the projected training samples by optimizing the Fisher criterion

$$J(\mathbf{w}) = \frac{\mathbf{w}^\top \mathbf{S}_B \mathbf{w}}{\mathbf{w}^\top \mathbf{S}_W \mathbf{w}}.$$

Here $\mathbf{S}_B$ and $\mathbf{S}_W$ are the between-class and within-class covariance matrices of the training samples. By differentiating $J(\mathbf{w})$ with respect to $\mathbf{w}$ it can be shown that the $J(\mathbf{w})$ is maximized by

$$\mathbf{w} \propto \mathbf{S}_W^{-1}(\mathbf{m}_1 - \mathbf{m}_{-1}),$$

where $\mathbf{m}_y$ denotes the mean of training samples in the respective class. Note that as $\mathbf{w}$ does not represent a separating hyperplane, but only a projection that maximizes class separation, LDA is in itself not a classification method. A linear classifier is usually constructed from $\mathbf{w}$ by choosing a threshold τ to separate the projected features:

$$H(\mathbf{s}) = \begin{cases} 1 & \text{if } \mathbf{w}^\top \mathbf{s} \leq \tau, \\ -1 & \text{otherwise.} \end{cases}$$

Wrapper methods often evaluate feature subsets by classification error using that subset, usually by the means of cross-validation. In the case of LDA this is not necessary: Provided that an optimal threshold was chosen, the classification error depends only on $\mathbf{w}$. Therefore $J(\mathbf{w})$ acts as a surrogate for the classifier performance. This observation motivates the following greedy feature selection method: Starting with an initial (empty) selection $\mathcal{S}_0 = \emptyset$, unselected features are iteratively added to maximize the Fisher criterion, i.e.

$$f_t = \arg\max_{f \in \overline{\mathcal{S}}_{t-1}} J(\mathbf{w}_t),$$

where $\mathbf{w}_t$ is computed using the feature f candidate and the selection of the last step $\mathcal{S}_{t-1}$. To ensure minimality of the feature set, the procedure may be extended by backward elimination: After each selection step, features may be unselected when removal has little impact on the classification performance.

2.3 Filter Methods

As mentioned above, wrapper methods select features that are optimal with respect to a given classifier, but there is no guarantee the selection will perform as well with other methods. This is especially problematic in the context of industrial applications, where the classifier is often not an elaborate method, but simple application of thresholds. In contrast, filter methods evaluate a given subset of features by means of some utility function that is independent of any classifier. Well known methods are based on information gain, Pearson's correlation coefficient or mutual information. Recently Brown et al. unified many of those methods in their Conditional Likelihood Maximisation framework [BPZL12], which will be briefly outlined below.

The framework is developed by maximization of the log-likelihood of a *hypothetical* predictive model q with parameters θ on the feature selection $\mathcal{S}$,

$$\ell = \frac{1}{N} \log \mathcal{L}(\mathcal{S}, \theta | \mathcal{T}) = \frac{1}{N} \sum_{i=1}^{N} q(y_i | \mathbf{f}_{\mathcal{S}}(\mathbf{s}_i), \theta).$$

They show that the log-likelihood can be decomposed into three terms,

$$\lim_{N \to \infty} -\ell = E_{\mathbf{f}y} \left\{ \log \frac{p(y|\mathbf{f}_{\mathcal{S}})}{q(y|\mathbf{f}_{\mathcal{S}}, \theta)} \right\} + I(F_{\overline{\mathcal{S}}}; Y | F_{\mathcal{S}}) + H(Y | F_{\mathcal{F}}),$$

where $F_{\mathcal{X}}$ and Y denote random variables corresponding to the feature vectors $\mathbf{f}_{\mathcal{X}}$ and class labels y respectively. The first term represents how well q can model the true distribution p. The conditional mutual information (CMI) term $I(F_{\overline{S}}; Y|F_S)$ encodes the amount of additional information about class labels that can be gained from the unselected features, given what is already known from the selected features. The last term, $H(Y|F_{\mathcal{F}})$, is the entropy of class labels conditioned on all features and represents the remaining uncertainty of the class labels, even when all features are considered.

Since the CMI term depends only on the feature selection, ℓ can be maximised independently of the model q by minimizing $I(F_{\overline{S}}; Y|F_S)$. Similar to the LDA approach, this is achieved by iterative greedy selection: In the selection step, the feature that maximizes the CMI with the labels is added to $\mathcal{S}$,

$$f_{t+1} = \arg\max_{f \in \overline{S}_t} I(F; Y|F_{S_t}) =: \arg\max_{f \in \overline{S}_t} J_{cmi}(f, S_t).$$

In the elimination step, a feature f_k may be unselected if the removal does not significantly decrease information content, i.e. if $I(F_k; Y|F_{S_t \setminus \{f_k\}}) < \tau$.

For further analysis, the criterion is decomposed into three terms that each encode different aspects of the selection method:

$$J_{cmi}(f_k, \mathcal{S}) = I(F_k; Y) - I(F_k; F_S) + I(F_k; F_S|Y).$$

The first term evaluates the relevance of the feature f_k to separate the classes, while the second term penalizes redundant features. The third term rewards redundant features, but only if those features show strong statistical dependency within classes[1]. Joint optimization of J_{cmi} is computationally intractable, so simplifying assumptions have to be made: For all unselected features f_k, it is assumed that (i) selected features are conditionally independent given f_k and (ii) selected features are conditionally independent given f_k and y. The criterion can then be approximated as

$$\hat{J}_{cmi}(f_k, \mathcal{S}) = I(F_k; Y) - \sum_{f_j \in \mathcal{S}} I(F_k; F_j) + \sum_{f_j \in \mathcal{S}} I(F_k; F_j|Y).$$

Using this formulation several well known methods can be reformulated to fit in this framework. The *Minimum-Reduncancy Maximum-Relavance* (MRMR) criterion proposed by Peng et al. [PLD05], for example, can be expressed as

$$J_{mrmr}(f_k, \mathcal{S}) = I(F_k; Y) - \frac{1}{|\mathcal{S}|} \sum_{f_j \in \mathcal{S}} I(F_j; F_k).$$

---

[1] Brown et al. note that this *conditional redundancy* term is often ignored in the literature [BPZL12].

This formulation can be interpreted such that MRMR assumes class-conditional pairwise independence of the selected features, therefore dropping the conditional redundancy term. As the selection grows, MRMR gradually adopts the additional assumption that the selected features are pairwise independent.

Yang and Moody's *Joint Mutual Information* (JMI) [YM99] expands MRMR by the conditional-relevancy term,

$$J_{jmi}(f_k, \mathcal{S}) = I(F_k; Y) - \frac{1}{|\mathcal{S}|} \sum_{f_j \in \mathcal{S}} \Big(I(F_j; F_k) - I(F_j; F_k | Y) \Big).$$

Unlike MRMR, JMI does not assume class-conditional pairwise independence from the start, but adopts this belief as the number of selected features increases.

Motivated by these interpretations, both methods can be modified to include prior knowledge derived from the use case: Two features are likely to be pairwise (and pair-wise class-conditionally) independent, if the corresponding optical filters do not overlap. This can be encoded by some similarity measure $s(f_j, f_k)$, where $s(f_j, f_k) = 0$ denotes no overlap, and $s(f_j, f_k) = 1$ means that f_j and f_k share the same transmission spectrum. The resulting criteria, similarity-MRMR and similarity-JMI, are computed as

$$J_{smrmr}(f_k, \mathcal{S}) = I(F_k; Y) - \sum_{f_j \in \mathcal{S}} s(f_j, f_k) I(F_j; F_k) \qquad \text{and}$$

$$J_{sjmi}(f_k, \mathcal{S}) = I(F_k; Y) - \sum_{f_j \in \mathcal{S}} s(f_j, f_k) \Big(I(F_j; F_k) - I(F_j; F_k | Y) \Big).$$

2.4 Embedded Methods

Embedded methods position themselves between wrappers and filters. Like wrappers, they utilize a model to select features. However, the selection is not based on predictive performance, but rather a direct result of the learning algorithm. In the following, an embedded method is derived from Freund and Schapire's AdaBoost algorithm [FS95].

In boosting, the decisions of several weak classifiers h_t are pooled to build a classifier H. Even though the individual h_t may perform barely better than chance, their collective vote will form a strong classifier. In AdaBoost, this classifier is of the form

$$H(\mathbf{s}) = \text{sign}\left(\sum_{t=1}^{T} \alpha_t h_t(\mathbf{s}) \right).$$

The weak classifiers h_t and corresponding weights α_t are selected in an iterative process: A distribution of weights W_t encodes the importance of each training sample (initially each training sample is equally important, $W_1(t) = \frac{1}{N}$). In the t-th iteration, h_t is selected to minimize the weighted error rate on the training samples, i.e.

$$h_t = \arg\max_h \left| \frac{1}{2} - \varepsilon(h) \right|, \quad \text{where}$$

$$\varepsilon(h) = \sum_{i=1}^{N} W_t(i) \big[h(\mathbf{s}_i) \neq y_i \big].$$

The corresponding weight α_t is computed from the weighted training error $\varepsilon(h_t)$, typically as log-odds of the (weighted) correct classification rate,

$$\alpha_t = \log \frac{1 - \varepsilon(h_t)}{\varepsilon(h_t)}.$$

Finally, the weight distribution is updated so that the training samples that h_t classified incorrectly will be more important in the next round:

$$W_{t+1}(i) = \exp\Big(\alpha_t \big[h_t(\mathbf{s}_i) \neq y_i \big] \Big) \frac{W_t(i)}{\sum_{i=1}^{N} W_{t+1}(i)}.$$

Iteration is stopped if either a maximum number of weak learners is selected, or if $\varepsilon(h_t)$ is not significantly different from a random choice.

By recalling the feature discretization in section 2.1 it is apparent how AdaBoost can be used for feature selection: Each discretized feature is itself a weak learner. The classifier ensemble H then represents the feature selection, where $|\alpha_t|$ encodes the importance of the feature f_t.

An interesting observation is that this technique could also be used for filter *design*: Since H represents a linear combination of filters, one could derive a global filter transmission function by choosing $f \in \mathcal{F}$ to represent suitable basis functions instead of physical filters. However, note that this may results in two filters, one corresponding to the positive, and one corresponding to the negative transmission coefficients.

3 Conclusion

Numerous works have shown the benefit of using optical filters derived from spectral analysis for visual inspection tasks. There are two general approaches to obtain suitable filters: design of a specialized transmission function and selection from a pool of possibilitiers. The design approach generally produces filters optimally suited for the task at hand, but the high manufacturing costs hamper application in an industrial setting. Selection, on the other hand, results in low costs due to the usage of off-the-shelve filters, although the solution may be suboptimal. While there are many methods suitable forfilter design, especially in the field of remote sensing, surprisingly few works are considered with automatic filter selection.

In a novel and comprehensive approach, filters selection is explicitly reduced to *feature* selection as it is known in the machine learning literature. The approach has been exemplified by a wrapper method based on LDA, a filter method using information theoretic measures, and by embedding the selection into the AdaBoost algorithm. Interestingly, the third method could also be extended to allow filter design.

Although targeted at visual inspection, the presented approach can also be used for band selection in remote sensing applications. Another interesting application arises when the filter pool does not only contain individual filters, but arbitrary combinations (e.g. monomials, which correspond to chains of filters) as well.

Bibliography

[BPZL12]   Gavin Brown, Adam Pocock, Ming-Jie Zhao, and Mikel Luján. Conditional likelihood maximisation: A unifying framework for information theoretic feature selection. *The Journal of Machine Learning Research*, 13:27–66, 2012.

[Bre01]   Leo Breiman. Random forests. *Machine learning*, 45(1):5–32, 2001.

[CCHP01]   Kuanglin Chao, YR Chen, WR Hruschka, and B Park. Chicken Heart Disease Characterization by Multi-spectral Imaging. *Applied engineering in agriculture*, 17(1):99–106, 2001.

[DBKDS05]   Steve De Backer, Pieter Kempeneers, Walter Debruyn, and Paul Scheunders. A Band Selection Technique for Spectral Classification. *Geoscience and Remote Sensing Letters, IEEE*, 2(3):319–323, 2005.

[FS95]   Yoav Freund and Robert E Schapire. A Decision-Theoretic Generalization of On-Line Learning and an Application to Boosting. In *Computational learning theory*, pages 23–37. Springer, 1995.

[FVG01]   Filip Feyaerts and Luc Van Gool. Multi-spectral vision system for weed detection. *Pattern Recognition Letters*, 22(6):667–674, 2001.

[GGDN06]   Baofeng Guo, Steve R Gunn, RI Damper, and JDB Nelson. Band Selection for Hyperspectral Image Classification Using Mutual Information. *Geoscience and Remote Sensing Letters, IEEE*, 3(4):522–526, 2006.

[KLD03]   O Kleynen, Vincent Leemans, and M-F Destain. Selection of the most efficient wavelength bands for 'Jonagold' apple sorting. *Postharvest Biology and Technology*, 30(3):221–232, 2003.

[Mac01]   Hugh Angus Macleod. *Thin-Film Optical Filters*. CRC Press, 2001.

[NNY12]   Shigeki Nakauchi, Ken Nishino, and Takuya Yamashita. Selection of optimal combinations of band-pass filters for ice detection by hyperspectral imaging. *Optics Express*, 20(2):986–1000, 2012.

[OKJ97]   Scott D Osborne, Rainer Künnemeyer, and Robert B Jordan. Method of Wavelength Selection for Partial Least Squares. *Analyst*, 122(12):1531–1537, 1997.

[Pal09]   Mahesh Pal. Margin-based feature selection for hyperspectral data. *International Journal of Applied Earth Observation and Geoinformation*, 11(3):212–220, 2009.

[Pal12]   Mahesh Pal. Multinomial logistic regression-based feature selection for hyperspectral data. *International Journal of Applied Earth Observation and Geoinformation*, 14(1):214–220, 2012.

[PLD05]   Hanchuan Peng, Fuhui Long, and Chris Ding. Feature Selection Based on Mutual Information: Criteria of Max-Dependency, Max-Relevance, and Min-Redundancy. *Pattern Analysis and Machine Intelligence, IEEE Transactions on*, 27(8):1226–1238, 2005.

[PLK+08]   Alexis Piron, Vincent Leemans, O Kleynen, Frédéric Lebeau, and M-F Destain. Selection of the most efficient wavelength bands for discriminating weeds from crop. *Computers and Electronics in Agriculture*, 62(2):141–148, 2008.

[YM99]   H Yang and John Moody. Feature Selection Based on Joint Mutual Information. In *Proceedings of International ICSC Symposium on Advances in Intelligent Data Analysis*, pages 22–25. Citeseer, 1999.

Optimizing Deflectometric Measurements for Visibility

Masoud Roschani

Vision and Fusion Laboratory
Institute for Anthropomatics
Karlsruhe Institute of Technology (KIT), Germany
masoud.roschani@kit.edu

Technical Report IES-2012-09

Abstract: Visibility is a general problem in visual inspection tasks. Especially in deflectometry, where the measurement area depends on how light is reflected on the surface, and thus of the shape of the surface itself. We consider the problem of finding an inspection plan such that the whole surface is completely covered. This problem is related to the classical set cover problem and is known to be NP-hard. We formulate the problem as a non-greedy optimization problem and investigate the usage of two global optimization algorithms and their combination for small sized problems.

1   Introduction

In deflectometry [Wer11] the test object is part of the measurement mapping and can only be observed indirectly through the reflection of the environment or pre-specified patterns. Depending on the size of the pattern generator and the surface shape only small regions of the test object may be observed. E.g. on a convex shaped object the light cone when observed from the camera, expand. Therefore the inspected area decreases with increasing convex curvature.

To reduce this problem a larger screen could be used. For example a so called cave could be used. The cave is a room where images can be projected onto its walls by means of a projector, i.e. the walls serve as the display. The test object is placed in the room and the reflection of of the walls can be viewed on the surface. Nevertheless it is not guaranteed that every possible surface can be fully observed. Here, we follow the approach of using a movable sensor (e.g. fixed on a robot arm). This makes it possible to plan for a whole coverage and to observe difficult locations on the surface. The challenge here is to select appropriate sensor configurations (i.e. position and orientation of the display and camera) for the deflectometric sensor.

Generally, it is possible to choose the sensor configuration manually. But in contrast to measuring with a camera sensor, the measurement areas in a deflectometric measurement can have nontrivial shapes, especially for complex shaped objects. This makes the procedure for a human non trivial and time consuming.

We investigate an automatic determination of sensor configurations for the deflectometric inspection task. We assume that the inspection surface can be represented as a function f and a reference surface is given (e.g. in form of a CAD model), which has only small deviations from the surface to be inspected. Then, the planning procedure can also be executed offline We choose a sequence of sensor configurations, also called a *plan*, which covers the whole surface.

This report is structured as follows: In Section 2 the set cover problem is introduced and its relation to surface inspection in deflectometry is established. Section 3 gives a short description of the deflectometric measurement/simulation model used in this report. Section 4 introduces to the planning problem and the next section to optimization algorithms used for solving it. The solution procedure is evaluated on several surfaces in a simulation in Section 6. Finally, we conclude in Section 7.

2   Covering Problem

The problem of surface inspection in deflectometry is related to the more general and well known set cover problem. In the classic set cover problem a finite set of elements $\mathcal{U}$ and a collection of subsets $\mathcal{S}$ is given. The problem is to find the smallest subcollection $\mathcal{S}' \subset \mathcal{S}$ of subsets such that their union contains all elements in the finite set. This subcollection is called the *minimal set cover*. It is well known that the set cover problem is NP-hard. An optimal solution can only be found for small sized problems or in some special cases. Practically, approximation algorithms have to be used. The performance γ of an approximation algorithm is measured by the quotient of the number of sets found by the approximization algorithm c_{approx} to the number of sets in the minimal cover c_{opt}:

$$\gamma = \frac{c_{approx}}{c_{opt}} \, .$$

For some approximation algorithms lower and upper bounds of the performance can be guaranteed.

This applies for example to the greedy algorithm. It is an iterative algorithm which picks in every iteration the set $S \in \mathcal{S}$ which covers the largest remaining elements of $\mathcal{U}$ until a cover is established. For the greedy algorithm an upper bound on its performance is given by [Sla96]

$$\frac{c_{greedy}}{c_{opt}} < \ln |\mathcal{U}| - \ln \ln |\mathcal{U}| + 0.78 , \tag{2.1}$$

where c_{greedy} is the number of sets in the cover found by the greedy algorithm. This bound is tight, because there exists a problem where the performance has the lower bound [Sla96]

$$\ln |\mathcal{U}| - \ln \ln |\mathcal{U}| - 0.31 < \frac{c_{greedy}}{c_{opt}} . \tag{2.2}$$

Furthermore it is shown that no greater improvements can be expected with a polynomial time algorithm [Fei98, LY94]. In the case when $\mathcal{S}$ is not finite a bound can be given by means of the VC-Dimension of $\mathcal{S}$ [BG95]. If the VC-Dimension for a problem is lower than $\mathcal{O}(log(|\mathcal{U}|))$, then the performance guarantees are better than (2.2) and (2.1). Unfortunately, even for simple inspection problems these requirements are not met as shown in [IKDV04] in the case for inspection with a camera.

General approximation algorithms beyond the greedy algorithm are Linear Programming or heuristic methods such as Genetic Algorithms [BC96] or Simulated Annealing algorithms [JB95]. For the interested reader we refer to the survey [CTF00] which provides an overview of recent and effective methods for the set cover problem.

The deflectometric planning problem can be seen as a set cover problem if the normal accuracy is neglected. The set $\mathcal{U}$ consists of the points of the surface and and the collection of sets $\mathcal{S}$ are the measurement areas. The difference to the classical formulation is, that $\mathcal{U}$ and $\mathcal{S}$ are not finite. If the problem is discretized by discretizing the surface in surface elements and also the sensor configurations, then there can only be a finite number of distinct measurement areas. Algorithms for the set cover problem usually require that the collection $\mathcal{S}$ is given explicitly. This is not the case in the deflectometric planning problem, because the measurement areas are defined implicitly by the sensor configurations. The presented method in this work will only discretize the surface and not the sensor configuration space. The optimization over the continuous sensor configurations is established by means of a heuristic method.

3 Deflectometric Simulator

A deflectometric setup consists of a display, a camera and the surface to be inspected. The display shows a set of patterns which decode every pixel on the screen. The reflection of the pattern is observed by the camera and the observed pattern is deformed due to the shape of the surface. The result of the measurement is a mapping from camera pixel to display pixels. With this mapping and the knowledge of the configuration of the deflectometric sensor the light path can be reconstructed and with it the normals of the surface.

From a measurement a partial differential equation can be formulated which solution space is generally an one dimensional manifold [Bal08]. This means that it is generally not possible to infer the shape of the surface from a single measurement. A regularization procedure is needed to choose one surface solution. Here we will focus on the visibility of the surface but not on the normals. With the assumption that a reference surface is given the visibility can be calculated unambiguously.

If the surface were diffuse, the intersection of the camera view cone with the surface would yield the measurement area. In the case of a specular surface not all those surface points are visible in the deflectometric sense. In a deflectometric setup a surface point is visible with respect to a sensor configuration if there exists a light path which passes from the display to the surface point and into the camera. Generally the measurement area can be arbitrary complicated depending on the shape of the surface.

For the planning procedure we need a simulator to calculate the measurement area of a deflectometric measurement. We use a ray tracing approach by sending rays from the camera pixel. To measure the coverage we discretize the surface by partitioning its domain into cells. In every cell the corresponding surface element is approximated by a plane. If a ray hits the plane its corresponding cell is assumed to be visible. Because this simulation will be executed frequently during the optimization procedure only a small subset of the rays are traced. The approximation quality is crucial because sending to few rays or choosing to large cells can lead to oversimplified measurement areas. The area which is visible after n measurement with sensor configurations $\theta_1, \ldots, \theta_n$ is denoted with $A(\theta_1, \ldots, \theta_n)$.

4 Planning Problem

A deflectometric sensor configuration consists of the position and orientation of the camera and the display. Additionally the intrinsic parameters of the camera can be considered. We choose a parametrization of the sensor configuration which takes the reference surface into account (see [RB12]). This has the advantage that we can always construct a sensor configuration with which at least one surface point is visible.

A measurement with a sensor configuration leads to a measurement area. The goal is to find a plan which provides a complete coverage of the surface. This can be formulated as an optimization problem

$$\min_{\theta_1,\ldots,\theta_n} n$$
$$\text{subject to} \quad A(\theta_1,\ldots,\theta_n) = |\mathcal{U}|.$$

An approximate solution can be found for example through the greedy algorithm. The sensor configuration θ_k is chosen such that

$$\theta_k = \arg\max_{\theta}\{A(\theta_1,\ldots,\theta_{k-1},\theta) - A(\theta_1,\ldots,\theta_{k-1})\} \,,$$

i.e. the configuration which covers the most remaining area is chosen. This algorithm terminates if full coverage is reached, i.e. $A(\theta_1,\ldots,\theta_{n_{greedy}}) = |\mathcal{U}|$. As discussed in Section 2 performance guarantees can be given for the solution of the greedy algorithm, but better solutions might be found through a heuristic search for moderate sized problems. We solve this problem by choosing a maximal number of possible measurements $n_{\max}$, where it can be guaranteed that there exists a solution such that the surface is fully covered. This can be done by means of the greedy algorithm. Then we set $\tilde{n} = n_{\max} - 1$ and solve the optimization problem

$$\max_{\theta_1:\theta_{\tilde{n}}} A(\theta_1,\ldots,\theta_{\tilde{n}}). \tag{4.1}$$

We reduce the number of measurements $\tilde{n}$ further and solve (4.1) until the optimization problem yields a solution which does not cover the surface fully.

5 Optimization Algorithms

The dimensionality of the optimization variable in Eq. (4.1) is $n \cdot d$, where d is the dimensionality of the sensor configurations. The number of measurements n can be very large and therefore an algorithm which optimizes the sensor configurations all at once converges slowly. This is illustrated in Fig. 5.1, where this effect can be seen after 400 iterations. Therefore we use the following method: We iterate over all sensor configurations $\theta_1,\ldots,\theta_n$. In each iteration the optimization (4.1) is solved with all the sensor configurations fixed except for one (say θ_j). The optimization algorithm is canceled early, so that the algorithm is not caught in a local maximum. In the following, such an iteration over all sensor configurations shall be called a *sweep*. The advantage of sweeps is that the inner optimization is over a low dimensional variable. This procedure is repeated till convergence or a specified number of sweeps.

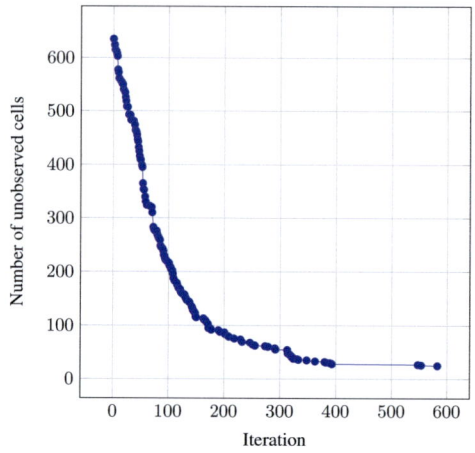

Figure 5.1: Number of unobserved cells depending on the number of iterations. The algorithm used is Nelder-Mead. It can be seen that the convergence is slow after 400 iterations.

The target function of the optimization problem has no simple closed form and multiple local minima. Furthermore a derivative can not be computed. Problems with these properties can be solved by derivate-free optimization algorithms.

Two well known algorithms in this field are the Nelder-Mead algorithm and the Simulated Annealing algorithm.

The Nelder-Mead algorithm [NM65] belongs to the so called simplex methods. It is an iterative algorithm that stores in each iteration a simplex, a set of $d+1$ points, and selects the point with the lowest and greatest function value. The point with the lowest function value is tried to be exchanged by another better point through a set of rules. If no improvements can be done the simplex is shrinked in the direction of the point with the greatest function value. This algorithm has proved successful in many practical applications.

Another well known optimization algorithm which does not need derivative information is the Simulated Annealing algorithm. It is motivated by a physical process of cooling: After a metal is heated it is cooled slowly such that stable crystals are build.

The algorithm works iteratively and in each iteration the current solution is perturbed randomly. If the new solution leads to a higher function value than it is accepted immediately otherwise it is accepted with a probability depending on the current temperature, i.e. in contrast to normal local optimization algorithms the solution can decrease in an iteration. The temperature is decreased in each iteration according to a cooling schedule. This algorithm has many free parameters for example the perturbation strategy, the acceptance function and the cooling schedule.

The perturbation strategy describes how the solution space is explored. The trivial way perturbing the solution is a random walk in the solution space by adding a small increment δx to the current solution x_k

$$x_{prop} = x_k + \alpha \delta x \,,$$

where α is a real valued variable describing the extent of the step and x_{prop} is the proposed solution. Another strategy is to partition the configuration vector into meaningful components (like the distance of the camera, the orientation of the camera etc.) and then choose one random component and only perturb this part of the vector randomly.

$$x_{prop} = x_k + \alpha Q_c \delta x_c \,,$$

where c is the component, δx_c is a random sample from the component space and Q_c maps the component into the sensor configuration space. In deflectometry the largest improvements in optimization are made by changing the distance of the camera or display. This can be incorporated in the optimization by assigning a higher probability to these important components and then decreasing them depending on the temperature.

As can be seen in Fig. 5.2 Simulated Annealing converges in a small number of steps to the optimum. The convergence speed is very high at the beginning of the optimization. However, Nelder-Mead decreases slowly due to flat regions in the optimization function (only the first 145 steps are shown). But one step of the Simulated Annealing algorithm is slower than one step of the Nelder-Mead algorithm (about 12 times slower in our case). Therefore we suggest to combine both algorithms by alternating between the two optimization algorithms. We start with the Simulated Annealing algorithm and optimize a number of steps. If the improvement of the new plan is not sufficient we switch the algorithms. This is repeated till convergence by adapting the threshold for improvement. The result of an experiment using this algorithm can be seen in Fig. 5.3. Although more steps

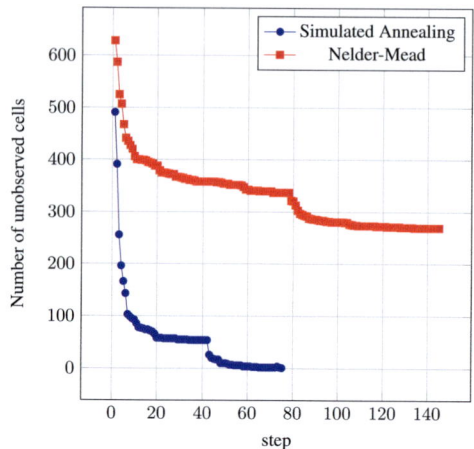

Figure 5.2: Number of unobserved cells in each step for the Nelder-Mead algorithm and the Simulated Annealing algorithm. Here a step is the optimization of one sensor configuration in a sweep. It can be seen that Simulated Annealing converges in a small number of steps. Nelder-Mead falls rapidly but then decreases slowly due to flat regions in the optimization function.

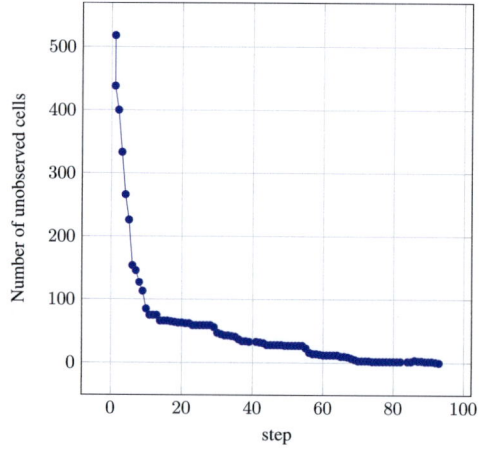

Figure 5.3: Number of unobserved cells in each step for the algorithm alternating Nelder-Mead and Simulated Annealing. About 25% of the steps are optimized with Nelder-Mead.

are needed for the optimization compared to Simulated Annealing in Fig. 5.2, the optimization converges faster due to faster steps of the Nelder-Mead algorithm.

6 Experiments

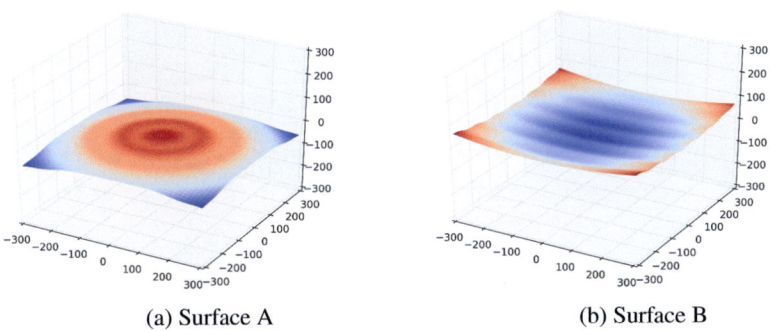

(a) Surface A   (b) Surface B

Figure 6.1: The two example surfaces denoted with A and B. The color encodes the heights of the surface from blue (lower values) to red (higher values).

We tested the presented method on several simple surfaces in a simulation. The surfaces are depicted in Fig. 6.1(a) and Fig. 6.1(b). Both surfaces are overlayed with a periodic wave such that the measurement areas are not trivial. The camera was approximated with maximal resolution of 40×30 pixels. The degree of approximation was adaptively changed during the optimization process. The display size was set to 17 Inch. In this example the starting value for the number of measurements was set heuristically but could also be found more systematically by using a greedy algorithm. Also note, that in this example the start values (Fig. 6.2(a) and Fig. 6.2(b)) of the sensor configuration were chosen such that the initial measurement areas are lying on a grid, but the optimization is robust against random start values due the Simulated Annealing optimization. The qualitative results are depicted in Fig. 6.2(c) and Fig. 6.2(d). For the first surface only four measurements suffice to cover it completely the second surface only needs two.

7 Conclusion

The deflectometric inspection task with known reference surface can be seen as a set cover problem. Theoretically it is known that the greedy algorithm already yields results which cannot be improved much further. Practically, for moderate

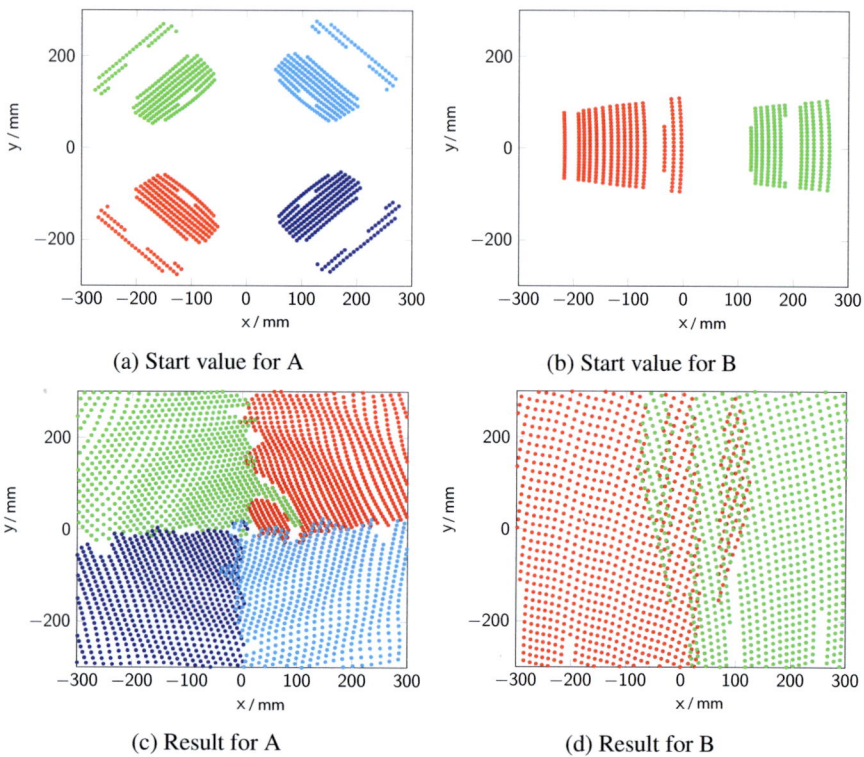

(a) Start value for A   (b) Start value for B

(c) Result for A   (d) Result for B

Figure 6.2: Results of the planning process for the example surfaces A and B. The startvalues of the measurement areas are depicted in (a)-(b) and the respective measurement areas after the optimization in (c)-(d). Points with different colors are measured with different sensor configurations.

sized problems and in bounded domains heuristics methods can be found which can yield better results. But these are not proved theoretically. We have seen that finding a plan of sensor configurations for the covering problem in deflectometry can be solved by an optimization algorithm. A combination of the Nelder-Mead algorithm with Simulated Annealing showed good results.

There are several points which need to be investigated to improve the results and applicability of the method. For a deflectometric measurement not only the visibility of a surface patch is important but also the uncertainty of the normal. This is ignored completely by the presented algorithm. But it could easily be incorporated for example by estimating the normal of every plane in the cell. Another problem is that the size of the cells is equal but should generally depend on the curvature or the size of the area it occupies, so that the approximation with a plane is justified. It needs to be investigated if Nelder-Mead and Simulated Annealing can be combined in a more natural way. Finally more tests should be made with more realistic surfaces and quantitative evaluations.

Bibliography

[Bal08]   Jonathan Balzer. *Regularisierung des Deflektometrieproblems - Grundlagen und Anwendung*. PhD thesis, 2008.

[BC96]   J.E Beasley and P.C Chu. A genetic algorithm for the set covering problem. *European Journal of Operational Research*, 94(2):392 – 404, 1996.

[BG95]   Hervé Brönnimann and Michael T. Goodrich. Almost optimal set covers in finite vc-dimension, 1995.

[CTF00]   Alberto Caprara, Paolo Toth, and Matteo Fischetti. Algorithms for the set covering problem. *Annals of Operations Research*, 98(1-4):353–371, 2000.

[Fei98]   Uriel Feige. A threshold of ln n for approximating set cover. *J. ACM*, 45(4):634–652, July 1998.

[IKDV04]   Volkan Isler, Sampath Kannan, Kostas Daniilidis, and Pavel Valtr. Vc-dimension of exterior visibility. *Pattern Analysis and Machine Intelligence, IEEE Transactions on*, 26(5):667–671, 2004.

[JB95]   Larry W. Jacobs and Michael J. Brusco. Note: A local-search heuristic for large set-covering problems. *Naval Research Logistics (NRL)*, 42(7):1129–1140, 1995.

[LY94]   Carsten Lund and Mihalis Yannakakis. On the hardness of approximating minimization problems. *J. ACM*, 41(5):960–981, September 1994.

[NM65]   J. A. Nelder and R. Mead. A Simplex Method for Function Minimization. *The Computer Journal*, 7(4):308–313, January 1965.

[RB12]   Masoud Roschani and Jürgen Beyerer. Planungsbasierte oberflächeninspektion in der deflektometrie bei gegebener referenzfläche mittels greedy-optimierung. In Prof. Dr.-Ing. Robert Schmitt, editor, *Tagungsband des XXVI. Messtechnisches Symposiums*, Aachen, September 2012. Shaker.

[Sla96]   Petr Slavík. A tight analysis of the greedy algorithm for set cover. In *Proceedings of the Twenty-eighth Annual ACM Symposium on Theory of Computing*, STOC '96, pages 435–441, New York, NY, USA, 1996. ACM.

[Wer11]   Stefan Bruno Werling. *Deflektometrie zur automatischen Sichtprüfung und Rekonstruktion spiegelnder Oberflächen*. PhD thesis, 2011.

Single Scattering Underwatter Imaging Model

Thomas Stephan

Vision and Fusion Laboratory
Institute for Anthropomatics
Karlsruhe Institute of Technology (KIT), Germany
thomas.stephan@kit.edu

Technical Report IES-2012-10

Abstract: Optical imaging under water represents a still unresolved problem. Poor visibility, blurred images and a limited signal-to-noise-ratio are the consequences of absorption and scattering dominating the properties of water. In order to enhance or even restore image content from underwater images, it is essential to understand and model the imaging process. In this technical report a new model is derived, taking into account three different components of light transportation. Thus most image degradation effects in underwater imaging can be described and therefore also removed.

1 Introduction

Most inspection and exploration tasks under water use acoustic imaging sensors instead of visual sensors such as cameras. This is because visual imaging under water hits its limits. Water interacts with light and therefore acts as an optical element. Thus, degradation effects like chromatic aberrations, blurring and loss of contrast appear in images taken under water. However, visual images are easy and cheap to obtain by cameras, the information density in terms of scene texture and object shapes is high and they are intuitively interpretable by human observers. Thus visual imaging can play an important role in the future of underwater inspection and exploitation.

In order to use visual imaging efficiently in underwater tasks image enhancement or image restoration is inevitable. Thus, image restoration has to be applied on underwater vision tasks. Therefore precise models and parameter estimation methods have to be developed in order to use visual imaging in underwater surroundings.

This technical report provides a new imaging model, based on linear, geometric ray propagation considering the reflection at scene surfaces, wavelength-dependent absorption and scattering in participating media. The derived model consists of different additive components of light transportation. This model can be easily adapted to the accuracy requirements of imaging tasks.

First we explain some radiometric quantities necessary for the derivation of the model. Next, different effects of light propagation are described in ascending complexity order. Finaly some conclusions are given.

2 Radiometry

To understand radiative transfer, some physical quantities have to be explained. These are in detail the radiant flux, the radiance, the irradiance and the radiant intensity. In this technical report the term 'light rays' is used equivalently to geometric beams of electromagnetic radiation.

2.1 Radiant Flux

The radiant flux Φ is the measure of the power of radiation passing through some surface A. Its unit is Watt $[W]$. If the surface A is a sphere around a light source, the corresponding radiant flux gives the emitted power of the light source. The figure to the right illustrates the concept of radiant flux $\Phi(A)$ through surface A.

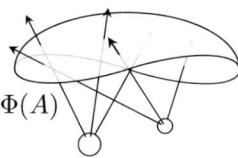

Figure 2.1: Illustration of the radiant flux

2.1.1 Radiance

An important quantity of radiometry is the radiance. It is best associated with a single light ray at a certain position propagating in a certain direction. The radiance L is the area-projection of the density of power coming from an area element $\mathrm{d}A$ radiated into a solid angle element $\mathrm{d}\omega$. The figure beside illustrates the radiance.

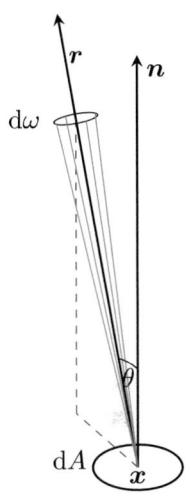

The relation between radiance and the radiant flux Φ is given by the integral over all solid angles and the area A.

$$\Phi = \int_\Omega \int_A L(r, x) \cos(\theta) \, \mathrm{d}A \, \mathrm{d}\omega \quad ,$$

where $x \in A$ denotes the position of radiance, r denotes the direction of radiance with its polar angle θ and $\omega \in \Omega$ denotes the solid angle corresponding to the direction r. Hence the unit of radiance is written as Watt per square meter and steradian $[\frac{W}{m^2 sr}]$.

Figure 2.2: Illustration of outgoing radiance from an area element $\mathrm{d}A$ in direction r into a solid angle element $\mathrm{d}\omega$.

2.2 Irradiance

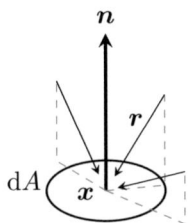

Figure 2.3: Illustration incoming irradiance at an area element $\mathrm{d}A$

The quantity of irradiance $E(x)$ describes the density of radiant flux Φ arriving at an area unit. Thus irradiance can be written as:

$$E(x) = \frac{\mathrm{d}\Phi}{\mathrm{d}A},$$

with its unit $[\frac{W}{m^2}]$. The relation between radiance $L(x, r)$ and irradiance $E(x)$ is given by the integral over all solid angles

$$E(x) = \int_\Omega L(x, r) \cos(\theta) \, \mathrm{d}\omega,$$

where θ is the angle between the normal vector n of the surface and the direction of the incident radiance r. The solid angle element $\mathrm{d}\omega$ corresponds to the direction r of the incident radiance $L(x, r)$.

2.3   Radiant Intensity

Whereas irradiance is the density of radiated power related to an area element dA, the radiant intensity $I(r)$ is the density of radiated power related to a solid angle element $d\omega$. Thus the radiant intensity can be defined as:

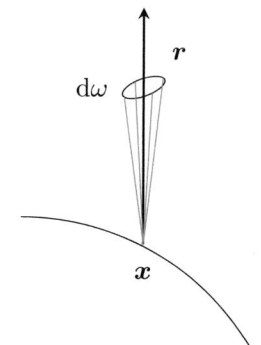

$$I(r) = \frac{d\Phi}{d\omega},$$

with its unit Watt per steradian $\left[\frac{W}{sr}\right]$. Hence the relations between radiance and radiant intensity are given as

Figure 2.4: Illustration of the outgoing radiant intensity into a solid angle element $d\omega$

$$I(x) = \int_A L(x, r) \cos(\theta)\, dx,$$

where θ is the angle between the normal vector of the surface and the direction of the outgoing radiance.

The concept of radiant intensity is useful to describe point sources, but it has not found much application in modeling radiative transfer under water except in the definition of the volume scattering function [Mob94, Cha60].

2.4   Scattering

A photon can be deflected by a particle into direction r divergent from origin direction r'. This process is called scattering. First of all scattering causes a decrease of radiance from direction r'. The decrease in radiance while crossing a volume element at x in direction r' due to scattering is proportional to the incident radiance. Thus loss of radiance due to scattering can be described by

$$r^T \nabla_x L(x, r') = -b(x) L(x, r')$$

Here $b(x)$ denotes the scattering coefficient.

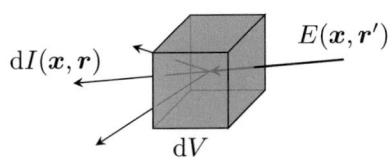

The loss of radiance in one direction by scattering do not cause a reduction of radiance in radiation field. The part of the energy lost from an incident light beam will reappear as scattered radiation in other directions. The distribution of angles of scattered radiation can be described by the volume scattering function $\beta(x, r)$, which is defined [Mob94] as

$$\beta(x, r' \leftrightarrow r) = \frac{dI(x, r)}{E(x, r')\, dV} ,$$

where dV denotes a volume element of scattering medium. The relation between volume scattering function $\beta(x, r)$ and the corresponding scattering coefficient b can be described by

$$b(x) = \int_\Omega \beta(x, r' \leftrightarrow r)\, d\omega(r)$$

as a consequence of conservation of energy in radiation field by scattering. Here $\omega \in \Omega$ denotes the solid angle corresponding to the direction r.

In summary, increase of radiance at location x in direction r by scattering can be written as

$$r^T \nabla_x L(x, r) = \int_\Omega \beta(x, r' \leftrightarrow r) L(x, r')\, d\omega' , \qquad (2.1)$$

where $r' \leftrightarrow r$ represents the change of direction from r' to r.

2.5   Reflection

Reflection is the change of the direction of a radiant beam on a surface. The law of specular reflection says that the angle of the incident radiance respective to the surface normal equals the angle of the reflected radiance.

Most objects do not have perfectly reflecting surfaces. Thus the angle of the reflected radiance differs from the incident angle. This phenomenon is called diffuse reflection. The properties of objects respect to their reflection can be described by the

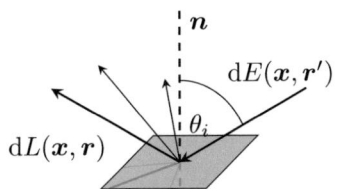

Bidirectional **R**eflectance **D**istribution
Function defined as

$$f(\boldsymbol{x}, \boldsymbol{r}', \boldsymbol{r}) = \frac{\mathrm{d}L\,(\boldsymbol{x}, \boldsymbol{r})}{\mathrm{d}E\,(\boldsymbol{x}, \boldsymbol{r}')} = \frac{\mathrm{d}L\,(\boldsymbol{x}, \boldsymbol{r})}{\mathrm{d}L\,(\boldsymbol{x}, \boldsymbol{r}')\cos(\theta')\,\mathrm{d}\omega'},$$

where $E\,(\boldsymbol{x}, \boldsymbol{r}')$ is the incident irradiance, θ' is the angle between surface normal
and direction $\boldsymbol{r}'$ and ω' is the solid angle corresponding to the incident direction
$\boldsymbol{r}'$. Thus the reflected radiance in direction $\boldsymbol{r}$ can be written as

$$L\,(\boldsymbol{x}, \boldsymbol{r}) = \int_{\Omega} f\,(\boldsymbol{x}, \boldsymbol{r}', \boldsymbol{r})\,L\,(\boldsymbol{x}, \boldsymbol{r}')\cos(\theta')\,\mathrm{d}\omega' \ .$$

3   Single Scattering Model

In this section the single scattering imaging model will be derived. This model
only takes into account the light rays scattered no more than once. The model
contains three components, which are the direct component, the backscattering
component and the blurring component. Figure 3.1 illustrate the properties and
the used variables.

We model the camera as a pinhole-
camera with its pinhole-position $\boldsymbol{p}$.
Pixels $\boldsymbol{u}$ are represented as scene
points in world coordinates. The scene
surface point, which corresponds to
the pixel $\boldsymbol{u}$ is denoted as $\boldsymbol{o}(\boldsymbol{u})$, where
the distance between the pinhole $\boldsymbol{p}$
and the scene surface point $\boldsymbol{o}(\boldsymbol{u})$ is
$d(\boldsymbol{u}) := \|\boldsymbol{p} - \boldsymbol{o}(\boldsymbol{u})\|$. For simplification of model description only one
emitting point light source at $\boldsymbol{\xi}$ is considered.

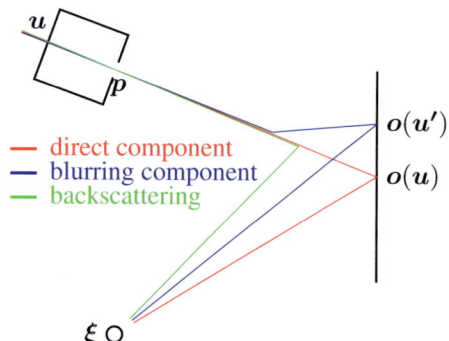

Figure 3.1:   Illustration scene and its
properties

Direct Component

The direct component is the unscattered part of the light rays, originating from
the light source $\boldsymbol{\xi}$ travelling through the water and is relected by the scene surface
point $\boldsymbol{o}(\boldsymbol{u})$ further pass it until it reaches the pinhole $\boldsymbol{p}$ and is projected at $\boldsymbol{u}$.

Backscattering Component

The backscattering component is the integration over all light rays, emitted from the light source and scattered at the sight line of the pixel u towards u. This part of the model does not contain any information about the scene surface. It acts only as an additive intensity during the imaging process.

Blurring component

The blurring component represents the light rays, which come from the scene surface $o(u')$ and are scattered into a line of sight of another pixel u. This part of the imaging model does contain information of the scene surface, but integrates information from neighboring pixels. As a consequence, the image appears blurred.

3.1 Light field of a point light source

In this section the character of a point light source will be discussed. A point light is a light source with defined radiant flux $\Phi > 0$ without any finite spatial extent. Hence, any emitted radiance, irradiance and radiant intensity spring from one infinitesimally small point. In nature there cannot be any real point light source, otherwise energy density would be infinite. In computer graphics infinitesimal point light sources are often used to reduce computational complexity.

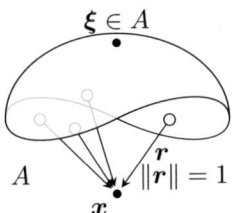

Figure 3.2: Illustration of point light

For further thoughts an empty space is considered, which only contains a point light source at the scene point ξ. For a scene point x with $\|x - \xi\| = 1$ the radiant intensity $E(x)$ and the irradiance $I(x)$ at x can be calculated in the same manner by integrating the radiance over a spherical cap A around the scene point x containing the light point source ξ

$$I(x) = \int_A L(x, r) \, dr.$$

Evidently the Irradiance $I(x)$ is independent of the area A of the spherical cap and depends only on the direction $x - \xi$

$$I(x) = S(x - \xi),$$

where $S(\cdot)$ is the radiant intensity of a point light in a donated direction. The boundary value

$$I(\boldsymbol{x}) = S(\boldsymbol{x} - \boldsymbol{\xi}) = \lim_{A \to 0} \int_A L(\boldsymbol{x}, \boldsymbol{r}) \, \mathrm{d}\boldsymbol{r}$$

and the sampling property of dirac delta function leads to the formulation of the radiance

$$L(\boldsymbol{x}, \boldsymbol{r}) = S(\boldsymbol{x} - \boldsymbol{\xi}) \delta(\boldsymbol{r} - \boldsymbol{x} + \boldsymbol{\xi}).$$

Analogous this can be extended to each scene point $\boldsymbol{x} \neq \boldsymbol{\xi}$

$$L(\boldsymbol{x}, \boldsymbol{r}) = S\left(\frac{\boldsymbol{x} - \boldsymbol{\xi}}{\|\boldsymbol{x} - \boldsymbol{\xi}\|}\right) \delta\left(\boldsymbol{r} - \frac{\boldsymbol{x} - \boldsymbol{\xi}}{\|\boldsymbol{x} - \boldsymbol{\xi}\|}\right),$$

where $\|\boldsymbol{r}\| = 1$. In 3.2 the explained scene is figured out.

3.1.1 Point light in participating media

The light field associated with a point light in an absorbing and scattering medium is completely different. Nevertheless, regarding only the direct part of the light field, that are light rays coming directly from the light source without being scattered into other directions, the light field can be depicted as

$$L(\boldsymbol{x}, \boldsymbol{r}) = S\left(\frac{\boldsymbol{x} - \boldsymbol{\xi}}{\|\boldsymbol{x} - \boldsymbol{\xi}\|}\right) \delta\left(\boldsymbol{r} - \frac{\boldsymbol{x} - \boldsymbol{\xi}}{\|\boldsymbol{x} - \boldsymbol{\xi}\|}\right) e^{-c\|\boldsymbol{x} - \boldsymbol{\xi}\|}. \tag{3.1}$$

The exponential factor stems from attenuation by combined out-scattering and absorption, which follows from the Lambert Beers law.

3.2 Reflection from scene surfaces

As described in section 2.5, reflection at scene surface points can be characterized by the BRDF

$$L(\boldsymbol{o}, \boldsymbol{l}) =$$
$$\int_\Omega f\left(\boldsymbol{o}, \frac{\boldsymbol{r}}{\|\boldsymbol{r}\|} \leftrightarrow \boldsymbol{l}\right) L\left(\boldsymbol{o}, \frac{\boldsymbol{r}}{\|\boldsymbol{r}\|}\right) \frac{\boldsymbol{n}^T \boldsymbol{r}}{\|\boldsymbol{r}\|} \, \mathrm{d}\omega(\boldsymbol{r}),$$

where $\boldsymbol{n}$ is the surface normal vector and $\mathrm{d}\omega(\boldsymbol{r})$ is the corresponding solid angle in direction $\boldsymbol{r}$. Instead of referencing the solid angle, area A is used to describe properties

$$L(o, l) =$$

$$\int_A f\left(o, \frac{r}{\|r\|} \leftrightarrow l\right) L\left(o, \frac{r}{\|r\|}\right) \frac{n^T r}{\|r\|} \frac{1}{\|r\|^2} \, dr \, .$$

This leads together with (3.1) to

$$L(o, l) = f\left(o, \frac{o - \xi}{\|o - \xi\|} \leftrightarrow l\right) S\left(\frac{o - \xi}{\|o - \xi\|}\right) \cdot$$

$$e^{-c\|o - \xi\|} \frac{n^T(o - \xi)}{\|o - \xi\|} \frac{1}{\|o - \xi\|^2} \, . \quad (3.2)$$

The reflected radiance depends on the cosine-angle of incoming light and on the reciprocal of the squared distance to the light source.

3.3   Direct Component

Regarding the direct component of light transportation, which are the non-scattered light rays travelling directly from light source via the scene surface to the camera sensor leads to

$$L\left(p, \frac{p - o}{\|p - o\|}\right) = L\left(o, \frac{p - o}{\|p - o\|}\right) e^{-c\|p - o\|} \, ,$$

which gives with (3.2)

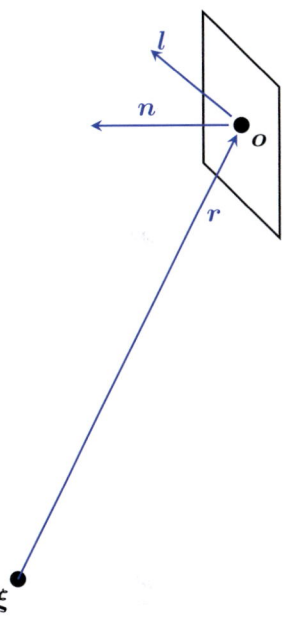

Figure 3.3: Illustration of surface reflectance

$$L\left(p, \frac{p - o}{\|p - o\|}\right) = f\left(o, \frac{o - \xi}{\|o - \xi\|} \leftrightarrow \frac{p - o}{\|p - o\|}\right) S\left(\frac{o - \xi}{\|o - \xi\|}\right) \cdot$$

$$e^{-c(\|p - o\| + \|o - \xi\|)} \frac{n^T(o - \xi)}{\|o - \xi\|} \frac{1}{\|o - \xi\|^2} \, . \quad (3.3)$$

3.4　Backscattering Component

Scattering in participating media is described by the volume-scattering-function (2.1). Referring to the area instead of solid angles scattering at a point x into direction l can be written as

$$\frac{\mathrm{d}}{\mathrm{d}\tau}L(x,l) =$$

$$\int_A \beta\left(x, \frac{r}{\|r\|} \leftrightarrow l\right) L\left(x, \frac{r}{\|r\|}\right) \frac{1}{\|r\|^2}\, \mathrm{d}r\,,$$
(3.4)

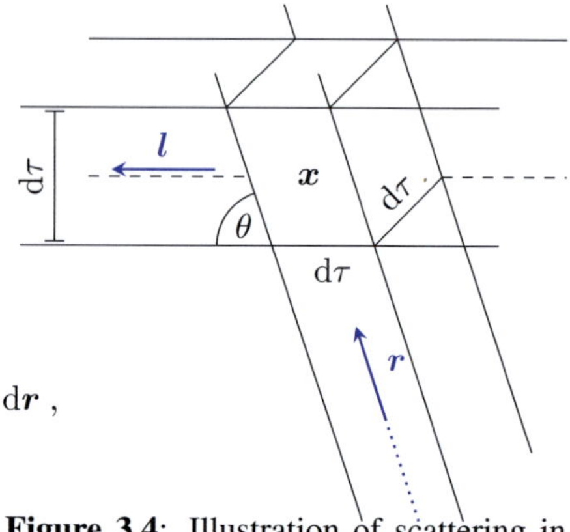

where the light beam incide from direction r and $\mathrm{d}V$. For better understanding figure 3.4 shows properties of given variables.

Figure 3.4: Illustration of scattering in volume elements

Regarding the incoming light from point light sources (3.1) leads to

$$\frac{\mathrm{d}}{\mathrm{d}\tau}L(x,l) = \beta\left(x, \frac{x-\xi}{\|x-\xi\|} \leftrightarrow l\right) S\left(\frac{x-\xi}{\|x-\xi\|}\right) \frac{e^{-c\|x-\xi\|}}{\|x-\xi\|^2}\,.$$
(3.5)

Hence, integrating the in-scattering (3.5) at all volume elements along the sight line gives the total backscattering component

$$L\left(u, \frac{u-p}{\|u-p\|}\right) = \int_0^{d(u)} \mathrm{d}L\left(p - \tau\frac{u-p}{\|u-p\|}, \frac{u-p}{\|u-p\|}\right) \mathrm{d}\tau\,,$$

where each point of the sight line of the pixel u can is described by $x(\tau) = p + \tau\frac{p-u}{\|p-u\|}$ and p is the pinhole of the camera. This leads to

$$L\left(u, \frac{u-p}{\|u-p\|}\right) =$$
(3.6)

$$\int_0^{d(u)} \beta\left(x(\tau), \frac{x(\tau)-\xi}{\|x(\tau)-\xi\|} \leftrightarrow \frac{u-p}{\|u-p\|}\right) S\left(\frac{x(\tau)-\xi}{\|x(\tau)-\xi\|}\right) \frac{e^{-c(\|x(\tau)-\xi\|+\tau)}}{\|x(\tau)-\xi\|^2}\, \mathrm{d}\tau\,.$$

3.5 Blurring Component

The blurring component consists of both, a direct illumination of a scene surface point and in-scattering of light into the sight line of one pixel. Hence, this component is a composition of both (3.6) (3.3). Beginning with the description of scattering at one scene point (3.4)

$$\frac{\mathrm{d}}{\mathrm{d}\tau}L(\boldsymbol{x},\boldsymbol{l}) = \int_A \beta\left(\boldsymbol{x}, \frac{\boldsymbol{r}}{\|\boldsymbol{r}\|} \leftrightarrow \boldsymbol{l}\right) L\left(\boldsymbol{x}, \frac{\boldsymbol{r}}{\|\boldsymbol{r}\|}\right) \frac{1}{\|\boldsymbol{r}\|^2}\,\mathrm{d}\boldsymbol{r}\,,$$

the radiance $L(\boldsymbol{x}, \frac{\boldsymbol{r}}{\|\boldsymbol{r}\|})$ is not caused by an infinite point light source, but by the illuminated object surface. This leads to

$$\frac{\mathrm{d}}{\mathrm{d}\tau}L(\boldsymbol{x},\boldsymbol{l}) = \int_A \beta\left(\boldsymbol{x}, \frac{\boldsymbol{x}-\boldsymbol{o}}{\|\boldsymbol{x}-\boldsymbol{o}\|} \leftrightarrow \boldsymbol{l}\right) L\left(\boldsymbol{x}, \frac{\boldsymbol{x}-\boldsymbol{o}}{\|\boldsymbol{x}-\boldsymbol{o}\|}\right) \frac{1}{\|\boldsymbol{x}-\boldsymbol{o}\|^2}\,\mathrm{d}\boldsymbol{o}\,,$$

where the integration has to be done over all scene surface points $\boldsymbol{o}$. With Lambert Beers' law this leads to

$$\frac{\mathrm{d}}{\mathrm{d}\tau}L(\boldsymbol{x},\boldsymbol{l}) = \int_A \beta\left(\boldsymbol{x}, \frac{\boldsymbol{x}-\boldsymbol{o}}{\|\boldsymbol{x}-\boldsymbol{o}\|} \leftrightarrow \boldsymbol{l}\right) L\left(\boldsymbol{o}, \frac{\boldsymbol{x}-\boldsymbol{o}}{\|\boldsymbol{x}-\boldsymbol{o}\|}\right) e^{-c\|\boldsymbol{x}-\boldsymbol{o}\|} \frac{1}{\|\boldsymbol{x}-\boldsymbol{o}\|^2}\,\mathrm{d}\boldsymbol{o}\,.$$

The radiance of scene surface point $\boldsymbol{o}$ illuminated by direct illumination is given by (3.2). Hence, the scattered part of radiance is

$$\frac{\mathrm{d}}{\mathrm{d}\tau}L(\boldsymbol{x},\boldsymbol{l}) = \int_A \beta\left(\boldsymbol{x}, \frac{\boldsymbol{x}-\boldsymbol{o}}{\|\boldsymbol{x}-\boldsymbol{o}\|} \leftrightarrow \boldsymbol{l}\right) f\left(\boldsymbol{o}, \frac{\boldsymbol{o}-\boldsymbol{\xi}}{\|\boldsymbol{o}-\boldsymbol{\xi}\|} \leftrightarrow \frac{\boldsymbol{x}-\boldsymbol{o}}{\|\boldsymbol{x}-\boldsymbol{o}\|}\right)$$
$$S\left(\frac{\boldsymbol{o}-\boldsymbol{\xi}}{\|\boldsymbol{o}-\boldsymbol{\xi}\|}\right) e^{-c(\|\boldsymbol{x}-\boldsymbol{o}\|+\|\boldsymbol{o}-\boldsymbol{\xi}\|)} \frac{1}{\|\boldsymbol{x}-\boldsymbol{o}\|^2}\,\mathrm{d}\boldsymbol{o}\,.$$

Transporting the radiance from $\boldsymbol{x}$ to the pinhole $\boldsymbol{p}$ and integrating all points over the sight line of $\boldsymbol{u}$ finaly leads to

$$L(\boldsymbol{u}, \frac{\boldsymbol{u}-\boldsymbol{p}}{\|\boldsymbol{u}-\boldsymbol{p}\|}) =$$
$$\int_0^{d(\boldsymbol{u})} \int_A \beta\left(\boldsymbol{x}(\tau), \frac{\boldsymbol{x}(\tau)-\boldsymbol{o}}{\|\boldsymbol{x}(\tau)-\boldsymbol{o}\|} \leftrightarrow \frac{\boldsymbol{p}-\boldsymbol{x}(\tau)}{\|\boldsymbol{p}-\boldsymbol{x}(\tau)\|}\right)$$
$$f\left(\boldsymbol{o}, \frac{\boldsymbol{o}-\boldsymbol{\xi}}{\|\boldsymbol{o}-\boldsymbol{\xi}\|} \leftrightarrow \frac{\boldsymbol{x}(\tau)-\boldsymbol{o}}{\|\boldsymbol{x}(\tau)-\boldsymbol{o}\|}\right)$$
$$S\left(\frac{\boldsymbol{o}-\boldsymbol{\xi}}{\|\boldsymbol{o}-\boldsymbol{\xi}\|}\right)$$

$$e^{-c(\|\boldsymbol{x}(\tau)-\boldsymbol{o}\|+\|\boldsymbol{o}-\boldsymbol{\xi}\|+\tau)} \frac{1}{\|\boldsymbol{x}(\tau)-\boldsymbol{o}\|^2} \, \mathrm{d}\boldsymbol{o} \, \mathrm{d}\tau \; . \qquad (3.7)$$

3.6 Other unconsidered Components

There are many other unconsidered components of radiative transfer like multiple scattering or illumination of scene surface by scattered light. These components increase the computational load. Because of linearity of geometric light transportation, each other component appends an additive contribution to the resulting image

$$L_{\text{total}}(\boldsymbol{u}, \frac{\boldsymbol{u}-\boldsymbol{p}}{\|\boldsymbol{u}-\boldsymbol{p}\|}) = \sum_{i=0}^{\infty} L_i(\boldsymbol{u}, \frac{\boldsymbol{u}-\boldsymbol{p}}{\|\boldsymbol{u}-\boldsymbol{p}\|}) \; . \qquad (3.8)$$

Every component is non-negative $L_i(\boldsymbol{u}, \frac{\boldsymbol{u}-\boldsymbol{p}}{\|\boldsymbol{u}-\boldsymbol{p}\|}) \geq 0$, furthermore assuming non-emitting volume and surface elements total amount of light energy is limited. As a consequence the equation (3.8) converges to a concrete value.

3.7 Affine Image Model

In this section a new imaging model is presented considering the derived single scattering model. This model allows describing many different imaging effects of underwater imaging, like loss of intensity, color-shift, loss of contrast and blurring. Therefore one channel of an image is regarded as column vector $\boldsymbol{g} \in \mathbb{R}^N$, where N is the total number of pixels. Hence, the model

$$\boldsymbol{g} = \boldsymbol{\Gamma}\boldsymbol{\rho} + \boldsymbol{b}$$

is an affine transformation of the signal vector $\boldsymbol{\rho} \in \mathbb{R}^N$, which represents the reflectance at the scene surface assuming lambertian surfaces. $\boldsymbol{\Gamma} = (\gamma_{ij}) \in \mathbb{R}^{N \times N}$ is the transportation matrix, which describes the direct and the blurring component of single scattering light transportation. $\boldsymbol{b} \in \mathbb{R}^N$ is the additive backscattering component.

The matrix diagonal elements γ_{ii} are the direct components derived from (3.3) with lambertian surfaces $f(\boldsymbol{o}_i, \boldsymbol{r} \leftrightarrow \boldsymbol{l}) = f(\boldsymbol{o}_i) = \rho_i$

$$\gamma_{ii} = S(\frac{\boldsymbol{o}_i - \boldsymbol{\xi}}{\|\boldsymbol{o}_i - \boldsymbol{\xi}\|}) e^{-c(\|\boldsymbol{p}-\boldsymbol{o}_i\|+\|\boldsymbol{o}_i-\boldsymbol{\xi}\|)} \frac{\boldsymbol{n}_i^T(\boldsymbol{o}_i - \boldsymbol{\xi})}{\|\boldsymbol{o}_i - \boldsymbol{\xi}\|} \frac{1}{\|\boldsymbol{o}_i - \boldsymbol{\xi}\|^2} \; ,$$

thereby o_i is the surface point corresponding to the image pixel g_i.

The other elements of transportation matrix Γ are caused by the blurring component (3.7). γ_{ij} quantifies the amount of light which comes from scene surface point o_j and is scattered into the sight line of u_i

$$\gamma_{ij} = \int_0^{d(u_i)} \beta(x(\tau), \frac{x(\tau) - o_j}{\|x(\tau) - o_j\|} \leftrightarrow \frac{p - x(\tau)}{\|p - x(\tau)\|})$$

$$S\left(\frac{o_j - \xi}{\|o_j - \xi\|}\right)$$

$$e^{-c(\|x(\tau) - o_j\| + \|o_j - \xi\| + \tau)} \frac{1}{\|x(\tau) - o_j\|^2} \, d\tau \ .$$

Vector b contains the additive backscattering component (3.6)

$$b_i =$$

$$\int_0^{d(u_i)} \beta(x(\tau), \frac{x(\tau) - \xi}{\|x(\tau) - \xi\|} \leftrightarrow \frac{u_i - p}{\|u_i - p\|}) S(\frac{x(\tau) - \xi}{\|x(\tau) - \xi\|}) \frac{e^{-c(\|x(\tau) - \xi\| + \tau)}}{\|x(\tau) - \xi\|^2} \, d\tau \ .$$

This formulation leads to a very clear mathematical description of imaging model. In case of lambertian surfaces and the considered components, light transportation can be explained as an affine transformation of scene surface reflectance, where the transformation depends on the optical properties of water, the shape of the surface and the location of light sources.

4 Conclusion

In this technical report a new imaging model for underwater imaging was derived, which is able to model different image degradation effects, like image blurring, color shift, decrease of signal intensity, loss of contrast. Mathematically it is an affine transformation of the scene reflectance. This formulation leads to a better understanding of underwater imaging and provides a straight forward access to the theme of image restoration.

4.1 Future Work

Formulating the process of image acquisition as an affine transformation allows to perform image restoration by established methods described in [Rie03]. Thus, underwater image restoration can be handled as standard linear inverse problem, where approaches like Tikhonov-Phillips regularization, Landweber iteration or conjugate gradient method can be used.

Bibliography

[Cha60]   Subrahmanyan Chandrasekhar. *Radiative transfer*. Dover, New York, 1960.

[Mob94]   Curtis D. Mobley. *Light and water: Radiative transfer in natural waters*. Academic Press, San Diego, 1994.

[Rie03]   Andreas Rieder. *Keine Probleme mit Inversen Problemen*, volume 1. Vieweg Wiesbaden, 2003.

A Frequentistic and a Bayesian Approach for Optimal Optical Filter Design.

Miro Taphanel

Vision and Fusion Laboratory
Institute for Anthropomatics
Karlsruhe Institute of Technology (KIT), Germany
miro.taphanel@kit.edu

Technical Report IES-2013-11

Abstract: This report discusses three merit functions to optimize optical interference filter coatings. The applications of these filters are intentionally optical 3D sensors, e.g. a chromatic confocal triangulation sensor. Optimizing these optical filters is done by minimizing the measurement uncertainty of the sensor. The measurement task is handled as a parameter estimation problem and the sensor is considered as a physical experiment. As part of the experimental design, the optical filters are optimized to achieve measurements with lower uncertainty. The first merit function is based on a frequentistic statistic utilizing the *Cramér-Rao* lower bound. An example is used to point out disadvantages and two alternative merit functions are proposed. Instead of a lower bound, the other merit functions incorporate a specific estimator function.

1 Introduction

Designing a sensor from scratch offers many degrees of freedom. The process is equal to setup an experiment and fixing all the design variables in the sense of an optimal experimental design. In literature [HK05],[Bos07], [Ber85],[CV95] experimental design is a well-studied topic. The basic idea is to apply estimation theory to model the outcome of an experiment. On top of this model optimality criteria are defined, which quantify the performance of the experiment. Finally, using these criteria as merit functions in an optimization framework will lead to improved experimental designs. In [Bos07],[VAdDVDvdB02] it is proposed to utilize the *Cramér-Rao* lower bound to quantify the variance of the experimental outcome. The *Cramér-Rao* lower bound is a general lower bound of the variance of an arbitrary estimator function [Bos07]. Because the purpose of this research is to optimize a measurement sensor, the variance of an estimator function is of special interest. According to [fS04], the uncertainty of a measurement is quantified by variances or standard deviations and the measurement itself is only an estimate of the value of the measurand. The main advantage of the *Cramér-Rao* lower bound is its compact closed form expression. Unfortunately, the *Cramér-Rao* lower bound implicit linearizes the physical model for a given set of design variables. This report emphasizes the resulting drawbacks for oscillating non-linear models. An example similar to [VDBCT03] is presented. To overcome this problem it is proposed to use a specific estimation function instead of a lower bound. For this purpose [MVDBB94] proposed to use the variance of a least square estimator. However, the sensor model had to be linearized. A general approach is Bayesian experimental design [HM13], [CV95],[VDBCT03], [Ber85]. In [HM13] the application of Bayesian experimental design is shown for nonlinear models. They optimize an experiment based on a merit function utilizing the *Kullback-Leibler* divergence. The *Kullback-Leibler* divergence is used as distance measure between the posterior and the priori and quantifies the information gain made by an experiment. The idea was originally proposed by [Lin56] and is derived from *Shannon* information theory. The principle approach was generalized [Lin72],[CV95] to allow other utility functions than the entropy as information measure. In section 3.3 this approach is used in combination with a variance like utility function. However this approach lead to experimental design, which are optimal on average. As an alternative in section 3.4 a merit function for experimental design is proposed, which optimizes always the worst case. In this case there is no risk that some working points of the experiment have higher uncertainty for the benefit for others.

2   Sensor Model

This section provides a rough sensor model. For simplification details are neglected but can be found in [THB13]. The intention of this section is to clarify the notation and the application. In the next section estimation theory is applied to the provided model.

The interference filters are optimized for a chromatic confocal triangulation (CCT) [TB12] sensor. In principle, interference filters can realize arbitrary transmission characteristics by customized thin film layer stacks. The scope of this research is to optimize the sensor by adjusting the thicknesses of these thin film layers, which in turn change the filter transmissions. Assume a CCT sensor with six filters corresponding to six camera channels. The gray values of each channel are organized in a vector and denoted as $\mathbf{g} = (g_1, \ldots, g_6)^\top$. Each filter is determined by its thin film layer stack. The characteristic thicknesses of each layer are organized as a parameter vector $\mathbf{p}_i$ and the index i specifies the corresponding optical filter. For simplification all filters are summarize in one long vector $\mathbf{p}$. In experimental design these parameters are sometimes called design variables.

The measurement procedure of a CCT sensor is to estimate a height, which is optical encoded by a wavelength λ, based on the gray values $\mathbf{g}$. Apart of a nonlinear relationship, height and wavelength λ are equivalent and instead of the height, λ is used as the parameter of interest. Assuming an arbitrary estimation function $f(.)$ the normal working procedure of a CCT senor can be formalized as:

$$\hat{\lambda} = f(\mathbf{g}; \mathbf{p}),$$

with the target to estimate the corresponding wavelength. In estimation literature the parameters $\mathbf{p}$ are denoted as nuisance parameter, because they are not of interest. In experimental design these parameter are the adjustment screws to gain better performance.

A requirement to apply powerful estimation functions, like the *Maximum Likelihood* estimation, is to specify the distribution of the measurements. The dominant non-systematic error source in the CCT sensor is the photon noise of the involved camera. For large number of photons the *Poisson* distribution can be approximated by the normal distribution. For this case the six channel camera gray value $\mathbf{g}$ is modeled as random variable G:

$$\mathrm{E}\{G\} = \mathbf{g}_\mu(\lambda; \mathbf{p}), \mathbf{g}_\mu : \mathbb{R} \to \mathbb{R}^6, \lambda \mapsto \mathbf{g}$$

$$G \sim \mathcal{N}\left(\mathbf{g}_\mu(\lambda; \mathbf{p}), \mathrm{diag}(\sigma_1^2(\lambda; \mathbf{p}), \dots, \sigma_6^2(\lambda; \mathbf{p}))\right), \text{ with}$$

$$\sigma(\lambda, \mathbf{p}) = \sigma_d + k\mathbf{g}_\mu(\lambda; \mathbf{p}), \sigma : \mathbb{R} \to \mathbb{R}^6, \lambda \mapsto \sigma = (\sigma_1, \dots, \sigma_6)^\top$$

$$p(\mathbf{g}|\lambda, \mathbf{p}) = \prod_{i=1}^{6} \frac{1}{\sqrt{2\pi}\sigma_i} e^{-\frac{1}{2}\left(\frac{g_i - g_{\mu,i}(\lambda; \mathbf{p})}{\sigma_i}\right)^2} \tag{2.1}$$

The sensor model $\mathbf{g}_\mu(\lambda; \mathbf{p})$ defines the expectation value of G. In [Bos07] this sensor model is called expectation model. The random variable G is assumed to be normal like distributed and each of the six camera channels is assumed to be statistically independent. The independence property results in a diagonal covariance matrix. The variance of each camera channel is a function of the sensor model again, to realize an approximation of the Poisson distribution.

For the Bayesian framework the deterministic parameter λ is considered as a random variable Λ. A non-informative a priori probability density function is assumed:

$$p(\lambda) = \begin{cases} \frac{1}{\lambda_{max} - \lambda_{min}}, & \text{if } \lambda_{min} \leq \lambda \leq \lambda_{max} \\ 0, & \text{else,} \end{cases}$$

which just expresses the knowledge that the wavelength will be within certain boundaries. Using the Bayes' theorem, the a posteriori probability density function is given by:

$$p(\mathbf{g}|\mathbf{p}) = \int p(\mathbf{g}|\lambda, \mathbf{p}) p(\lambda) d\lambda$$

$$p(\lambda|\mathbf{g}, \mathbf{p}) = \frac{p(\mathbf{g}|\lambda, \mathbf{p}) p(\lambda)}{p(\mathbf{g}|\mathbf{p})}$$

$$= \begin{cases} \frac{p(\mathbf{g}|\lambda, \mathbf{p})}{\int_{\lambda_{min}}^{\lambda_{max}} p(\mathbf{g}|\lambda, \mathbf{p}) d\lambda}, & \text{if } \lambda_{min} \leq \lambda \leq \lambda_{max} \\ 0, & \text{else.} \end{cases}$$

3 Optimizing the Experimental Sensor Design

In this section merit functions are derived to optimize the sensor performance. Optimizing the performance of such a sensor aims to minimize the measurement uncertainty. According to [fS04] the measurement uncertainty is defined as standard deviation (or variance) of the measurement result, while the measurement is only an estimation of the true value. Because the measurement process is an estimation procedure, the optimization tries to minimize the variance of the estimation. The following subsections define different design criteria, which propose optimal design parameters $\mathbf{p}^\star$ for optimal experimental design settings.

3.1 Cramér-Rao Lower Bound Approach

The *Cramér-Rao* lower bound is a fundamental lower bound for the variance of any estimator. Because the lower bound is a function of the experimental design parameters, too, it is a easily accessible way to improve an experiment. The assumption behind this approach is that estimators are available, which reach this lower bound at least asymptotically. A famous example is the *Maximum Likelihood* estimator[Bos07] (p. 81). According to [Bos07] the *Cramér-Rao* lower bound for normal distributed observations is defined as:

$$\text{Var}\{f(\mathbf{g}; \mathbf{p})\} \geq \left(\frac{\partial \mathbf{g}^\top(\lambda, \mathbf{p})}{\partial \lambda} \mathbf{C}^{-1} \frac{\partial \mathbf{g}(\lambda, \mathbf{p})}{\partial \lambda} \right)^{-1},$$

with a covariance matrix C. In the CCT sensor application only one parameter λ is of interest, this scalar variance measure can directly be used as a merit function to optimize the experimental design. Because a sensor is only as good as its worst working point, a *Minimax* optimization is proposed:

$$\mathbf{p}^\star = \arg \min_{\mathbf{p}} \max_{\lambda} \text{Var} \left\{ f \left(\mathbf{g}(\lambda, \mathbf{p}) \right) \right\},$$

which concentrates on minimizing the highest variance whithin the measurement range.

As comparison in [THB13] several merit functions were presented. To link this result to these, a slightly different noise model (2.1) is assumed. For this comparison the covariance matrix $\text{Cov} = \sigma^2 \mathbf{I}$ is modeled with constant standard deviation σ and identity matrix $\mathbf{I}$. In this case the *Cramér-Rao* lower bound can be expressed as:

$$\text{Var}\{f(\lambda)\} = \left(\frac{\partial \mathbf{g}^\top(\lambda, \mathbf{p})}{\partial \lambda} (\sigma^2 \mathbf{I})^{-1} \frac{\partial \mathbf{g}(\lambda, \mathbf{p})}{\partial \lambda} \right)^{-1}$$

$$= \frac{1}{\sigma^2} \left(\left\| \frac{\partial \mathbf{g}(\lambda, \mathbf{p})}{\partial \lambda} \right\|_2^{-1} \right)^2, \tag{3.1}$$

which is identical to the proposed "sensitivity" merit function in [THB13] and reflects the result in a different light.

Unfortunately, this kind of experimental optimization will fail due to the non-linearity of the CCT sensor model. The model $\mathbf{g}(\lambda, \mathbf{p})$ is highly non-linear and has in particular an oscillating character. Optimizing only the lower bound of the estimation variance will lead to an ill-posed estimation problem. The well posed property will be lost, because the oscillating character of $\mathbf{g}(\lambda, \mathbf{p})$ will cause ambiguities. To clarify the problem, an example is provided in the next section.

3.2 Example - Effect of Non-Linear Models

The following example is intent to emphasize the problem of a non-linear CCT sensor model. Especially, the oscillating function character leads to ambiguities and causes the estimation problem to be ill-posed. The example is adapted from [VDBCT03]. Instead of investigating the CCT sensor model an simplified sensor model is assumed:

$$g_\mu(\lambda, \mathbf{p}) = \frac{1}{2} \sin \left(p_1 (\lambda - p_2) \right) + \frac{1}{2}, \tag{3.2}$$

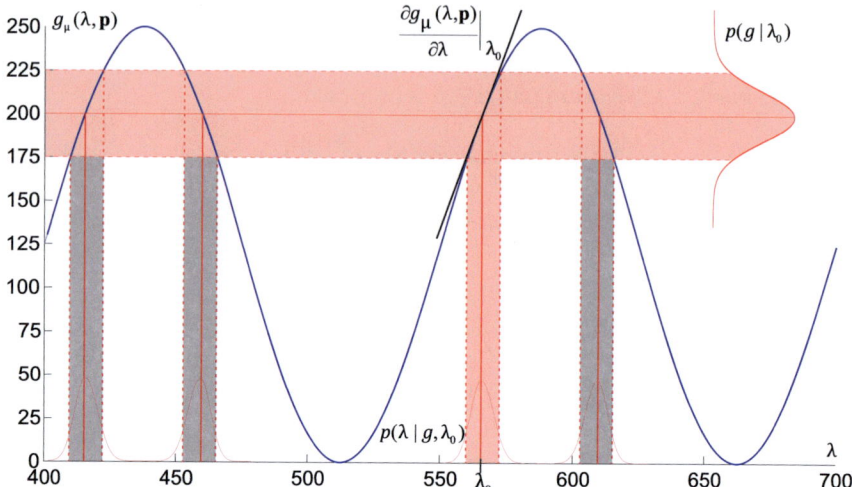

Figure 3.1: Blue graph depicts the non-linear (sinus like) relationship between the gray value $g_\mu(\lambda, \mathbf{p})$ and λ. Furthermore, the normal distribution $p(\mathbf{g}|\lambda_0)$ is depicted and the gradient at λ_0 as part of the *Cramér-Rao* lower bound. Finally, the posteriori probability density function is illustrated, too. The posteriori shows four peaks with equal probability. However, this ambiguity is not recognized by the gradient used to calculate the *Cramér-Rao* lower bound. The example is adapted from [VDBCT03].

with clear oscillating character. The model is depicted in Fig. 3.1 as blue graph. This model lead to an estimation process which is ill-posed due to ambiguities. Assuming a measurement (observation) of $\mathbf{g} = 200$, there is no evidence to prefer one of the four estimates: $\hat{\lambda} \in \{415, 460, 565, 610\}$. The task of a experimental design is to remove the ill-posed property and too ensure measurements with low uncertainty. The key idea is, that this can be done in parallel if the current estimation variance is minimized. Ambiguities in the estimation process increase the uncertainty of the estimate and thus the variance of the estimator.

Assume that the frequency p_1 and the offset p_2 in the example model (3.2) would be adjustable design parameters of the experiment. Then, an optimal solution for a setup with well posed estimation process is shown in Fig. 3.2. The depicted solution is optimal, because every higher frequency p_1 would introduce an ambiguity. On the other side, a lower frequency would decrease the gradient $\partial g_\mu/\partial\lambda$ and according to the *Cramér-Rao* lower bound increase the variance of the estimation. The step between the result depicted in Fig. 3.1 and the proposed preferred

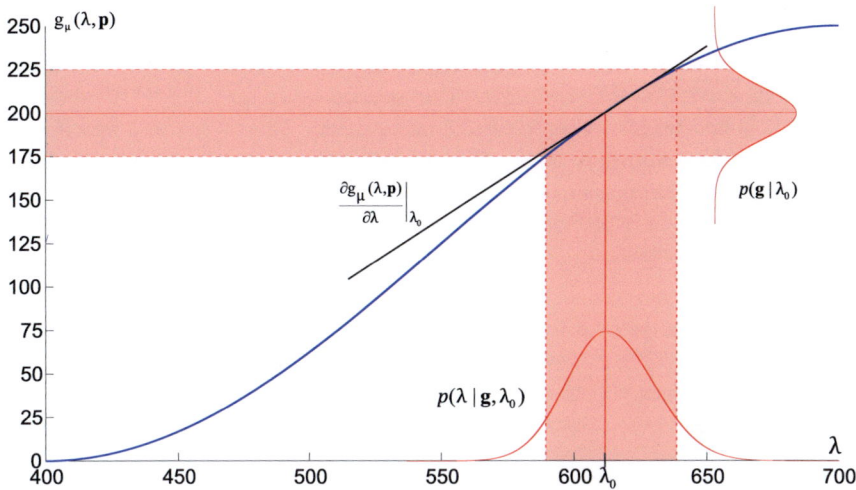

Figure 3.2: Blue graph shows a sensor model $g(\lambda)$ in optimal experimental settings. The estimation problem is well-posed and the uncertainty for this case is minimal.

result in Fig. 3.2 is optimizing the experimental design. However, the *Cramér-Rao* lower bound approach will lead to a contrary result. According to equation (3.1), the lower bound involves a sensor model gradient. With view to the example model (3.2) an optimized design would increase the frequency p_1 to infinity, because:

$$\frac{\partial \mathbf{g}(\lambda, \mathbf{p})}{\partial \lambda} = \frac{1}{2}\cos(p_1(\lambda - p_2))p_1 \leq \frac{1}{2}p_1.$$

This shows clearly that ambiguities are not recognized by the local gradient.

In the following two sections experimental design approaches are presented, which incorporate a specific estimation function. If e.g. an *Maximum-a-Posteriori Probability* (MAP) estimator is used, the estimate is just the maximum of the posteriori probability density $p(\lambda|g, \lambda_0)$. As depicted in Fig. 3.1 the posteriori probability density function consists of four asymmetric gaussian like distributions. These four peaks contain the information of an increased measurement uncertainty, caused by ambiguities due to the non-linear sensor model. Utilizing the MAP estimator variance will prevent the experimental design optimization to turn into an ill-posed problem.

3.3   Bayesian Experimental Design

The last two sections show that the *Camér-Rao* lower bound variance measure is
not suitable for non-linear models. This section overcomes the disadvantages of
a lower bound by involving a estimation function. Restricting to a specific estimation function allows to access the variance without approximation. As shown
in example 3.1, ambiguities heavily increase the estimation variance. Minimizing
this variance in an experimental design optimization will prevent ambiguities in
the estimation process.

The idea to incorporate a concrete estimation function in experimental design does
not justify to change over from a frequentistic to a Bayesian approach. It's rather
a free decision of the author. In [CV95] a general approach of Bayesian experimental design was presented. An experimental design is defined by the design
variables $\mathbf{p}$ and observations $\mathbf{g}$ which will be made in the experiment. Based on $\mathbf{g}$
an estimation function $\hat{\lambda} = f(\mathbf{g}; \mathbf{p})$ estimates the unknown parameter of interest
λ. Then, the best Bayesian experimental design is given by [CV95]:

$$\mathbf{p}^\star = \arg\min_{\mathbf{p}} \min_{f \in \mathcal{F}} \int \int u(f, \lambda, \mathbf{p}, \mathbf{g}) p(\lambda|\mathbf{g}, \mathbf{p}) p(\mathbf{g}|\mathbf{p}) \mathrm{d}\lambda \mathrm{d}\mathbf{g}. \qquad (3.3)$$

The utility function $u(f, \lambda, \mathbf{p}, \mathbf{g})$ reflects the purpose of the experiment and with
the idea of a variance measure it is chosen to $u(f, \lambda, \mathbf{p}, \mathbf{g}) = (\lambda - \hat{\lambda})^2$. The double
minimization takes into account, that both, a suitable estimation function f out of
a set of estimation function $\mathcal{F}$ and the best design parameters $\mathbf{p}$ must be chosen.
Suitable estimation function are e.g. the *Bayesian* estimator:

$$\hat{\lambda} = \int \lambda p(\lambda|\mathbf{g}, \mathbf{p}) \mathrm{d}\lambda$$

and the *Maximum a posteriori* (MAP) estimator:

$$\hat{\lambda}_{\mathrm{MAP}} = \arg\max_{\lambda} p(\lambda|\mathbf{g}, \mathbf{p}).$$

Without prove, the MAP estimator is preferred, because the non-linear model will
cause an asymmetric posterior probability density function which will cause a bias
for the Bayesian estimator. Although, the Bayesian estimator is proven to have the
lowest variance [Ber85](p.136).

3.4   Worst Case Experimental Design

The approach of the Bayesian experimental design (section 3.3) contains a hidden
risk. The integral over λ causes an averaging over all possible working points.

Thus an experimental design can be improved by increasing the measurement uncertainty of a single working point for the benefit for others. However, a sensor is only as good as its worst working point and this behavior is undesirable. In literature, the worst case optimization in combination with experimental design is rarely studied. A related idea *Maximum Mean Squared Error* optimization was proposed by [SSW89] and [SWMW89]. In [Coh96],[SHL12] an similar idea was discussed. As a side note, the following formulation of a merit function is neither purely frequentistic nor Bayesian. For a given working point λ_0, the squared difference of an estimator function $\hat{\lambda} = f(\mathbf{g})$ is given by:

$$u(f, \lambda_0, \mathbf{p}, \mathbf{g}) = (\hat{\lambda} - \lambda_0)^2,$$

as a function of the observations $\mathbf{g}$ and its corresponding random variable G. According to [Coh96] the expected mean squared error (MSE) is given by:

$$\mathrm{E}_{\mathrm{MSE}}\{G\} = \int (\hat{\lambda} - \lambda_0)^2 p(\mathbf{g}|\lambda_0, \mathbf{p})\mathrm{d}\mathbf{g}.$$

This equation evaluates the expected MSE at the working point λ_0. The best worst case experimental design is then given by:

$$\mathbf{p}^\star = \arg\min_{\mathbf{p}} \max_{\lambda_0} \int (\hat{\lambda} - \lambda_0)^2 p(\mathbf{g}|\lambda_0, \mathbf{p})\mathrm{d}\mathbf{g}.$$

In contrast to (3.3) the optimization of the selected estimation function was neglected.

4 Conclusion

The research points out, that the *Cramér-Rao* lower bound implicit linearizes a sensor model. Using the lower bound to optimize the experimental setup for nonlinear models is problematic. For the application to optimize interference filters for a CCT sensor, the optimized experimental design results in a ill-posed estimation task. To avoid this problem an alternative approach is proposed. Specifying a concrete estimator, the estimation variance can directly be minimized. Open questions are an experimental validation with a comparison between the Bayesian experimental design and the proposed worst case experimental design. In an former publication [THB13] the problem of an ill-posed estimation process was avoided by an additional merit function. A comparison with this approach would be interesting, too. Another open question is the selection of a suitable estimation function.

A topic that was not tackled is the numerical realization in an optimization framework. Due to the non-linearities, the overall optimization problem is highly nonconvex. The found optimized experimental design will be a local optimum with high probability. For this reason, the calculation complexity will influence the quality of experimental design, too. For the application itself, the calculation speed is of great importance.

Bibliography

[Ber85]   James O. Berger. *Statistical Decision Theory and Bayesian Analysis*. Springer, August 1985.

[Bos07]   Adriaan van den Bos. *Parameter Estimation for Scientists and Engineers*. John Wiley & Sons, August 2007.

[Coh96]   David A. Cohn. Neural network exploration using optimal experiment design. *Neural Networks*, 9(6):1071–1083, August 1996.

[CV95]   Kathryn Chaloner and Isabella Verdinelli. Bayesian experimental design: A review. *Statistical Science*, 10(3):273–304, August 1995. ArticleType: research-article / Full publication date: Aug., 1995 / Copyright © 1995 Institute of Mathematical Statistics.

[fS04]   International Organization for Standardization. *Guide to the expression of uncertainty in measurement (GUM)-Supplement 1: Numerical methods for the propagation of distributions*, volume ISO draft guide DGUIDE99998. International Organization for Standardization, Geneva, 2004.

[HK05]   Klaus Hinkelmann and Oscar Kempthorne. *Design and Analysis of Experiments: Advanced experimental design*. Wiley, April 2005.

[HM13]   Xun Huan and Youssef M. Marzouk. Simulation-based optimal bayesian experimental design for nonlinear systems. *Journal of Computational Physics*, 232(1):288–317, January 2013.

[Lin56]   D. V. Lindley. On a measure of the information provided by an experiment. *The Annals of Mathematical Statistics*, 27(4):986–1005, December 1956. ArticleType: research-article / Full publication date: Dec., 1956 / Copyright © 1956 Institute of Mathematical Statistics.

[Lin72]   D. V. Lindley. *Bayesian Statistics, A Review*. SIAM, January 1972.

[MVDBB94]   M. A O Miedema, A. Van Den Bos, and A. H. Buist. Experimental design of exit wave reconstruction from a transmission electron microscope defocus series. *IEEE Transactions on Instrumentation and Measurement*, 43(2):181–186, 1994.

[SHL12]   Antti Solonen, Heikki Haario, and Marko Laine. Simulation-based optimal design using a response variance criterion. *Journal of Computational and Graphical Statistics*, 21(1):234–252, 2012.

[SSW89]   Jerome Sacks, Susannah B. Schiller, and William J. Welch. Designs for computer experiments. *Technometrics*, 31(1):41, February 1989.

[SWMW89]   Jerome Sacks, William J. Welch, Toby J. Mitchell, and Henry P. Wynn. Design and analysis of computer experiments. *Statistical Science*, 4(4):409–423, November 1989. Mathematical Reviews number (MathSciNet): MR1041765; Zentralblatt MATH identifier: 0955.62619.

[TB12]   M. Taphanel and J. Beyerer. Fast 3D in-line sensor for specular and diffuse surfaces combining the chromatic confocal and triangulation principle. In *Instrumentation and Measurement Technology Conference (I2MTC), 2012 IEEE International*, pages 1072–1077, May 2012.

[THB13]   Miro Taphanel, Bastiaan Hovestreydt, and Jürgen Beyerer. Speed-up chromatic sensors by optimized optical filters. pages 87880S–87880S, May 2013.

[VAdDVDvdB02]   S. Van Aert, A.J. den Dekker, D. Van Dyck, and A. van den Bos. Optimal experimental design of STEM measurement of atom column positions. *Ultramicroscopy*, 90(4):273–289, April 2002.

[VDBCT03]   Jojanneke Van Den Berg, Andrew Curtis, and Jeannot Trampert. Optimal nonlinear bayesian experimental design: an application to amplitude versus offset experiments. *Geophysical Journal International*, 155(2):411–421, 2003.

A Texture Modulation Model to Describe Structural-Statistical Textures

Markus Vogelbacher

Vision and Fusion Laboratory
Institute for Anthropomatics
Karlsruhe Institute of Technology (KIT), Germany
markus.vogelbacher@kit.edu

Technical Report IES-2013-12

Abstract:

Many existing methods describe structural or statistical textures. For the transition region, the structural-statistical textures, only very few dedicated methods are known. In this report, a texture model is presented that allows the description of certain structural-statistical textures. The way of looking at modulation from communications technology is applied to textures. A structural texture may be subject to a variation of the gray value, i.e., amplitude modulation, or primitive, i.e., frequency modulation. This is based on the description of the modulated texture using an extended two-dimensional Fourier series. This enables not only the representation of modulated textures, but also the demodulation with the help of a presented phase-locked loop. Thus, an assessment of a modulated texture is achieved.

1 Introduction

In the field of image processing, the analysis of textures is an important area. Textures are described as two-dimensional distinct structure with certain deterministic or statistical regularities. Structural, structural-statistical and statistical texture types can be distinguished, depending on how much knowledge of a texture exists. Structural textures are characterized by a texture primitive that is repeated in a fixed local arrangement scheme. If the primitive or the arrangement scheme is subject to certain stochastic variations, we speak of a structural-statistical texture type. If no primitive or arrangement scheme is visible, we talk about a statistical texture type. Depending on which type of texture is present, there are different methods of analysis. The methods for statistical textures are mainly related to differences

 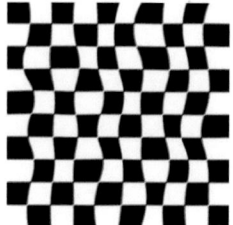

(a) AM of a texture   (b) FM of a texture

Figure 1.1: Examples of the analysis of structural-statistical textures similar to the communications technology.

in the statistics of first and second order. Histogram features such as the mean, the variance, or the autocorrelation function may be used for evaluation. Known methods for this type of texture also determine the co-occurrence matrix (GLCM) and the associated Haralick features [HSD73, Har79, Bey11] or the use of local binary patterns [WH89]. Furthermore, statistical properties can be mapped with the help of an AR-model [MJ92]. For structural textures the primitive can be determined for example using the GLCM, the autocorrelation function or the Renyi entropy [GP03] and the arrangement scheme by looking at the Fourier transform [RH99]. For the analysis of structural-statistical textures the methods for purely structural or statistical textures are often combined. Methods that are explicitly used for the structural-statistical texture type don't exist.

In this report, an approach will be further developed, which has been proposed in [Vog12] and allows a structural-statistical description of textures. The concept of modulation, as known from communications technology, is introduced for textures. A variation of the gray value corresponds to an amplitude modulation (AM) (1.1(a)) and the changes in the shape of the primitive or the frequential arrangement of the primitives corresponds to a frequency modulation (FM) (Fig. 1.1(b)). The step from communications technology to modulated textures is achieved with the help of an extended two-dimensional Fourier series (EFS). This report considers particularly the area of FM and presents a proposal for solution for demodulation with the help of a phase-locked loop.

The report is organized as follows: In Section 2 the modulation model from the communications technology is first derived for arbitrary signals and a phase-locked loop is described which allows demodulation of frequency modulated textures. Section 3 shows different results of this demodulation. Summary and outlook are given in Section 4.

2 Modulated Texture

2.1 The modulation model: From communications technology to arbitrary signals

The modulation in the communications technology allows to transmit a desired signal or modulating signal $v(t)$ by a suitable carrier $x(t)$. The information of the desired signal can be introduced in the amplitude (AM) $x_{AM}(t)$ or frequency (FM) $x_{FM}(t)$ of the carrier signal:

$$x(t) = a_0 \cos(2\pi f_0 t + \varphi_0),$$
$$x_{AM}(t) = [a_0 + a_1 v(t)] \cos(2\pi f_0 t + \varphi_0),$$
$$x_{FM}(t) = a_0 \cos(2\pi f_0 t + \Delta\Omega\, V(t) + \varphi_0),$$
$$\text{with } V(t) = \int_0^t v(t')\, dt' \text{ and } \Delta\Omega = \text{frequency deviation}$$

The creation of the analytic signal using the Hilbert transform and the complex envelope permits demodulation, i.e., the recovery of the desired signal $v(t)$ from the modulated carrier signal ($x_{AM}(t)$ or $x_{FM}(t)$) [Kam11].

In [Vog12] it is shown how this approach can be expanded for any periodic one- and two-dimensional signals by using Fourier series. The unmodulated structural texture, described by a complex 2D-Fourier series, can be used as two-dimensional carrier signal:

$$f(x,y) = \sum_{m=-\infty}^{\infty} \sum_{n=-\infty}^{\infty} E_{mn}\, e^{j(m 2\pi f_x x + n 2\pi f_y y)},$$
$$\text{with } f_x = \frac{1}{T_x},\ f_y = \frac{1}{T_y}\ , \text{and}$$
$$E_{mn} = \frac{1}{T_x T_y} \int_{-T_y}^{T_y} \int_{-T_x}^{T_x} e^{-j(m 2\pi f_x x + n 2\pi f_y y)} f(x,y)\, dx\, dy$$

E_{mn} denotes the Fourier coefficients, which are obtained from the primitive texture. f_x and f_y are the fundamental frequency in x- and y-direction of the arrangement scheme. A structural-statistical texture can be generated by introduction of modulation. Specifically for the FM, which will be examined in more detail below, this means introducing modulation terms $V_x(x,y)$ and $V_y(x,y)$ for

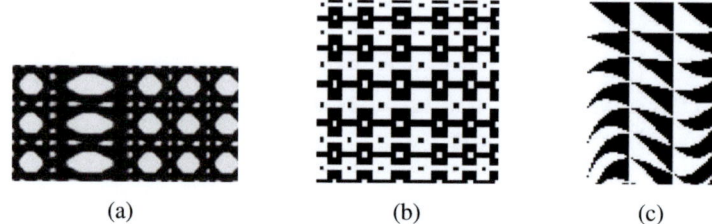

| (a) | (b) | (c) |

Figure 2.1: Structural-statistical textures generated by the modulation approach: (a) Modulation only in x-direction ($V_x(x, y) = V_x(x)$, $V_y(x, y) = 0$), (b) Independent modulation in x- and y-direction ($V_x(x, y) = V_x(x) = V_y(x, y) = V_y(y)$), (c) Combined x-y-modulation ($V_x(x, y) = 0$, $V_y(x, y)$).

the corresponding fundamental frequencies and thus leads to the EFS:

$$f_{FM}(x, y) = \sum_{m=-\infty}^{\infty} \sum_{n=-\infty}^{\infty} E_{mn} \, e^{j(m(2\pi f_x x + V_x(x,y)) + n(2\pi f_y y + V_y(x,y)))}$$

Fig. 2.1 shows some examples of structural-statistical textures that can be described with the help of the modulation approach and the EFS. Likewise, inclined modulation can be guaranteed by the dependence of the modulation terms of both x and y (Fig. 2.1(c)).

2.2 Demodulation using a phase locked loop

With the approach described in Section 2.1 structural-statistical textures with known modulated arrangement scheme can be represented. A simple demodulation analogous to the communications technology is no longer possible due to the summation of the Fourier series. But just because this area is in the analysis of modulated textures of special interest, a method presented below enables the demodulation and the determination of the modulation terms $V_x(x, y)$ and $V_y(x, y)$. This method involves the use of a phase-locked loop (Fig. 2.2), which allows recursive determination of the modulation terms using the EFS as a reference model $f_M(x, y, V_x(x, y), V_y(x, y))$. Variables to be regulated are the modulation terms $V_x(x, y)$ and $V_y(x, y)$:

$$f_M(x, y, V_x(x, y), V_y(x, y)) =$$
$$\sum_{m=-\infty}^{\infty} \sum_{n=-\infty}^{\infty} E_{mn} \, e^{j(m(2\pi f_x x + V_x(x,y)) + n(2\pi f_y y + V_y(x,y)))}$$

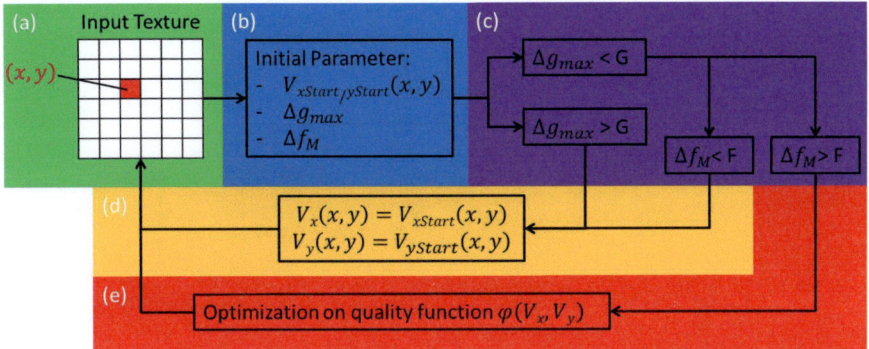

Figure 2.2: Phase-locked loop for demodulation of modulated textures.

As the first component the texture $g(x, y)$ to be demodulated is coupled in the control loop as an input variable (Fig. 2.2 (a)). Thus, the Fourier coefficients for the reference model can be determined first. The subsequent determination of the modulation terms occurs recursively for every pixel. In the next step the start parameters for the further regulation are derived for the subject pixel (x, y) (Fig. 2.2 (b)). As first start parameter the initial values for the modulation parameters $V_{xStart}(x, y)$ and $V_{yStart}(x, y)$ are calculated with the help of the preceding neighbors:

$$V_{xStart/yStart}(x, y) = \frac{V_{x/y}(x - 1, y) + V_{x/y}(x, y - 1)}{2}$$

The second start parameter contains the maximum gray value jump Δg_{max} within the neighborhood U (Fig. 2.3):

$$\Delta g_{max} = max\big(\, |g(x, y) - g(x - 1, y - 1)|,$$
$$|g(x, y) - g(x - 1, y)|, ..., |g(x, y) - g(x, y - 1)|\,\big)$$

The consideration of the gray value jump Δg_{max} is necessary because, especially for EFS with a few number of Fourier coefficients E_{mn}, a large gray jump can lead to a higher model deviation or requires a setting time. The model deviation Δf_M reached with the help of the previously defined start parameters denotes the third and last start parameter:

$$\Delta f_M = |g(x, y) - f_M(x, y, V_{xStart}(x, y), V_{yStart}(x, y))|$$

The calculated start parameters are compared below with previously defined thresholds (Fig. 2.2 (c)). If the gray value jump is too high $\Delta g_{max} > G$, which

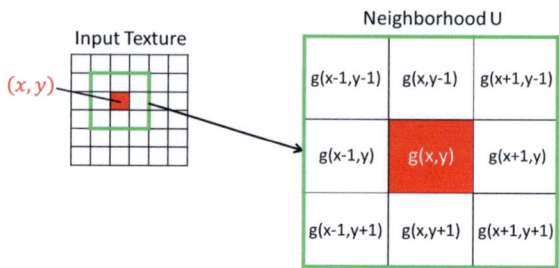

Figure 2.3: Neighborhood U for determining the gray level jump.

can't be covered by the model or reached within a pixel transition due to the setting time, the previously determined start values of the modulation parameters are taken directly for the current pixel (Fig. 2.2 (d)). This is to prevent the modulation parameters to vary too much especially at edges. If there is no high gray value jump, next the model error is considered, which is reached with the start values of the modulation parameters. If this one is located within a range of tolerance $\Delta f_M < F$ a further adaption of the modulation parameters is not required and the start values can again be used directly for the current pixel (Fig. 2.2 (d)). An optimization using a qualitiy function $\varphi(V_x, V_y)$ to determine the modulation parameters is subsequently necessary if the constrains described above, i.e., $\Delta g_{max} < G$ and $\Delta f_M > F$, do not apply (Fig. 2.2 (e)). The required quality function $\varphi(V_x, V_y)$ can be defined differently:

- Model deviation:

$$\varphi(V_x, V_y) = |g(x, y) - f_M(x, y, V_x(x, y), V_y(x, y))|$$

- Model deviation for neighborhood

$$\varphi(V_x, V_y) = \sum_{(k,l) \in U} |g(x - k, y - l) - f_M(x - k, y - l, V_x(x, y), V_y(x, y))|$$

- Model deviation + Penalty term for parameter changes

$$\varphi(V_x, V_y) = |g(x, y) - f_M(x, y, V_x(x, y), V_y(x, y))| \\ + |V_x(x, y) - V_{xStart}| + |V_y(x, y) - V_{yStart}|$$

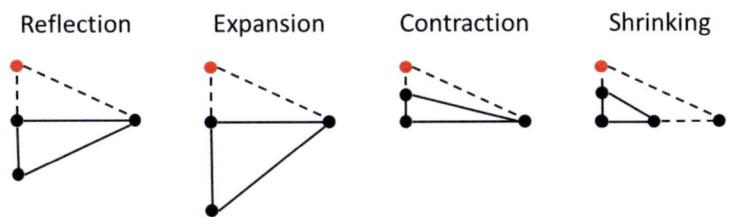

Figure 2.4: Choice of a new optimization point at the Downhill-Simplex algorithm (red: worst point).

- Model deviation for neighborhood + Penalty term for parameter changes

$$\varphi(V_x, V_y) = \sum_{(k,l) \in U} |g(x - k, y - l) - f_M(x - k, y - l, V_x(x,y), V_y(x,y))|$$

$$+ |V_x(x,y) - V_{xStart}| + |V_y(x,y) - V_{yStart}|$$

An optimization/minimization of the selected quality function is carried out with the Downhill-Simplex algorithm according to J. Nelder and R. Mead [NM65, LRWW98]. Based on the start values of the modulation parameters three starting points are selected, for example $[(V_{xStart} + \Delta, V_{yStart}), (V_{xStart}, V_{yStart} + \Delta), (V_{xStart}, V_{yStart} - \Delta)]$. For the starting points the corresponding function values $[\varphi(V_{xStart} + \Delta, V_{yStart}), \varphi(V_{xStart}, V_{yStart} + \Delta), \varphi(V_{xStart}, V_{yStart} - \Delta)]$ are calculated and checked whether the lowest function value is within the range of tolerance. If this is the case, the modulation parameters of the associated start point can be entered for the current pixel. If the smallest function value is outside the range of tolerance, the worst point is replaced by a new point (Fig. 2.4) and with the new point constellation the calculation is performed as to the three starting points. This procedure is repeated until an optimum point is found or as long as a certain number of iterations is reached. Thus, a calculation of the modulation parameters is achieved by means of optimization for the current pixel. This procedure is performed for all pixels of the texture to be examined $g(x, y)$. As a result, the modulation parameters $V_x(x, y)$ and $V_y(x, y)$ are obtained.

It should be noted that in the presented control loop different variable values are provided, which can influence the quality and the result of the determination of the modulation parameters. The variable parameters are the threshold values for the gray value jump G and the model error F, the choice of the quality function $\varphi(V_x, V_y)$ and the distance between the starting points Δ at the Downhill-Simplex algorithm.

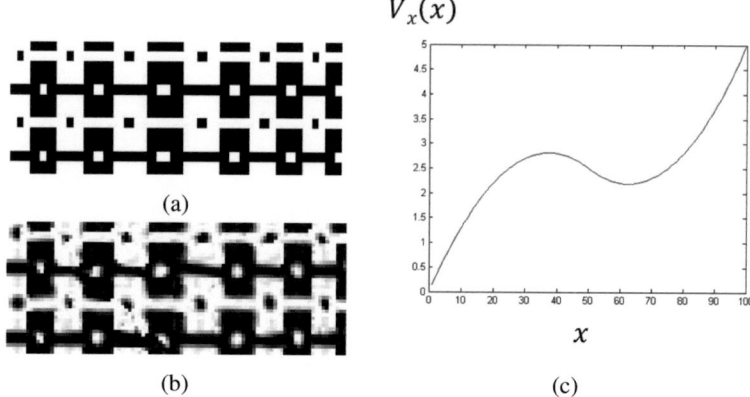

$V_x(x)$

(a)

(b)   (c)

Figure 3.1: Modulated texture example 1: (a) Original modulated texture, (b) Synthesized texture with the modulation parameters $V_x(x,y)$ and $V_y(x,y)$ from the phase-locked loop, (c) Ideal profile of the modulation parameter $V_x(x,y) = V_x(x)$ ($V_y(x,y) = 0$).

3   Results

This section shows some results of the phase-locked loop presented in Section 2.2 for the analysis of modulated textures. The two examples in Fig. 3.1(a) and Fig. 3.2(a) show a purely in x-direction modulated texture, i.e., $V_y(x,y) = 0$ and $V_x(x,y) = V_x(x)$ (3.1(c) or 3.2(c)). The investigation of the texture by the phase-locked loop, i.e., demodulation, delivers the estimated modulation parameters $V_x(x,y)$ and $V_y(x,y)$ whereby a synthesized texture can be created (3.1(b) or 3.2(b)). To get an idea of the profiles of the modulation parameters from the phase-locked loop, in Fig. 3.3-3.5 the results are shown row-wise.

It can be seen that the ideal profile of the modulation parameter is not achieved by the determination with the phase-locked loop. The profiles show strong variations and jumps. However, the basic shape of the ideal profile can be seen if we consider the superimposed line by line profiles (Fig. 3.3(d) and Fig. 3.5). The existing jumps are not desirable and should be addressed in future extensions of the control loop. The partially significant variations suggest that the optimization problem is not clearly identified or the description of the modulated texture with the current EFS is not unique. Nonetheless a synthesis of the texture is possible by means of the estimated modulation parameters.

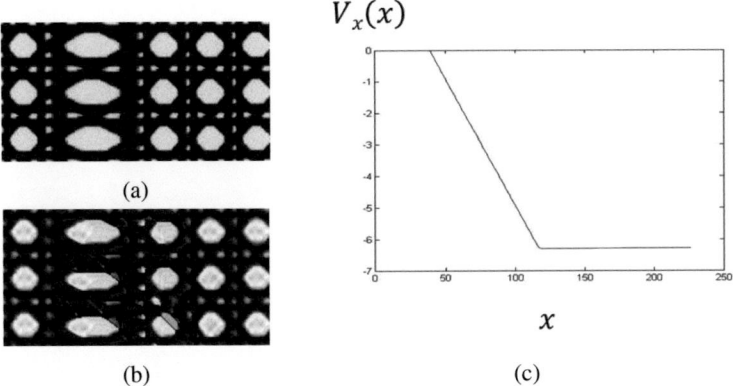

$V_x(x)$

x

(a)

(b)   (c)

Figure 3.2: Modulated texture example 2: (a) Original modulated texture, (b) Synthesized texture with the modulation parameters $V_x(x, y)$ and $V_y(x, y)$ from the phase-locked loop, (c) Ideal profile of the modulation parameter $V_x(x, y) = V_x(x)$ $(V_y(x, y) = 0)$.

The problem of nonunique description using the EFS also becomes apparent when we look at an example with combined x-y modulation (Fig. 3.6). The results of the phase-locked loop for the modulation parameters are seen in Fig. 3.7 and have a distinctly different profile with respect to the ideal profile (Fig. 3.6(c)). However, the synthesized texture from the determined modulation parameters (Fig. 3.6(b)) is comparable to the original input texture with a few failures. By varying the various variable parameters of the control loop, it is possible to determine modulation parameters, which produce a synthesized texture that perfectly corresponds to the input texture. But the profiles of this modulation parameters deviate even more clearly from the ideal profile.

The results indicate that with the help of the phase-locked loop a basic demodulation of frequency modulated textures is possible. However, the determined modulation terms can vary considerably from the modulation parameters used for modulation of the original texture. To what extent this issue affects the analysis of modulated textures must be considered in further studies. Possible approaches for improving the results could be achieved by making changes at the control loop or by introducing additional conditions, for example for the prevention of outliers. Through a better usage of neighborhood relations also smoother modulation profiles would be possible. Another important issue involves the uniqueness of the EFS model. It is necessary to investigate how far the EFS model has to be changed

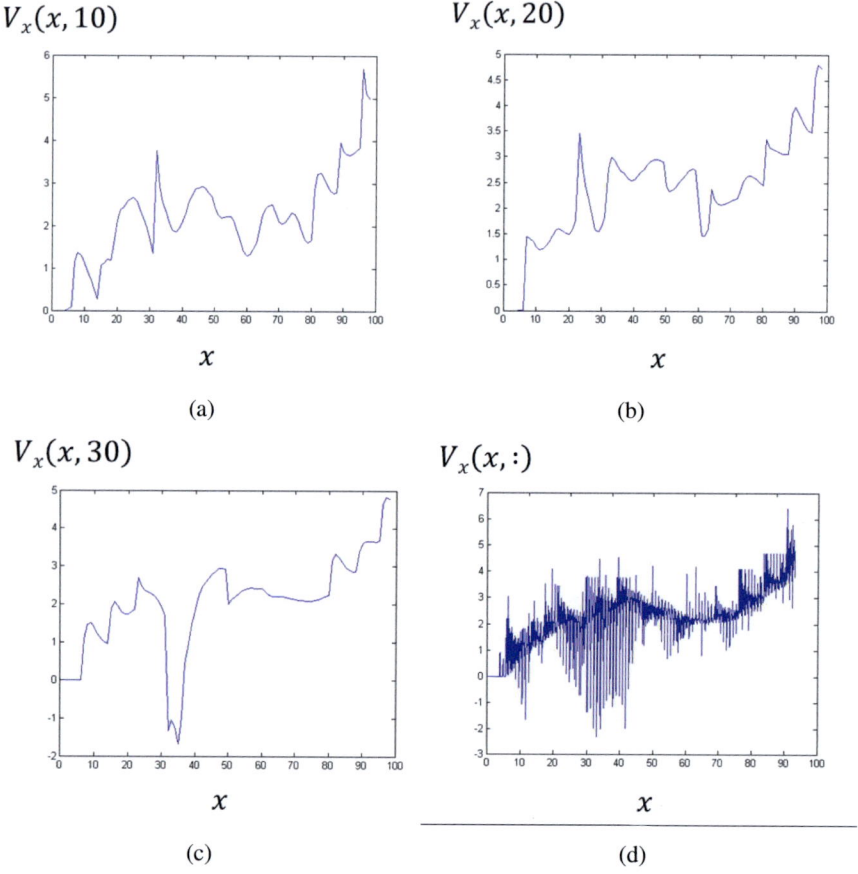

Figure 3.3: Selection of row-wise results of the modulation parameter $V_x(x, y)$ for example texture 1 (Fig. 3.1): (a) Line 10, (b) Line 20, (c) Line 30, (d) Superposition of all row-wise profiles for the example texture.

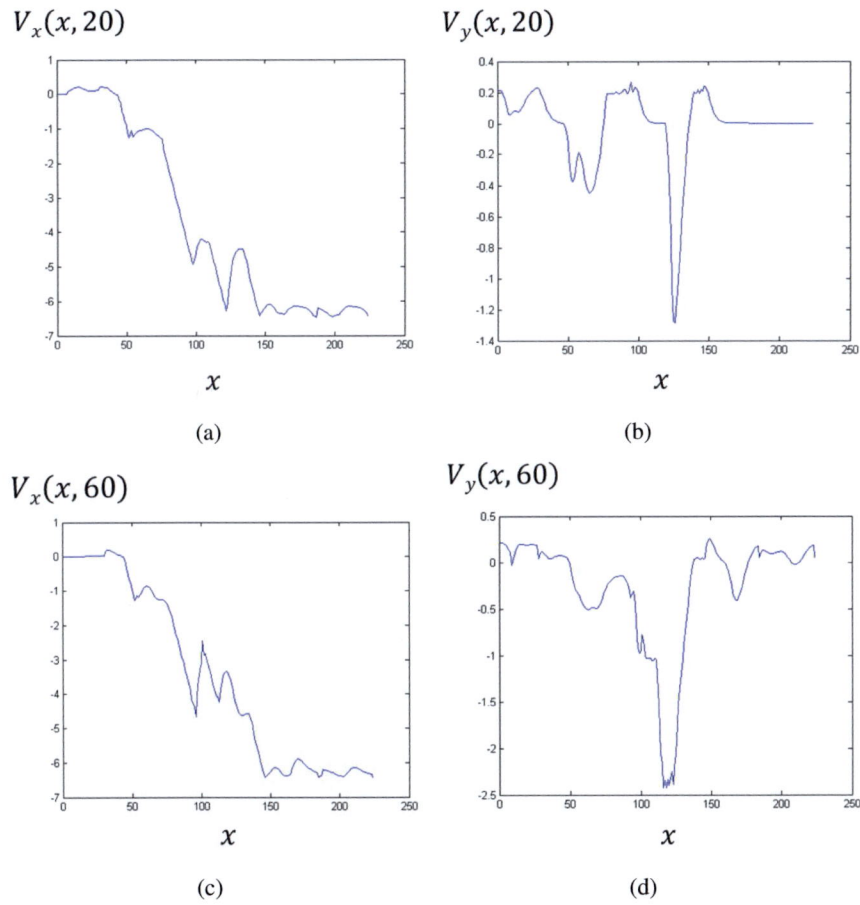

Figure 3.4: Selection of row-wise results of the modulation parameters $V_x(x, y)$ and $V_y(x, y)$ for example texture 2 (Fig. 3.2): (a) $V_x(x, y)$ for Line 20, (b) $V_y(x, y)$ for Line 20, (c) $V_x(x, y)$ for Line 60, (d) $V_y(x, y)$ for Line 60.

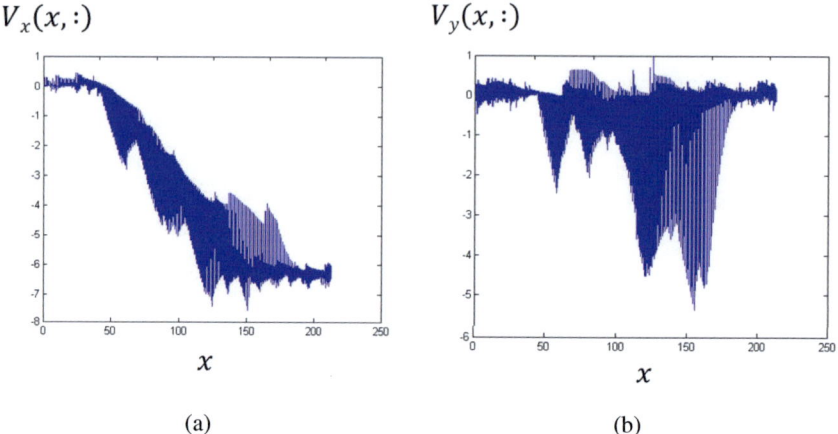

$V_x(x,:)$ $V_y(x,:)$

(a)   (b)

Figure 3.5: Superposition of all row-wise profiles of the modulation parameters $V_x(x,y)$ and $V_y(x,y)$ for the example texture 2 (Fig. 3.2): (a) $V_x(x,y)$, (b) $V_y(x,y)$.

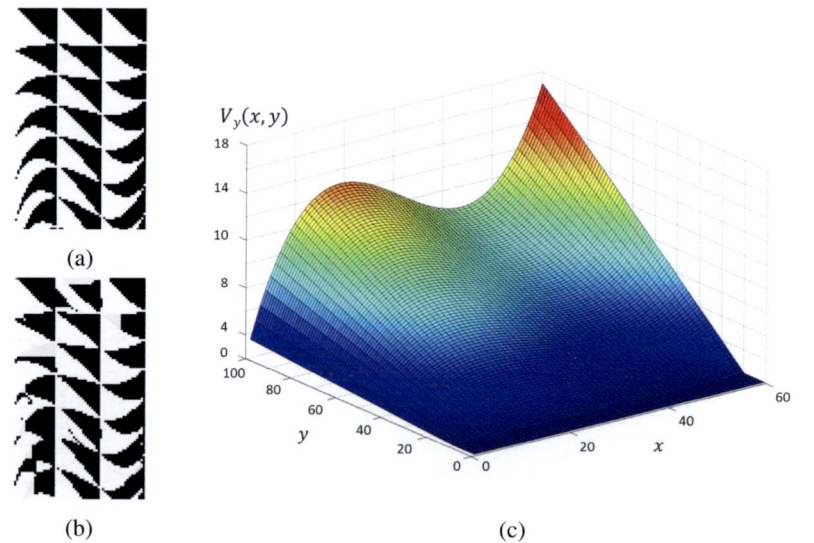

$V_y(x,y)$

(a)

(b)   (c)

Figure 3.6: Modulated texture example 3: (a) Original modulated texture, (b) Synthesized texture with the modulation parameters $V_x(x,y)$ and $V_y(x,y)$ from the phase-locked loop, (c) Ideal profile of the modulation parameter $V_y(x,y)$ ($V_x(x,y) = 0$).

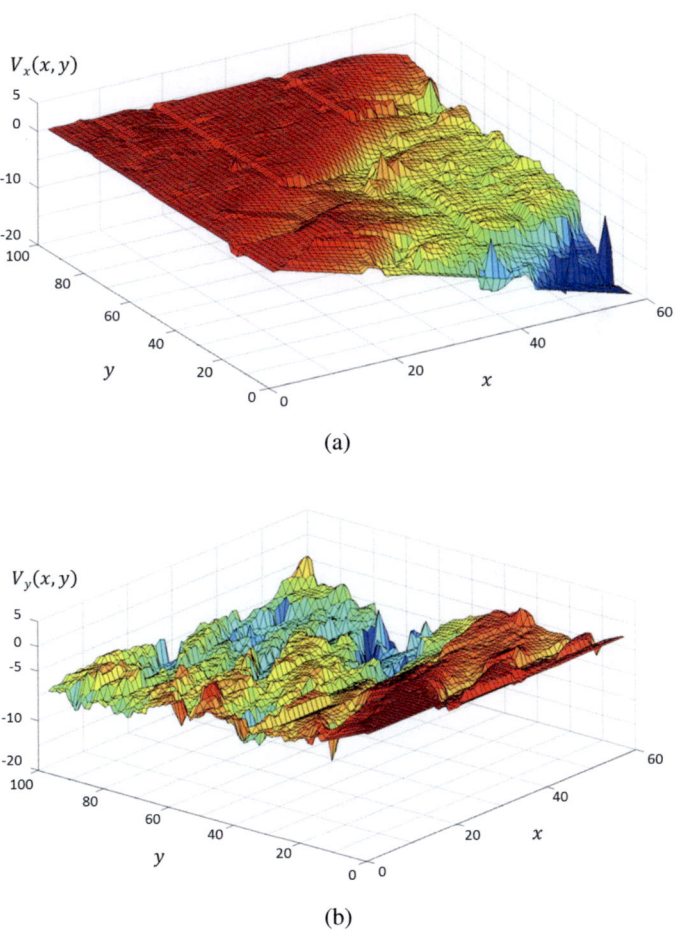

(a)

(b)

Figure 3.7: Modulation parameter $V_x(x,y)$ and $V_y(x,y)$ for example texture 3 (Fig. 3.6): (a) $V_x(x,y)$, (b) $V_y(x,y)$.

or simplified to get a unique solution. The reduction to one modulation parameter could be the first stage of development.

4 Conclusion and Outlook

This report deals with the description of structural-statistical textures with the help of the modulation approach from the communications technology. The variation of the gray value, the variation of the primitive or the arrangement scheme can therefore be seen as amplitude or frequency modulation. For this, the EFS was introduced as a new structural-statistical texture model.

Further, a phase-locked loop has been presented which allows demodulation. Using the observation of examples it was demonstrated by comparison with synthesis results that the determined modulation parameters reflect the modulation. It also turned out that this modulation parameters do not necessarily have to be unique, i.e., for a modulated texture different profiles for the two modulation parameters are conceivable. Furthermore, the results depend strongly on the choice of the variable parameters of the control loop and can be subject to wide fluctuations and jumps.

Overall, the basis for the description and analysis of structural-statistical textures was created. It now applies to future work to use the first experiences with the model and the phase-locked loop to achieve uniqueness of the optimization problem and to prevent jumps and fluctuations of the modulation parameters by suitable extensions. First ideas and approaches are presented in this report.

Bibliography

[Bey11] J. Beyerer. Lecture: Automatische Sichtprüfung und Bildverarbeitung. *Karlsruher Institut für Technologie, Lehrstuhl für Interaktive Echtzeitsysteme*, 2011.

[GP03] S.E. Grigorescu and N. Petkov. Texture analysis using Renyi's generalized entropies. *International Conference on Image Processing*, 2003.

[Har79] R.M. Haralick. Statistical and structural approaches to texture. *Proceedings of the IEEE*, 67(5):786 – 804, 1979.

[HSD73] R.M. Haralick, K. Shanmugam, and I. Dinstein. Textural features for image classification. *IEEE Transactions on Systems, Man and Cybernetics*, SMC-3(6):610–621, 1973.

[Kam11] K.D. Kammeyer. *Nachrichtenübertragung*. Vieweg+Teubner Verlag, 2011.

[LRWW98] J.C. Lagarias, J.A. Reeds, M.H. Wright, and P.E. Wright. Convergence properties of the Nelder-Mead simplex method in low dimensions. *SIAM Journal on Optimization*, 9:112–147, 1998.

[MJ92]   J. Mao and A.K. Jain. Texture classification and segmentation using multiresolution simultaneous autoregressive models. *Pattern Recognition*, 25(2):173–188, 1992.

[NM65]   J.A. Nelder and R. Mead. A simplex method for function minimization. *Computer Journal*, 7:308–313, 1965.

[RH99]   T. Randen and J.H. Husoy. Filtering for texture classification: A comparative study. *IEEE Transactions on Pattern Analysis and Machine Intelligence*, 21(4):291–310, 1999.

[Vog12]   Markus Vogelbacher. Review and outlook for texture analysis methods. Technical report, Vision and Fusion Laboratory, Institute for Anthropomatics, Karlsruhe Institute of Technology (KIT), 2012.

[WH89]   L. Wang and D.C. He. Texture classification using texture spectrum. *Pattern Recognition*, 23(8):905–910, 1989.

Empirical Comparison of Defect Classifiers on Specular Surfaces

Mathias Ziebarth

Vision and Fusion Laboratory
Institute for Anthropomatics
Karlsruhe Institute of Technology (KIT), Germany
mathias.ziebarth@kit.edu

Technical Report IES-2013-13

Abstract:
Today the inspection of specular surfaces, especially in the automobile sector, is often done by humans. An automated inspection would be preferable for reasons such as reproducibility, reliability, and objectivity. However it is problematic to replace humans by machines in this field. The main reasons for this are their greater flexibility for changes in the production process and their ability not only to find defects but to decide whether a customer would complain about those defects. With the deflectometric principle, there is a measurement method for specular surfaces that is fast and accurate enough to compete with humans. Open problems are the necessary expenses for the parameterization of the defect detection and the missing link to the human perception of defects. The first problem is addressed in this paper. An overview of methods capable of detecting and classifying defects of different shapes and scales on unknown surface shapes is given. Then all methods are compared empirically on real measurement data.

1 Introduction

The automated visual inspection of specular surfaces is a practical problem with many applications. Today, there are methods known to get precise measurements of specular surfaces, ranging from small glossy mobile devices up to large lacquered automobile bodies. One measurement principle is deflectometry which can be used for specular to partially specular surfaces. It has the advantage of being especially sensitive to changes in the surface curvature. This corresponds to the human perception of specular surfaces is therefore often used for the inspection of surfaces that have to "look good". Additionally deflectometry can be used to obtain metric measurements of functional specular surfaces like mirrors.

A typical surface inspection consists of several steps, as follows:

1. Measurement: the acquisition of the objects surface,

2. Detection: the determination of defect locations,

3. Classification: the assignment of defects to defect classes,

4. Assessment: the rating of the defects visibility,

5. Decision: whether to accept or reject the surface.

In this paper, at first, the surface topology is measured using the deflectometric method. Then possible defect locations are detected and each defect is assigned to a specified class. Beyond the content of this paper, based on this classification, the severeness of each defect has to be estimated. Finally, combining the information of all surface defects, the decision, whether to accept or reject the object, has to be made.

In the following sections multiscale features are introduced and compared to get useful information for the detection and classification task. Hence, two classifiers, a Bayesian classifier and a Support Vector Machine (SVM), are used to learn the regions in feature space that correspond to the defect classes. For training and testing of each feature and classifier, several datasets were created. These datasets were acquired from flat lacquered metal sheets with several pimple and dent defects. For each metal sheet a ground truth was manually created. Then the dataset was divided in two independent datasets, to evaluate the generalizing properties of each feature-classifier combination.

2   Related Work

In the past several studies were made to evaluate the inspection qualities of human inspectors. Schoonard et al. [SGM73] studied influencing aspects for the inspection of small integrated circuits. They found that the more accurate the inspectors were, the less eye fixations during the inspection task they had, resulting in a higher accuracy and a faster completion of the inspection task. Additionally, they observed that the rate of missed defects of the inspectors was quite high, while only a few defects were mistakenly detected. Furthermore, they observed that a variation of the given inspection time by factor 6 only led to variation in accuracy by less than factor 2. Finally, changes in the inspection setup had small influence on the inspection results. As a consequence for this technical report, an automated inspection has to compete with the inspector's flexibility to adapt to changes in the setup and their low false negative rate finding defects. In addition it has the potential to exceed the inspectors with an lower false positive rate and objective, repeatable results.

The detection, classification and evaluation of surface defects is a rather general task with many applications and accordingly a lot of studies exist in this field. The studied applications range from the evaluation of auto-body panels [And09, Fer13], assessing scratch damages in bulk materials and coatings [HWP03], scratch visibility on polymers [RSW+03, JBH+10, LBS+11] and defects on machined and painted surfaces [PK06].

The standard approach to detect surface defects is to find changes between the measured surface and the surface model. The matching of the measurements with the surface model as well as the interpretation of changes between both are difficult. Li and Gu [LG05] used some special points on the surface to align the measurement data with the CAD model and defined a maximum tolerance for the deviations based on the tolerance of the manufacturing process. Savio et al. [SCS07] summarized the state of the art for a general free-form inspection based on a reference model. They structured the matching algorithm in several stages. First of all, multiple overlapping measurements have to be aligned. Depending on the necessary accuracy this can be computational expensive. Alternatively the surface can be marked with reference points which can be used for the alignment. Then a filtering operation has to separate between measurement noise, geometrical surface features and the surface form. Now the measurement data has to be aligned with the model, which is in general split into a coarse and a fine alignment step. The result of the alignment depends on the chosen merit function, usually the mean squared differences are minimized. The final evaluation of all deviations from the model also depends on some function to describe the deviations and region dependent maximum tolerances of this function. Another possibility is to match derivatives of surface instead of the surface itself, like Kase et al. [KMN+99] did, matching the surface curvature. This simplifies the evaluation of changes, because the curvature is invariant to deviations in the absolute height.

3 Methods

In this section a short introduction to deflectometry, wavelets, support vector machines, and Bayes classification is given, as these methods are used in the following experiments. Furthermore, methods used for extracting the feature vectors from deflectometric measurements of specular surfaces are presented.

3.1 Deflectometry

Deflectometry is a method for topography measurements of specular surfaces. Due to the specularity of the surface optical measurement methods relying on a diffuse reflection of a projected pattern are not applicable. In contrast, deflectometric methods exploit the specularity of the surface. Furthermore, if the objective is to find defects that are disturbing for a human, the perception of a human has to be considered. Since the surface itself is only visible through its reflection of the surrounding area, the optical aberrations caused by the surface are more perceptible than the surface itself. The virtual image of the surrounding area, which is visible in the specular surface, is determined by the shape of the surface, or more precisely by the surface curvature. The curvature can be calculated from the derivative of surface normal field. To obtain this surface normal field, a sequence of patterns, uniquely coding each point on a screen P_L, is observed over the reflection at the surface, using a camera with an image plane P_I. Based on these observations, geometric information about the light path from the camera to the screen is known and saved in the deflectometric registration l, which implies information about the surface:

$$l : P_I \mapsto P_L, \; l[u,v] = (x_L, y_L),$$

where u and v are points on the camera sensor and x_L an y_L are points on the screen. The deflectometric registration itself can be used as non-metric measurement to characterize the surface and to detect defects, since it is similar to the gradient field of the surface and therefore its derivative corresponds to the human perception. Alternatively the surface can be reconstructed, so that an estimated metric representation of the surface topography can be used for measurement purposes. For the reconstruction, additional knowledge, e.g. the distance between camera and surface, is required. Balzer [Bal08] proposed two approaches to obtain additional regularizing information of the surface that lead to a unique reconstruction. The field was extensively researched in the past ten years, see [HAN00, LKKG05, SCP05, BSG06, LBRB08, WMHB09, BHWB10].

3.2   Wavelet Transform

The wavelet transform is related to the Fourier transform, as it represents signals in the frequency domain. As the Fourier transform is a global transform, local changes in the signal affect the whole frequency domain of the signal. The reason for this are the periodically oscillating sine and cosine functions with infinite support which are used as basis functions for the transform. On the contrary, the wavelet transform uses small wavelets with finite support both in spatial and in frequency space. This results in a good localization in both spaces. Something similar is achieved with the short time Fourier transform, which has a fixed width window function that is multiplied with the basis sine and cosine functions. Due to the fixed size of this window the short time Fourier transform has a limited frequency resolution. Using a short window function, the resolution in spatial space (called localization) is good but in frequency space the resolution is limited to higher frequencies. In contrast, wavelets have an adaptive window length and with the best possible localization in spatial space and in frequency space. The idea behind the wavelet transform is clear when looking at the definition of the continuous wavelet transform (CWT). It is defined as the inner product of a signal $f(x)$ with a wavelet ψ in varying scales s and translations t:

$$F(s, u) := \mathcal{W}\{f(x)\} =< f, \psi_{s,u} >, \text{ with } \psi_{s,u}(x) = \frac{1}{\sqrt{s}}\phi\left(\frac{x - u}{s}\right).$$

In practice the more computational efficient discrete wavelet transform (DWT) is used instead. Additional requirements to the wavelet function assure that only dyadic scales and integer translation have to be considered. By defining a scaling function ϕ, the signal $f(x)$ can be approximated in various scales s:

$$a_s[u] = \int_{-\infty}^{\infty} f(x)\frac{1}{\sqrt{2^s}}\phi\left(\frac{x - 2^s u}{2^s}\right) dx, \ (s, u) \in \mathbb{Z}^2.$$

The scaling function has a low-pass characteristic, which results in a loss of high-frequency information of $f(x)$ with increasing scale. Furthermore, the scaling function is required to be orthogonal to the wavelet function, which allows the multiresolution analysis. The wavelet function, which has a high-pass characteristic, captures the details that are lost from one scale to the next. For an efficient calculation of the approximations and details, instead of the scaling and wavelet function, filter banks are used. Starting with an approximation of the signal in scale s (wavelet crime: $a_0[x] := f[x]$), the next coarser approximation is calculated with low-pass h. The details are calculated with a high-pass filter g. Multidimensional functions are calculated separately in each dimension, resulting in one approximation space and three detail spaces for the 2-dimensional signal $f(x, y)$:

$$a_{s+1}[u, v] = \sum_{m=-\infty}^{\infty} h[m - 2u] \sum_{n=-\infty}^{\infty} h[n - 2v] a_s[m, n], \qquad (3.1a)$$

$$d_{s+1,1}[u, v] = \sum_{m=-\infty}^{\infty} h[m - 2u] \sum_{n=-\infty}^{\infty} g[n - 2v] a_s[m, n], \qquad (3.1b)$$

$$d_{s+1,2}[u, v] = \sum_{m=-\infty}^{\infty} g[m - 2u] \sum_{n=-\infty}^{\infty} h[n - 2v] a_s[m, n], \qquad (3.1c)$$

$$d_{s+1,3}[u, v] = \sum_{m=-\infty}^{\infty} g[m - 2u] \sum_{n=-\infty}^{\infty} g[n - 2v] a_s[m, n]. \qquad (3.1d)$$

One more difference between the wavelet and the Fourier transform is the freedom of choice for the basis functions. It is possible to choose a wavelet out of existing families of wavelet functions with special properties or to define a new wavelet. A good overview over the theory and applications of wavelets is given by Mallat [Mal09].

Although the DWT allows a perfect reconstruction of the signal, there is a major drawback of the transform: due to the subsampling of the signal, precise locations of local irregularities are lost in higher scales. When the same signal is translated with a translation operator τ_t by t the whole scale space may change $\mathcal{W}\{\tau_t f(x)\} \neq \tau_t \mathcal{W}\{f(x)\}$. It is not translation invariant. By leaving out the subsampling, the undecimated or stationary wavelet transform (SWT) circumvents this problem by introducing additional redundancy. This results in increased memory requirements and increased computational efforts. Nevertheless, the translation invariance is indispensable for the given application.

3.3   Support Vector Machine

The classification is performed by a support vector machine (SVM) as described by Vapnik [CV95]. As the standard SVM only discriminates between two classes the SVM has to be extended for separation of more than two classes. In the following experiments the free library LIBSVM by Chang and Lin [CL11] was used. Amongst others, they provide an implementation of Vapnik's SVM with an extension to combine several two-class SVMs to one multiclass SVM. Moreover they implement an extension that allows the SVM to give probability estimates for each classification.

3.4   Bayes Classifier

Another classification method is the direct application of Bayes law as described in Duda et al. [DHS00],

$$p(\boldsymbol{\mu}_i, \boldsymbol{\Sigma}_i | \mathbf{d}) = \frac{p(\mathbf{d} | \boldsymbol{\mu}_i, \boldsymbol{\Sigma}_i) p(\boldsymbol{\mu}_i, \boldsymbol{\Sigma}_i)}{p(\mathbf{d})}.$$

Depending on the prerequisites a probability density function representing the likelihood has to be chosen. Here, a normal density is assumed that describes the mean $\boldsymbol{\mu}_i$ and the covariance $\boldsymbol{\Sigma}_i$ of the data $\mathbf{d}$ for each class i. In some cases, where the individual features are class conditional independent, the probability density function simplifies to several univariate densities for each feature dimension.

3.5   Features

In the following section features and classifiers that are used to detect and classify defects on specular surfaces are shown. The feature extraction methods share the similarity of being applicable in different scales depending on a scaling parameter.

3.5.1   High-pass

The high-pass filter approximates an ideal high-pass filter with a defined cutoff frequency ω_c with a finite number of coefficients in spatial space. To avoid spectral leakage effects the filter coefficients are multiplied with a Hamming window of the same length as the filter function. Depending on the scale s, the filter length $n = s + 1$ and the number of cutoff frequencies $\omega_c \in \{ \frac{i\pi}{s+1} \mid i \in 1 \ldots s \}$ were varied.

3.5.2   Gradient

The gradient filter calculates the Euclidean norm of the gradient magnitude

$$g_\sigma(\mathbf{x}) = \sqrt{d_\sigma^x(\mathbf{x})^2 + d_\sigma^y(\mathbf{x})^2}$$

at each point $\mathbf{x}$. Each gradient direction is approximated by the first partial derivative of a Gaussian $h_\sigma(\mathbf{x})$ with variance σ^2

$$d_\sigma^x(\mathbf{x}) = -\frac{\partial h_\sigma(\mathbf{x})}{\partial x} = \frac{\mathbf{x}}{2\pi\sigma^2} e^{-\frac{\|\mathbf{x}\|^2}{2\sigma^2}}.$$

Depending on the parameter σ of the Gaussian, edges in different scales are detected. The discrete filter has a radius $r = 2\sigma$.

3.5.3 Laplacian-of-Gaussian

The Laplacian-of-Gaussian (LoG) filter [BPLF12] approximates the sum of all second partial derivatives of the smoothed signal. It is obtained by calculating the Laplacian of a Gaussian $h_\sigma(\mathbf{x})$

$$l_\sigma(\mathbf{x}) = -\frac{\partial^2 h_\sigma(\mathbf{x})}{\partial x^2} - \frac{\partial^2 h_\sigma(\mathbf{x})}{\partial y^2} = \frac{2\sigma^2 - \|\mathbf{x}\|}{2\pi\sigma^6} e^{-\frac{\|\mathbf{x}\|^2}{2\sigma^2}}.$$

Depending on the parameter σ of the Gaussian, edges in different scales are detected. The discrete filter has a radius $r = 2\sigma$.

3.5.4 Wavelets

In Hahn et al. [HZHR13] several wavelet families with different support sizes were studied for the detection and classification task. The best families were the family of Symmlets and Biorthogonal Spline wavelets, especially those with a small support. The reason for this could be that a larger support leads to a worse detection but should have better invariance properties for curved surfaces. In the experiment only flat surfaces were studied, so the invariance properties weren't necessary.

Only wavelets from the Symmlet family were studied in this paper. Symmlets are nearly symmetric and have invariance properties, called vanishing moments, which depend on the length of the wavelet's filter function. These vanishing moments define the ability of the wavelet to suppress parts of the analyzed signal. Functions with a degree smaller than the number of vanishing moments of the wavelet do not appear in the detail space. For surfaces which are represented by cubic splines, all surface properties of lower order, i.e. the surface shape, are suppressed.

4 Experimental Setup

For the experimental evaluation of the methods above, five independent datasets were used. Each dataset was acquired from black flat lacquered metal sheet using a deflectometric measurement setup and a FEM-based reconstruction of the surface. Two surfaces have two defect types (dent and pimple), the rest has one defect type (pimple). Defects of the type pimple are characterized by a small lateral extent and a steep gradient. The dent defects have a larger extent and a low gradient.

All defects were labeled by hand to provide a ground truth. Each point within the extent of a defect was labeled as belonging to this defect. For large defect extents it was difficult to definitely decide which points belong to the defect area. In these cases, the defect extent was chosen 50% smaller, to ensure that defect-free areas were not marked as defect.

For testing the ability of the feature-classifier combination to differentiate between trained defect classes and an unknown surface shape, some synthetic surfaces were generated from the real measurements. As most real world inspection problems have to deal with surface curvature, it is an interesting property of the inspection system to be adaptable to unknown or changed curvatures. The synthetic surface was generated from the sum of a measurement dataset and function generating some surface model. Here two models were assumed. The first model was a sine function with amplitude one and one period over the whole the surface area in one direction. The second model was product of two sine functions with amplitude one and one period over the whole surface area in both directions.

The feature set $\mathbf{d}$ for a point $\mathbf{x}$ on the surface S is given by selected coefficients from the SWT in 5 scales or by multiple evaluations of the other features described above calculated in 5 scales at the same point. Now each of the classifiers decides, based on the feature vector, which class the point on the surface belongs to.

Three different classifiers were evaluated in this experiment. Two classifiers were Bayesian and use parametric density functions. As a third classifier a parameter free SVM as described above was used.

For the first Bayesian classifier class conditional independence of all features is assumed, i.e. the feature for each scale is class conditional independent of the other scales. While this assumption holds for orthogonal wavelets [ZLGH12], it is most likely violated by the other features. The classifier is defined by two parameter vectors $\boldsymbol{\mu}_i$ and $\boldsymbol{\sigma}_i$, representing mean and standard deviation of each feature in class C_i. Consequently the probability for a feature vector $\mathbf{d}$ belonging to class C_i is determined by Bayes' rule:

$$p(\boldsymbol{\mu}_i, \boldsymbol{\sigma}_i | \mathbf{d}) = \frac{p(\mathbf{d} | \boldsymbol{\mu}_i, \boldsymbol{\sigma}_i) \, p(\boldsymbol{\mu}_i, \boldsymbol{\sigma}_i)}{p(\mathbf{d})}.$$

Tests [ZLGH12] have shown that the coefficients are often Laplace distributed. Hence the likelihood for class C_i is modeled as product of univariate Laplace

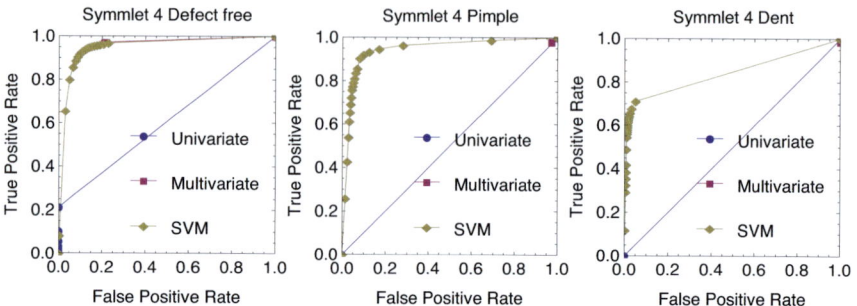

Figure 4.1: Comparison of classifiers using the Symmlet wavelet on a flat surface.

distributions:

$$p(\mathbf{d}|\boldsymbol{\mu}_i, \boldsymbol{\sigma}_i) = \prod_k \frac{1}{\sigma_{i,k}\sqrt{2\pi}} \exp\left(-\frac{1}{2}\frac{|d_k - \mu_{i,k}|}{\sigma_{i,k}^2}\right).$$

The parameters $\boldsymbol{\mu}_i$ and $\boldsymbol{\sigma}_i$ are chosen such that for each class C_i the likelihood for the training set is maximized. The prior is chosen as uniform distribution over all classes.

The second classifier uses a multivariate normal density with a mean vector $\boldsymbol{\mu}_i$ and a covariance matrix $\boldsymbol{\Sigma}_i$ to describe the likelihood of the data for each class

$$p(\mathbf{d}|\boldsymbol{\mu}_i, \boldsymbol{\Sigma}_i) = \frac{1}{|\boldsymbol{\Sigma}_i|^{\frac{p}{2}}(2\pi)^{\frac{p}{2}}} \exp\left(-\frac{1}{2}(\mathbf{d}-\boldsymbol{\mu}_i)^T\boldsymbol{\Sigma}_i^{-1}(\mathbf{d}-\boldsymbol{\mu}_i)\right).$$

For the training of this classifier the parameters $\boldsymbol{\mu}_i$ and $\boldsymbol{\Sigma}_i$ were chosen such that the first two moments of the estimated density match the first two moments of the data.

The SVM classifier uses a radial basis function $e^{-\gamma|u-v|^2}$ as kernel function. Besides the necessity for training data the SVM needs to be parametrized with two parameters: a regularization parameter for weighting the costs of misclassifications C and the width of the kernel function γ. The optimization of these parameters $\gamma \in \{2^{i/2}\}, C \in \{2^{j/2}\}, i \in \{-4,\ldots,40\}, j \in \{-24,\ldots,24\}$ was realized using a five fold cross validation with 200 feature vectors for each class and a grid search as proposed in [HCL10].

To compare the performance of the classifiers and features, the receiver operating characteristics was plotted for each combination of classifier, feature, training and

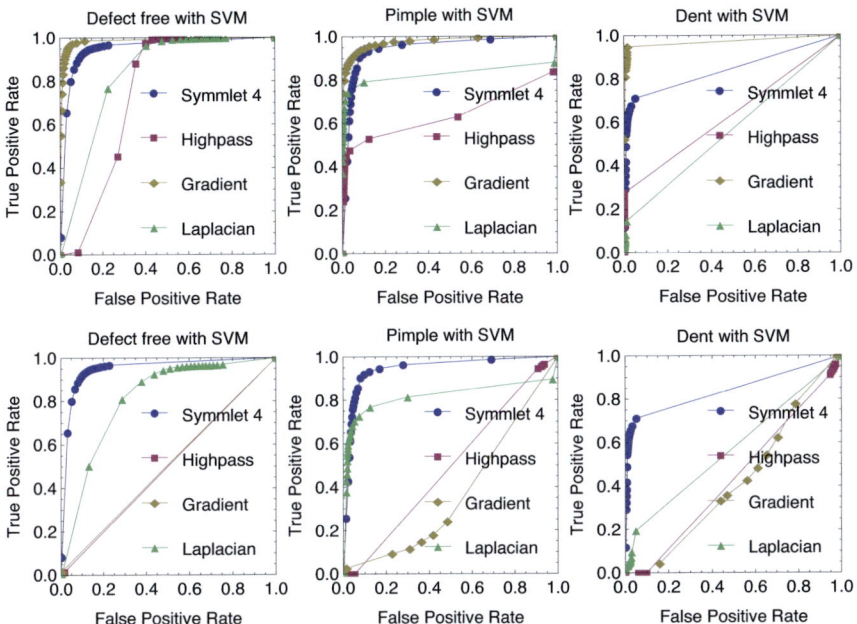

Figure 5.1: Comparison of trained SVM with 5-scale feature vectors on a flat surface with pimples and dents (first row) and the corresponding curved surface (second row).

testing dataset and defect class. All studied classification methods return probability values for each of the three respectively two classes. Now the decision value can be varied between 0 and 1, which results in different false and true positive rates.

5 Results & Discussion

The comparison of the three classifiers using the Symmlet 4 wavelet (Fig. 4.1) shows that the SVM clearly outperforms the other two classifiers. While the multivariate Bayes classifier still discriminates between defect free and defect areas, the naive Bayes classifier fails. The ROC curves of the Bayes classifiers only consist of a few points with a false positive rate between 0 and 1. This is due to the

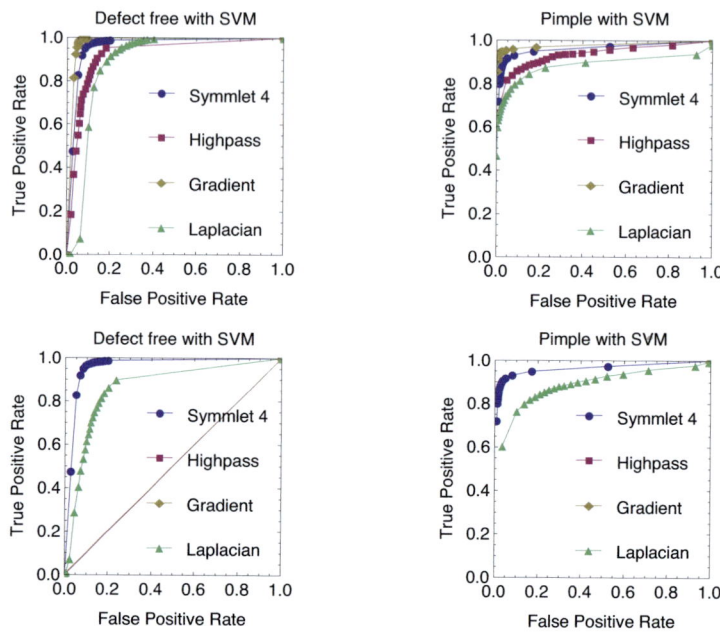

Figure 5.2: Comparison of trained SVM with 5-scale feature vectors on a flat surface with pimples (first row) and the corresponding curved surface (second row).

fact, that those classifiers have a narrow band of probability values for all classified points on the surface and a change in the decision threshold leads to either an acceptance or a rejection of all points on the surface.

To compare the features, only the results obtained with the SVM classifier are shown here. The classifier was always trained with on feature extraction method on a flat surface and was then tested on other surfaces with the same defect types. The comparison of the feature extraction methods (Fig. 5.1), shows that on flat surfaces the gradient feature outperforms the other features in all the classification rate of all three classes. Both, the Laplacian and the high-pass feature have a bad classification performance. The performance of the SVM in combination with the Symmlet 4 feature is lower compared to the gradient feature but still leads to good classification results. The performance of all features but the Symmlet 4 and the Laplacian feature changes dramatically, when the classifier is tested on a curved surface. While the performance of the Laplacian feature gets slightly worse, the

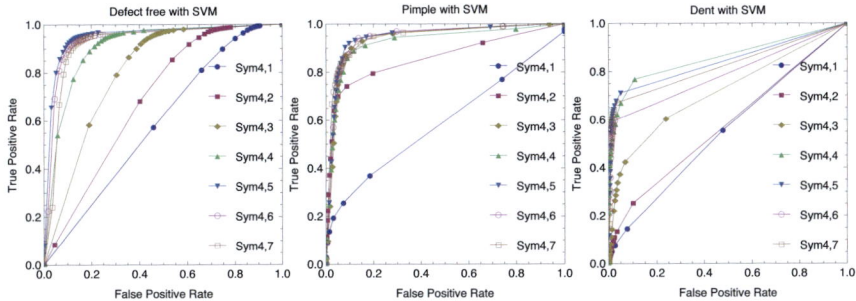

Figure 5.3: Scale dependency of a Symmlet 4 feature vector and the SVM classifier on a flat surface with pimples and dents.

performance of the Symmlet 4 feature stays on the same level. The same effect can be observed on the other data set with only 2 defect classes in Fig. 5.2.

As shown in Fig. 5.3 the classification performance of the Symmlet 4 feature increases as the number of scales that are included in the feature vector increases. Starting with 5 scales, the classification performance only slowly increases by adding more scales to the feature vector.

6   Conclusion

In this paper methods for the inspection of specular surfaces were proposed and compared. The classification method is not the crucial factor here, but the evaluation has shown that the naive Bayes and the multivariate Bayes classifiers with the given density assumptions had a worse performance than the SVM. Two of the proposed features, the Symmlet 4 and the gradient feature led to good classification results in combination with a SVM classifier, when both, the training and the testing dataset were flat surfaces. As soon as the testing dataset differs from the training dataset significantly in surface shape, only with Symmlet 4 feature, the classification results kept good. This is an important property of the wavelet features, due to their vanishing moments, that differentiates them from the other proposed features. Additionally the wavelet transform is more efficient than the other features, as the length of filter function stays constant over the scales. Therefore the combination of an appropriate wavelet in combination with a SVM has a high practical relevance for real inspection problems. The invariance of the wavelets to the surface shape allows a deflectometric measurement system to be adapted faster to new product types and allows a robust classification of several defect classes on specular surfaces.

Bibliography

[And09]   A. Andersson. Evaluation and visualisation of surface defects on auto-body panels . *Journal of Materials Processing Technology*, 209(2):821–837, 2009.

[Bal08]   J. Balzer. *Regularisierung des Deflektometrieproblems – Grundlagen und Anwendung.* PhD thesis, Universität Karlsruhe (TH), Universitätsverlag Karlsruhe, 2008.

[BHWB10]   J. Balzer, S. Höfer, S. Werling, and J. Beyerer. Optimization on Shape Curves with Application to Specular Stereo. In *Pattern Recognition – DAGM Symposium*, 2010.

[BPLF12]   J. Beyerer, F. Puente León, and C. Frese. *Automatische Sichtprüfung: Grundlagen, Methoden und Praxis der Bildgewinnung und Bildauswertung.* Springer, Berlin Heidelberg, 2012.

[BSG06]   T. Bonfort, P. Sturm, and P. Gargallo. General specular Surface Triangulation. *Proceedings of the Asian Conference on Computer Vision*, II:872–881, 2006.

[CL11]   Chih-Chung Chang and Chih-Jen Lin. LIBSVM: A library for Support Vector Machines. *ACM Transactions on Intelligent Systems and Technology*, 2:27:1–27:27, 2011.

[CV95]   C. Cortes and V. Vapnik. Support-vector networks. *Machine Learning*, 20:273–297, 1995.

[DHS00]   R. Duda, P. Hart, and D. Stork. *Pattern Classification.* Wiley, 2000.

[Fer13]   K. Fernholz. Quantifying the Visibility of Surface Distortions in Class "A" Automotive Exterior Body Panels. *Journal of Manufacturing Science and Engineering*, 135:011001–1, 2013.

[HAN00]   R. Höfling, P. Aswendt, and R. Neugebauer. Phase reflection – a new solution for the detection of shape defects on car body sheets. *Optical engineering*, 39:175–182, 2000.

[HCL10]   C.-W. Hsu, C.-C. Chang, and C.-J. Lin. *A Practical Guide to Support Vector Classification*, 2010.

[HWP03]   I. Hutchings, P. Wang, and G. Parry. An optical method for assessing scratch damage in bulk materials and coatings. *Surface and Coatings Technology*, 165(2):186–193, 2003.

[HZHR13]   A. Hahn, M. Ziebarth, M. Heizmann, and A. Rieder. Defect Classification on Specular Surfaces Using Wavelets. In *Scale Space and Variational Methods in Computer Vision*, volume 7893 of *Lecture Notes in Computer Science*, pages 501–512. Springer, Jun 2013.

[JBH+10]   H. Jiang, R. Browning, M. Hossain, H-J. Sue, and M. Fujiwara. Quantitative evaluation of scratch visibility resistance of polymers. *Applied Surface Science*, 256(21):6324–6329, 2010.

[KMN+99]   K. Kase, A. Makinouchi, T. Nakagawa, H. Suzuki, and F. Kimura. Shape error evaluation method of free-form surfaces. *Computer-Aided Design*, 31(8):495–505, 1999.

[LBRB08]   J. Lellmann, J. Balzer, A. Rieder, and J. Beyerer. Shape from Specular Reflection and Optical Flow. *International Journal of Computer Vision*, 80:226–241, 2008.

[LBS+11]   P. Liu, R. Browning, H-J. Sue, J. Li, and S. Jones. Quantitative scratch visibility assessment of polymers based on Erichsen and ASTM/ISO scratch testing methodologies. *Polymer Testing*, 30(6):633–640, 2011.

[LG05]   Y. Li and P. Gu. Inspection of free-form shaped parts. *Robotics and Computer-Integrated Manufacturing*, 21:421–430, 2005.

[LKKG05] S. Lowitzsch, J. Kaminski, M. Knauer, and G.Häusler. Vision and Modeling of Specular Surfaces. In *Vision, Modeling and Visualization 2005 - Proceedings*. Akademische Verlagsgesellschaft Aka GmbH, Berlin, 2005.

[Mal09]   S. Mallat. *A Wavelet Tour of Signal Processing: The Sparse Way*. Elsevier / Academic Press, 2009.

[PK06]   F. Puente León and S. Kammel. Inspection of specular and painted surfaces with centralized fusion techniques. *Measurement*, 39(6):536–546, 2006.

[RSW+03] P. Rangarajan, M. Sinha, V. Watkins, K. Harding, and J. Sparks. Scratch visibility of polymers measured using optical imaging. *Polymer Engineering & Science*, 43(3):749–758, 2003.

[SCP05]   S. Savarese, M. Chen, and P. Perona. Local Shape from Mirror Reflections. *International Journal of Computer Vision*, 64:31–67, 2005.

[SCS07]   E. Savio, L. De Chiffre, and R. Schmitt. Metrology of freeform shaped parts. *CIRP Annals - Manufacturing Technology*, 56(2):810–835, 2007.

[SGM73]   J. Schoonahd, J. Gould, and L. Miller. Studies of Visual Inspection. *Ergonomics*, 16(4):365–379, 1973.

[WMHB09] S. Werling, M. Mai, M. Heizmann, and J. Beyerer. Inspection of Specular and Partially Specular Surfaces. *Metrology and Measurement Systems*, 16:415–431, 2009.

[ZLGH12] M. Ziebarth, T.-T. Le, T. Greiner, and M. Heizmann. Inspektion spiegelnder Oberflächen mit Wavelet-basierten Verfahren. In *Forum Bildverarbeitung 2012*, pages 167–180. KIT Scientific Publishing, Nov 2012.

Karlsruher Schriftenreihe zur Anthropomatik
(ISSN 1863-6489)

Herausgeber: Prof. Dr.-Ing. Jürgen Beyerer

Die Bände sind unter www.ksp.kit.edu als PDF frei verfügbar
oder als Druckausgabe bestellbar.

Band 1   Jürgen Geisler
         Leistung des Menschen am Bildschirmarbeitsplatz. 2006
         ISBN 3-86644-070-7

Band 2   Elisabeth Peinsipp-Byma
         **Leistungserhöhung durch Assistenz in interaktiven Systemen
         zur Szenenanalyse.** 2007
         ISBN 978-3-86644-149-1

Band 3   Jürgen Geisler, Jürgen Beyerer (Hrsg.)
         Mensch-Maschine-Systeme. 2010
         ISBN 978-3-86644-457-7

Band 4   Jürgen Beyerer, Marco Huber (Hrsg.)
         **Proceedings of the 2009 Joint Workshop of Fraunhofer IOSB and
         Institute for Anthropomatics, Vision and Fusion Laboratory.** 2010
         ISBN 978-3-86644-469-0

Band 5   Thomas Usländer
         Service-oriented design of environmental information systems. 2010
         ISBN 978-3-86644-499-7

Band 6   Giulio Milighetti
         **Multisensorielle diskret-kontinuierliche Überwachung und
         Regelung humanoider Roboter.** 2010
         ISBN 978-3-86644-568-0

Band 7   Jürgen Beyerer, Marco Huber (Hrsg.)
         **Proceedings of the 2010 Joint Workshop of Fraunhofer IOSB and
         Institute for Anthropomatics, Vision and Fusion Laboratory.** 2011
         ISBN 978-3-86644-609-0

Band 8   Eduardo Monari
         **Dynamische Sensorselektion zur auftragsorientierten
         Objektverfolgung in Kameranetzwerken.** 2011
         ISBN 978-3-86644-729-5